Word Perfect

Pittsburgh Series in Composition, Literacy, and Culture
David Bartholomae and Jean Ferguson Carr, Editors

Academic Discourse and Critical Consciousness
Patricia Bizzell

Eating on the Street:
Teaching Literacy in a Multicultural Society
David Schaafsma

Fragments of Rationality:
Postmodernity and the Subject of Composition
Lester Faigley

Literacy Online:
The Promise (and Peril) of Reading and Writing with Computers
Myron C. Tuman, Editor

Word Perfect:
Literacy in the Computer Age

Myron C. Tuman

University of Pittsburgh Press

UK   The Falmer Press, 4 John St., London WC1N 2ET
USA   University of Pittsburgh Press, 127 North Bellefield Avenue, Pittsburgh, Pa. 15260

First published 1992 by The Falmer Press

Published in the United States by the University of Pittsburgh Press, Pittsburgh, Pa. 15260

A catalogue record for this book is available from the British Library

Library of Congress Catalog Card Number 92-50273

Library of Congress Cataloging in Publication Data are available on request

ISBN 0-8229-3735-2
ISBN 0-8229-5489-3 (pbk)

Jacket design by Benedict Evans
Typeset in 9.5/11pt Bembo
by Graphicraft Typesetters Ltd., Hong Kong

Printed in Great Britain by Burgess Science Press, Basingstoke on paper which has a specified pH value on final paper manufacture of not less than 7.5 and is therefore 'acid free'.

Contents

Introduction   *vii*

Preface   *x*

Chapter 1   Two Literacies   1

Chapter 2   The Technology of Print   23

Chapter 3   The New Reading   52

Chapter 4   The New Writing   81

Chapter 5   Imagining the Future   109

Bibliography   139

Index   148

Related Titles   151

For Ginny

Introduction

Literacy is a social technology. That is, literate communities develop varied social, linguistic and cognitive practices with texts. These require the development and use of implements, ranging from plumes and ball point pens to keyboards. The objects and products of such practices and tools are recoverable texts arrayed on tablets, notebooks or other visual displays.

The social uses and consequences of literacy extend far beyond the relatively straightforward storage, retrieval and transmission of information. In Western literate cultures, texts and textual practices have become central means for the making of tradition and authority, identity and agency. Accordingly, access to and control of textual archives is crucial — whether those archives are legal and economic records, laws and covenants, or sacred and profane literature; whether they are magnetically encoded files, or written on paper. What will count as significant information? Who should have access to information? Who should be 'inputting', constructing and interpreting that information? Insofar as it is forcing a reorganization and reappraisal of these matters, the advent of microchip technology marks a significant juncture in the history of literacy. But exactly how, to what ends and in whose interests are urgent matters for investigation, argument and debate.

In this context, literacy education continues to be a key site for the brokering of each generation's access to texts and knowledge, information and power. In spite of its nature-like appearance in literate communities, literacy does not 'develop' as part of some sort of inevitable technological 'evolution' or 'revolution' (the terms themselves are metaphors for how history works). It would be erroneous, then, to construe 'becoming literate' as an arbitrary, natural or individual procedure. Even the lone (Romantic) reader and writer is reliant on the codes and sanctions of interpretive communities, codes and sanctions taught and learned in institutions like schools and universities. This teaching and learning of what can and what cannot, what should and what should not be done with the technology of writing has been and continues to be elaborated as part of larger social and cultural, political and economic strategies and agendas.

Yet a persistent folk wisdom about literacy maintains that the written word has an intrinsic movement which transcends particular interpretive communities, particular cultures and particular epochs. At the heart of much contemporary teaching — traditional and progressive, classical and child-centred — is a belief in an inexorable will of the literate and literature towards Truth, Beauty and the Good. It is as if we and other literate cultures have developed cargo cults around this particular technology. The book has been assigned variously mystical and spiritual, healing and hermeneutic powers. It is associated by its users with a range of moral and cognitive, social and political properties and effects.

Technological determinism has a history probably as long as that of technology. We can trace the emergence of a cross-disciplinary discourse on literacy to the innovative early and mid-twentieth century work of Lewis Mumford, Harold A. Innis, and later Marshall McLuhan. Their writings tell a very different history of literacy, one which turns on breathtaking claims about the cultural and intellectual 'bias' of particular commmunications media. Unlike traditional works by literary and narrative historians, no longer is Western Man (*not* Woman) the major protagonist. In this story, the technology of writing itself becomes a prime engine of cultural and social transformation.

Much of the current debate on computers and education is built on technological determinist arguments, often in the form of recycled industrial-era claims about print literacy. Teachers have had to deal with two broad premises about the advent of computer technology: first, the human capital rationale that 'high tech' societies (and competitive late-capitalist economies) demand ever higher levels of 'computer literacy' from all; and second, the claim that microchip technology is alternately a threat to traditional print based schooling, and a 'magic bullet' for alleviating many of the longstanding problems of that same system. A few voices of caution — among them Myron Tuman, Chet Bowers, Chris Bigum — have raised ethical, political and epistemic questions about such claims and their related applications in policy and curriculum. But by and large, educational applications presuppose that the characteristics and effects of computer-driven instruction are value and ideology neutral.

The educational promises made on behalf of this and other emergent communications technologies echo those made by Reformation and Industrial-era reformers about print literacy. It would appear that archetypal 'literacy myths' are being reinflected across technologies and educational generations, in the face of ample evidence that the same old patterns of inequality affiliated with twentieth century print literacy education persist. Women, ethnic minorities, the urban poor, indigenous peoples — the historic outsiders of technologies of power — are forming up the ranks of new regional global underclasses of the information and technology 'poor'. Already the possibilities and limits of new technologies have been tied directly to multinational political economies which control the marketplace of ideas and information in particular corporate interests.

Word Perfect is an 'essay on criticism' for the new literacies. As such, it models those exploratory, critical aspects of print traditions which Tuman argues are worth vindicating and reconstructing. Tuman here begins from a recognition that word processing is but a more sophisticated form of text handling, heralding a change in implements but not in the conventional characteristics of print literacy. The key challenges to modernist textuality and discourse relations he locates in the 'on-line literacy' of data bases and telecommunications, and in hyper-text technology which allows multiple pathways through text, user-driven pastiche, simulation and the construction of virtual realities.

Tuman thus begins by examining how word processing has influenced the psychology and social relations of composition, a central question in the rapidly expanding field of college composition and writing. But he is more focally concerned with how the technology itself, and its pedagogic programs and activities lead to a reconstruction of traditional notions and practices of 'reading' and 'writing'. In a critical review of university curricular experiments that range from putting the traditional literary canon on screen, to on-line interaction over student writing, Tuman argues that these new technologies have reopened questions about what will count as 'authorship', 'text' and 'criticism' — concepts which he traces from Barthes' and Foucault's reworkings of the author function to Baudrillard's and Lyotard's commentaries on the significance of electronic texts in postmodern culture.

The task, then, for university writing and literature courses and literacy education in schools alike is somewhat more complex than the use of the technology for more efficient introduction of canonical knowledge, or for the enhancement of 'product' in student writing. The educational questions are ultimately normative and ideological, involving the selection and exclusion of particular textual practices and relations. Such selection, Tuman would argue, requires that we come to grips with what from critical print literate practices and traditions should and can be viably preserved. Tuman thus sets out to articulate a critical, humanist literary model of the potential of on-line literacy — one that is skeptical of technological determinism, and that keeps a clear eye fixed on social consequences and concomitants.

Literate traditions, as Tuman recognizes, perhaps only secondarily reside in a textual corpus, a literary canon — a point often missed by cultural literacy advocates and progressives alike. Reproduced cross-generationally in institutions like schools, universities and churches are textual practices undertaken by classes and communities of literates, particular ways of using the technology. There is no doubt that microchip technologies set out material conditions for the emergence of new relations of power and knowlege, that they enable differing social and textual relations, and indeed that they encourage new kinds of social and cultural theorizing, itself textual work. Yet, to return to my initial contention, neither new nor old communications technologies have 'natural' lives, destinies and legacies of their own.

They have the potential, however, of being used to reconstruct agency and authority, tradition and power in ways which appear 'nature-like'. Straddling the boundaries of the modern and postmodern, industrial and postindustrial — we are in a position to debate, reassess and challenge critical criteria for judging the practices, the implements, and indeed the on-line/on-screen artifacts of these new technologies. If none of these are intrinsic or inevitable, what seems absolutely crucial is to consider how the uses of these techonologies are being shaped, by whom and in whose interests. *Word Perfect* lays out prospects and perspectives for beginning that work, on-line and off.

Allan Luke
Townsville, Australia
October, 1991

Preface

This book can be considered an elaboration of Durkheim's claim that major debates about pedagogy are always an indicator of underlying social change. Its immediate concern is charting the enormous impact computers are having on how we read and write, how we teach reading and writing, and, more generally, how we define *literacy*, subjects that could not be fully covered in many books this size. Yet there is another, even larger concern here — namely, how technology generally affects not just specific language practices and policies but our most basic understanding of what it means to be literate or to be educated, even to think. The guiding thesis of this work is that how we as a society generate wealth has a great deal to do with how we relate to each other and to ourselves and, in complex ways that we seldom consider, how we organize education.

Although seemingly in the form of a critical analysis, this book can be seen as a grand narrative recounting the transition from one historical epoch to another — from a modern age both rooted in the unprecedented industrial expansion of the last hundred years and committed to the reading and writing of books to a postmodern age rooted in the equally unprecedented expansion in the ability to manage information and, as will be suggested here, probably just as committed to reading and writing with computers. Here in simple but dramatic terms is a story of epic proportion — the struggle between two competing models of literacy: one based in print and, for better or worse, largely responsible for our current situation, and one based in new computer technology and, depending on one's perspective, poised to save or ruin us over the next century.

This is a story where the computer occupies center stage but only so far as technical innovations seem to be leading to new ways of thinking about literacy. Thus there are whole chapters devoted to hypertext (as the basis for a new model of reading) and networking (as the basis for a new model of writing) but little about word processing, less about the latest hardware developments, and nothing whatsoever about such fascinating topics as artificial intelligence, computer-aided instruction, or many other new programs for processing language. Meanwhile figures like Alvin Gouldner and E.D. Hirsch have important roles because their work, despite saying little or nothing directly about computers, elucidates a major theme — the central, complex interrelationship between technology and critical thinking.

This is also a story taking place outside as well as inside the text, with all of us as readers, as central characters. Computers are a powerful new technology, equal to the steam turbine in their capacity to transform the world and how we think about our place in it. Even now they are changing our most basic attitudes about reading and writing, about authors and texts, and about the purpose and value of an education. Anyone with the skill and the inclination to read a book like this is already deeply implicated in print culture, and thus has much to lose or gain in this real-life drama — all readers and writers of such texts will be changed, some willingly as they become champions of new models of literacy, perhaps like the one described in these pages, others unwillingly as their allegiance to older models, perhaps like the one embodied in this book itself, remains firm while the world around them changes, infusing their own normative activities with an antiquarian air.

Finally, this is indirectly an autobiography, a story of my own struggle to shape an image of the future that builds upon, rather than simply rejects, the best of a print tradition that, although under increasing strain, continues to give purpose to my professional life as an English teacher. This is a story about the future that is very much rooted in the past, a story about the twenty-first century very much rooted in the nineteenth, one whose origins can be traced at least as far back as the mid-1960s when as an undergraduate I encountered three fabulous professors of nineteenth-century British literature: William H. Marshall, the first to teach me that we are all Romantics, Clyde Ryals, the first to try to tone down my still sometimes inflated rhetoric, and Morse Peckham, hovering somewhere in my unconscious as the archetypal literate.

More recently a number of other people played roles in helping me complete this project, and I want to thank them now: Dick Lanham for taking my views so seriously and with such good humor; Dwight Eddins for talking through with me, on a Florida beach, what became the central ideas of Chapter 5; Cully Clark for being a good administrator and ignoring my ranting; Ralph Bogardus for being a good friend and not ignoring it; Don Langham for editorial assistance throughout the last year; and Sarah Bane Wood for an unusually close, sympathetic, and timely reading of the manuscript.

Finally a word of thanks for my family: for my three children, Jeremy, Kathryn, and Dawn, for knowing when to humor and when to avoid me during the final months of this project; and especially for Ginny, to whom this book is dedicated, for not knowing — not the last few months, nor the last thirty years.

Myron Tuman
Tuscaloosa, Alabama
August 1, 1991

Chapter 1

Two Literacies

> In our images of the machine, we project our attitudes toward those internalized structures of repression which both confine and focus our energies.
>
> Eric Leed,
' "Voice" and "Print" '

At times we must wonder: why all the fuss over computers and literacy? We are by now all accustomed to the marvels, and the terminology, of word processing. We routinely *boot* computers, *load* programs, *open* files, *block* and *merge* text, *download* soft fonts, and, before printing, *spellcheck* our document and *preview* it on the screen. Our computer screens have become, in William Zinsser's words, 'a dancing sea of revisions and repairs': 'Long sentences suddenly vanished, but left no hole — the remaining sentences closed the gap and rearranged themselves as if nothing had been removed. Everything was instantly made tidy' (1983, p. 17).

Yet just how different, we must ask, is Zinsser's response from the account of another writer's first encounter with an earlier kind of word processor?

> I am trying to get the hang of this new fangled writing machine, but I am not making a shining success of it. However this is the first attempt I have ever made & yet I perceive I shall soon & easily acquire a fine facility in its use.... The machine has several virtues. I believe it will print faster than I can write. One may lean back in his chair & work it. It piles an awful stack of words on one page. It don't muss things or scatter ink blots around. Of course it saves paper.... (Blivens, 1954, p. 61).

That Mark Twain, the author of this 1874 letter, went on to submit the first typed manuscript to a publisher is today little more than a footnote to the history of literacy and technology — as is the entire history and development of typing. There are only a handful of historical studies of the typewriter (that older form of word processing) and these mostly located in business libraries, suggesting their importance in the history of office automation, not in our understanding and practice of writing. While individual writers over the years have extolled the value of their high school typing class (in part as an indirect means of criticizing the rest of their schooling), typing has remained a part of vocational education: it is a skill that one hires, usually at low wages, to place the original thought of others in more legible form. A composition handbook, for example, like the tenth edition of the best-selling *Harbrace Handbook*, (1986), a work designed for profession-bound college students, those intended to create or author, rather than merely reproduce texts, barely touches on the larger issue of manuscript preparation, devoting a scant nine pages (out of over 500) to the topic, with only a single six-sentence paragraph devoted to the issue of typing. This section, entitled 'Legible Typing', includes directions about checking the quality of the ribbon and the type, double-spacing, and not overstriking to make corrections.

Typing for the past 120 years has been a mere adjunct to literacy. It has been seen as a device for producing clean copy as a service to the reader, usually the course instructor, and not for generating superior content. College writing instructors, while often requiring students to type out-of-class essays, regularly caution students against making a fetish of neatness, especially for in-class writing. Here the routine advice is to cross out where necessary (not bothering with correction fluid) and to make changes in the margins or between lines. Behind this advice lies the basic assumption of higher literacy instruction embedded in college-level composition and literature classes — that what we mean by writing has little to do with the transcription of letters and far more to do with the ability to create a text containing original thought. Typing has had such little impact on this higher-level literacy over the last 120 years precisely because it is not perceived as having anything substantial to do with literacy, that is, with creating or comprehending the content, rather than the physical form, of texts. Why then should we expect so much more from computers? Are computers really designed to do anything more than to facilitate our entering text, in the words of Robert Lucky, 'remov[ing] the overhead in writing and bring[ing] us closer to fluency in expression' (1989, p. 167)? Are computers really anything more than turbocharged typewriters?

To begin to answer this question we need to recognize that any discussion of literacy and computers begins on something of a slippery slope where the footing — our sense of the stability of the terms under discussion — is likely to give way with little notice. It would be comforting, for example, to be able to depend on the basic definition of literacy as 'the ability to read and write', but the meanings of *reading* and *writing* are themselves unstable. Even worse, their meanings have shifted in the past, and may shift again in the future, precisely in response to technological change, so that questions concerning the impact of technology on literacy can quickly become circular: how do we study the impact of a new technology on literacy when our understanding of literacy is itself shaped by an existing technology, often in ways that are not fully conscious? In the *Phaedrus*, for example, Plato has Socrates question the detrimental impact of the new technology of writing on memory and public speaking — the preferred means of storing and communicating important material, hence the forms of 'literacy' that were being transformed by a new technology. Two thousand years later, at the beginning of the modern age of literacy, the playwright Richard Sheridan in *The Rivals* has the Tory patriarch Sir Anthony Absolute issue a series of admonitions about the dangers of novel reading, especially for young women, citing the same reasons as those used for widely advocating the study of literature in the twentieth century — that it helps break down traditional models of understanding and social roles, making the individual more open to new ways of being in the world. In Sir Anthony's pre-modern and pre-industrial world, the value of literacy lay elsewhere, in its ability to teach obedience, and conformity to traditional patterns of social existence.

New technologies for reproducing text can be seen as threats to literacy; they can also be ignored. The Chinese, for example, had access to moveable type as early as the eleventh century, but preferred the technology of full-page blocks for meeting the existing need of reprinting a few important works. Likewise in the West, the system of scribes continued for decades after the introduction of moveable type, given the need of supplying only a few readers with a selected number of texts. As Marshall McLuhan jokingly speculated about the sceptical reception the printed book must have received by an 'harassed sixteenth century administrator':

> Could a portable, private instrument like the new book take the place of the book one made by hand and memorized as one made it? Could a book which could be read quickly and even silently take the place of a book read slowly aloud? Could students trained by such printed books measure up to the skilled orators and disputants produced by manuscript means? (1962, p. 145).

It is easy for us to dismiss McLuhan's sixteenth-century administrator as a hopeless Luddite, someone lacking the insight to see how the new technology of print was going to create entirely new uses for reading and writing, indeed, an entirely new world of texts. It seems obvious now that handwriting and eventually print were going to do more than extend the traditional practices of oral or manuscript culture. Writing, and eventually printed books, played key roles in the formation of modern culture, allowing for the expression of individual, hence multiple, experience. 'More than any other single invention', writes Walter Ong, 'writing has transformed human consciousness' (1982, p. 78). It is tempting to see such a change as entirely positive, failing to recognize how, in creating this new sense of self, print technology adversely affected various traditional reading and writing practices. For example, to the extent that we accept the importance of the diligence required to copy and memorize, and the reflection produced by reading slowly and aloud — or, like Sheridan's Sir Anthony, to the extent that we value obedience and respect for tradition in our children — then we may have reason to lament that such pre-modern literacy skills as memorizing and transcribing may well have declined with the ascendancy of print. Similarly, is it not just as likely that at least some of the skills nurtured in the age of the mass reproduction of books will themselves become less important in the future? With the advent of writing, Socrates laments, what is to become of the ancient art of memorizing; with the advent of romance novels and circulating libraries, Sir Anthony laments, what is to become of feminine modesty? With the advent of computers, two millennia after Socrates and two centuries after Sheridan, Gore Vidal (1984) asks, 'What is to become of that written literature which was for two millennia wisdom's only mold? What is to become of the priests of literature, as their temples are abandoned?'

What is at issue here is how the computer, like the printing press, will create entirely new forms of communication and subtly alter the development of related communication skills, all in the name of *literacy*. Consider, for example, how computers, unlike typewriters, may already be changing the nature of writing, at least as defined by college composition this century. There the goal of writing has been producing an essay, a work usually defined in terms of its structure or wholeness (its introduction, body, and conclusion all supporting the development of a central thesis) and its content (that its thesis is original or somehow insightful). Until recently most discussions of computers and writing have concentrated on the effect computers have on students' ability to compose such organized, insightful essays. Underlying much of this research has been the sense that the computer has been oversold, that its impact on students' ability to write such essays is neither obvious nor always positive. Christina Haas, in one such study (1989), notes the various problems people who compose at a computer have in reading, or 'getting a sense' of their text, difficulties involving proofreading, large-scale revisions using block moves, and, most damaging of all, acquiring the sense of the whole necessary to direct such revisions. Given the task of producing an essay, the contemporary counterpart of McLuhan's sixteenth-century administrator will rightly ask how the ability either to manage different fonts and margins or to retrieve, search, merge, and save chunks of text — features offered by entry-level word processing programs today — will necessarily lead to 'better' (more organized, more insightful) writing.

The implications for literacy, however, change markedly if the paradigmatic text in college composition becomes something other than the individual essay, becomes, for example, a newsletter, a type of writing that even in miniature form requires mastery of columns, headlines, captions, and graphics — all features associated with desktop publishing, not critical thinking. Is it not possible that the design features of word processors will lead us away from a concern with the generation and development of complex thought and in the direction of more effective communication of widely shared or collectively generated information (the common content of newsletters)? Or what if the paradigmatic text moves in an entirely different direction, becoming, for example, a research report generated from a carefully structured search of the new electronic storehouse of collected wisdom (and information), a modern electronic database? Or moves in a third direction, where the paradigmatic text is no longer a text at all but an electronic conversation in which different parties read and respond to each other instantly (in *real-time*) and informally over a computer network? Would not any of these new computer-based forms of writing place more emphasis on abilities other than shaping disparate thoughts into a unified document? Indeed, with electronic conversations and different forms of online documentation and electronic presentations, there is no printed form, no document, no unified text. Then the paradigmatic text of this new age becomes, in Richard Lanham's words, the 'polyvocal, interactive, volatile' computer file (1990, p. xv), a form of expression that has already become the primary site of writing in the workplace, and, the alarms of traditional English professors notwithstanding, may eventually dominate the schools as well.

Essays have been at the center of school-based literacy this century in large measure because as miniature books they reflect the commitment of print culture to the task of generating and comprehending such focused texts. The central question before us is not whether books or essays will disappear entirely with the advent of computers — neither is likely to disappear even as writing moves in the direction of document design and file transfer and manipulation; it is whether or not books, or essays, will become marginal to the central project of literacy education, much as the formerly dominant practices of memorizing texts or copying manuscripts have in the last 200 years become menial tasks that students still routinely perform, albeit usually only in support of other, more central concerns. Books are themselves a wonderful technology, providing for the compact, inexpensive, portable storage of tens of thousands of words and hundreds of illustrations in a format that can be easily browsed and, with suitable margins, annotated. Is there any better format, one might ask, for reading? Or to phrase this question in its classic format, can one imagine lugging a computer to the beach in order to read a novel?

Surprisingly, the best answer to this rhetorical question might be that it depends on what one means by 'read', for just as the modern age of print culture has nurtured the sense that writing involves the ability to generate and to organize something worth saying, so too it has nurtured the sense that reading involves the ability to understand whatever is unique about the text. Our goal in reading a novel like Dickens' *Our Mutual Friend* in the modern age has been to fathom the special insights densely embedded into the structure and imagery of the work. Reading in this modern sense is directly connected to the intensity of our personal relationship with the text. The portability of the text becomes all-important — we want to be able to take the text with us to a place that will support such an intense relationship, a place like the beach where we will be undisturbed for hours at a time. But what happens if instead of just 'reading' *Our Mutual Friend* by plumbing its depth in an intensely personal experience we were required, as in a graduate seminar, to 'read up' on the novel, that is, to learn as much as we could about it — when and under what circumstances Dickens composed it, its publication history, contemporary and subsequent critical responses, its major sources, its relation to Dickens' other works, to the history of the English novel, to Victorian economic and social history, and so forth? Then we may want more than just the text itself, even if it is a Norton critical edition with annotations and ample critical materials. What we want then is access to all the annotations of all editions, and then to all the materials to which these annotations refer, and then to all the annotations in these materials ... and so on in an ever-widening circle of references. To read *Our Mutual Friend* in this second sense, what today we might refer to as doing research, or 'reading up' on the novel, we would not be satisfied with any single printed copy. Instead, our 'reading' ('reading up') would require us to move physically through the card catalogues, stacks, and various collections of a major research library. Accordingly, were we going to the beach to 'read up' *Our Mutual Friend*, we would in fact be much better off with our computer if via a modem we could access all the material about Dickens, the history of the novel, Victorian England — and eventually all human experience — that is increasingly being stored in computer databases.

Technologies of communication have little social import, Raymond Williams writes, until they are 'consciously developed for particular social uses' (1983, p. 129). It is the particular use we make of a technology, from the many possible uses it affords us, that defines its role. It is usually a mistake to assume that a new technology will be used to extend, rather than transform, an existing practice.

The telephone, for example, was initially designed, not to facilitate voice and now data exchange between two parties, but as a one-way transmission device, an improvement on the rope-pulls and other signalling devices whereby masters or managers summoned or gave orders to workers; or, as an advertisement of 1878 put it, 'all pulling, tugging and the grating noises occasioned by the cranks and consequent breaking of the wires are done away with' (Cherry, 1985, p. 61). A year later the Chief Engineer of the British Post Office reported to the House of Commons that 'here we have a superabundance of messengers, errand boys and things of that kind ... if I want to send a message — I use a sounder or employ a boy to take it.' As Cherry notes, it was the introduction of not the telephone itself but the telephone exchange with its facility of allowing any one person to contact anyone else that transformed communicative practice.

To understand how computers may change our present understanding of literacy, therefore, we need to look less at the technology itself and more at existing practices of reading and writing. One such backward glance over the last two centuries reveals that our modern notion of literacy has depended no more on the invention of printing than on the possibility of privacy, access to a metaphorical space of one's own — what sociologist Alvin Gouldner refers to as 'a sphere that did not routinely have to give an accounting of itself, either by providing information about its conduct or justification for it' (1976, p. 103). There is a connection here, to be elaborated upon in Chapter 2, between the mass, public circulation of books, and the accompanying growth in urban life over the past 400 years and the private experience of written language. As Elizabeth Eisenstein notes, it was the informal essay, perfected by Montaigne, that first assured 'the solitary reader' that the author shared his or her 'sense of singularity' (1983, p. 57). While there are great literary traditions associated with oral recitation and public performance, from the epics of Homer and the odes of Pindar to the plays of Shakespeare and the speeches of Edmund Burke, our defining image of literacy in the age of the mass production of books has been that of the solitary writer, often the unrecognized literary genius like Emily Dickinson, Franz Kafka, or John Kennedy Toole whose success is largely posthumous, or a solitary reader like Abraham Lincoln, Richard Wright, or Richard Rodriguez whose struggle to master the world of books lacks the immediate support of home or environment. What unites such readers and writers is the intense privacy of their respective experiences of literacy.

It was not, in other words, the invention of printing that created the modern practices of reading and writing. The first uses of new print techniques were to expand manuscript culture, even to the point of printing texts that looked like they were hand-lettered. Nor did printing immediately change reading, which remained an oral and largely social event (often in the form of Bible reading) until the industrial expansion of the eighteenth and nineteenth centuries. What transformed literacy was not the printing press, but profound changes in the organization of society brought on by the experience of industrialism. As Ian Watt explains in his classic study, *The Rise of the Novel*, it was a largely new, urban, aspiring middle class that was so passionately attracted to the intimacy of detail, the shared privacy of such genre-defining novels as Samuel Richardson's *Pamela* and *Clarissa*. There are, as Watt articulates, at least two apparent ironies connected to this cultural transformation: that this new intensity of identification with characters and other worlds 'should have been produced by exploiting the qualities of print, the most impersonal, objective and public of the media of communication' (1957, p. 206); and that a new literary genre that was 'less concerned with the public and more with the private side of life than any previous one' should have been the product of urbanization. With this new literary form came a new experience of reading. Readers of Richardson's novels, alone in their own quarters, learned more details about the private lives of his heroines than they often knew about members of their own family. It is not a coincidence that large numbers of new urban readers began for the first time in history recording their own intimate thoughts in another new literary form, the diary.

Although Richardson's narratives had a public dimension — news of Pamela's wedding was greeted with the ringing of church bells throughout England — the power of her story comes from its sense of shared intimacy. The picture here is of readers, secure in their closets, sharing the thoughts that Pamela and Clarissa, secure in their closets, have written down in diary-like letters. This sharing of secrets between writer and reader can be taken as a model of literate exchange in the age of print: with the diaries and personal reminiscences, the poems, stories, and novels, even the essays and philosophical discourses that comprise so much of the modern literate tradition, all seen as a vast series of Chinese puzzles in which the deeply felt, intensely private thoughts of one person are artfully packaged for others to read, or unfold, in their own time and in their own private place. The physical arrangement of urban life, with its provision for a private, inner sanctum, parallels the structure of the new literate text, what Milton in 'The Areopagitica' called the 'good book[,] ... the precious lifeblood of a master spirit, embalmed and treasured up on purpose to a life beyond life'.

The myriad workings of this parallelism between literacy and physical space is exemplified in Charlotte Brontë's intensely autobiographical novel, *Villette*. The novel itself is the outer package, with the trials of its heroine, Lucy Snow, as a governess at a boarding school for girls in Belgium carefully reproducing much of the author's own ordeal some ten years earlier at the Pensionnat Héger, although with the novelistic transformation of M. Héger, the object of authorial desire, from forbidden husband to the eligible suitor, M. Paul. But the layers of wrappings go much deeper than veiled autobiography, for in Lucy Snow's own experience with writing, Charlotte Brontë dramatizes the interiority of this new experience of literacy. Protestant and English in Catholic Belgium, Lucy feels herself not just unappreciated and isolated but under the constant surveillance of the school's proprietor Madame Beck. Although she eventually establishes a friendship with a local physician, Dr John, for a time imagining that she is in love with him, only when she receives a letter from him — what she rhapsodically describes as 'a morsel of real solid joy' (p. 318) — does she feel as if her self-worth (Eisenstein's 'sense of singularity') has been recognized.

Such a treasure, one she compares to the venison that the dying Isaac demanded of Esau, is not to be consumed lightly, nor in public. Her first thought then is to secure the letter in what little privacy was afforded her as a live-in governess.

> I stole from the room, I procured the key of the great dormitory which
> was kept locked by day. I went to my bureau; with a sort of haste and
> trembling lest Madame should creep upstairs and spy me, I opened a

drawer, unlocked a box, and took out a case, and — having feasted my eyes with one more look, and approached the seal, with a mixture of awe and shame and delight, to my lips — I folded the untasted treasure, yet all fair and inviolate, in silver paper, committed it to the case, shut up box and drawer, reclosed, relocked the dormitory, and returned to class, feeling as if fairy tales were true and fairy gifts no dream (p. 319).

While the letter may be temporarily safe — inside a case inside a box, inside a drawer, inside a locked dormitory — a public room was hardly an adequate place for the reading of something of such import. For this purpose, Lucy must find space further inside the hidden recesses of the house itself and further from the wakeful public world:

Taking a key whereof I knew the repository, I mounted three staircases in succession, reached a dark, narrow, silent landing, opened a worm-eaten door, and dived into the deep, black, cold garret. Here none would follow me — none interrupted — not Madame herself! (pp. 323–24).

Meanwhile the description of Lucy's actual reading of the letter plays the inner richness of the most solitary and arduous experience of the text against outer comforts of worldly pleasure. 'The poor English teacher in the frosty garret, reading by a dim candle guttering in the wintry air ... was happier than most queens in palaces.'

Yet, in ways that prove instructive for the fate of literacy in the twentieth century, the privacy that Lucy Snow so deliberately seeks turns out to be illusory. She is startled by an intruder while reading in the garret, and, more to the point, she discovers that Madame Beck, in an effort to exercise complete control over all happenings in her household, repeatedly searches Lucy's belongings, riffling through what has grown to be a small stack of letters. Madame Beck's takes on characteristics of an encroaching totalitarian state, one that attempts to control its inhabitants completely by denying them, if not the privacy of their own thoughts, then at least the space necessary for the reading and writing of such thoughts. 'In what corner of this strange house,' asks Lucy, 'was it possible to find security or secrecy? Where could a key be a safe-guard, or a padlock a barrier?' (p. 379).

Some hundred years later another English literary protagonist, George Orwell's Winston Smith, has an even more difficult time finding such a private 'safe-guard'. Everyone in Oceania is under continual surveillance, as if an extension of the domestic spying at Madame Beck's — 'The family had become in effect an extension of the Thought Police' (p. 111) — and, more to our purpose, by the latest in electronic technology, the telescreen, the harbinger of the contemporary closed-circuit video camera:

How often, or on what system, the Thought Police plugged in on any individual wire was guesswork. It was even conceivable that they watched everybody all the time. But at any rate they could plug in your wire whenever they wanted to. You had to live — did live, from habit that became instinct — in the assumption that every sound you made was overheard, and, except in darkness, every movement scrutinized. (pp. 6–7).

Here is Madame Beck's pension writ large. What has made *1984* such a foreboding image for modern society is the ruthlessness and totality to which it has committed all the resources of modern technology, not just to monitoring illicit activities, but to destroying the very condition of privacy necessary for any kind of independent thought. The ultimate objective here is to control thinking by controlling language itself — to limit written messages, for example, to 'printed postcards with long lists of phrases', from which the sender 'struck out the ones that were inapplicable' (p. 92):

> [T]he whole aim of Newspeak is to narrow the range of thought[.] In the end we shall make thoughtcrime literally impossible, because there will be no words in which to express it. Every concept that can ever be needed will be expressed by exactly *one* word, with its meaning rigidly defined and all its subsidiary meanings rubbed out and forgotten…. The Revolution will be complete when the language is perfect (pp. 46–47).

Oceania represents the triumph of totality, the creation of a world unified by a single system of belief. In *1984*, each of the traditional sources of resistance to such overweening social control fails Winston Smith — the unruliness of the working class (the 'proles'), the restorative power of the English countryside, the deep personal commitment of romantic love, and, most important for our purpose, a tradition of independent thought based on the permanence of written records.

Closely aligned with the control of language and thought in Oceania is the centralization of records in a system with a number of similarities to a modern electronic database, specifically the ability to perform the kind of global search-and-replace and global deletion that today we regularly perform with a word processor on our own individual documents. It is a world without an independent past: 'The past not only changed, but changed continuously' (p. 68), depending, of course, on the whims of the present. 'For how could you establish even the most obvious fact,' agonizes Orwell's hero, 'when there existed no record outside your own memory?' (p. 33).

Orwell's answer to this rhetorical question would seem to be that argued by Goody and Watt in their classic article, 'The Consequences of Literacy' (1963) — namely, that it is only the existence of written records, hence literacy itself, that makes possible countervailing intellectual positions and finally theoretical knowledge itself. Shakespeare may have proclaimed, 'Not marble, nor the gilded monuments/Of princes, shall outlive this powerful rhyme' (Sonnet 55), but George Orwell's Oceania is precisely a world where monuments live and words die. The triumph of totality in Oceania represents the end of literacy, not so much by the elimination of reading and writing — there is written language everywhere in Oceania — but by the elimination of the social conditions that have made literacy possible, including both the preservation of texts and the accessibility to privacy.

As developed by Eric Havelock in a series of elegant tracts culminating in *The Muse Learns to Write* (1986), our modern notion of theoretical knowledge is grounded in alternative ways of considering the world that do not have to be memorized or believed by society as a whole to retain their validity. Prose, writes Havelock, unlike the epic poetry of oral culture, became for classical Greece 'the vehicle of a whole new universe of fact and of theory' (p. 110), first seen, he notes, in 'the creation of "history" as essentially a prosaic enterprise'. There is history too in Oceania, Orwell would contend, but it is modeled after the earlier, oral Greek model of poetic accounts of the past as confirmation of widely shared social beliefs and practices. Although stored in written form, the records of the past have no permanence: 'Past events, it is argued, have no objective existence, but survive only in written records and in human memories. The past is whatever the records and the memories agree upon' (p. 176). And, as we have seen, both records and memories change instantly to fit current needs.

In such a world print literacy becomes not the expression and comprehension of anomalous ways of being in the world, but the ultimate act of subversion. While Smith's rebellion includes an illicit sexual relationship, it is his commitment to 'obsolete' ideas of books, and, in the form of his diary, to the technology of books themselves that most clearly marks his resistance to the new totality. As with Charlotte Brontë, there is in Orwell a passionate attachment, almost a fetish, for the materials of writing, to his pen described as 'an archaic instrument, seldom used even for signatures' (p. 9) and to his diary: 'A peculiarly beautiful book. Its smooth creamy paper, a little yellowed by age, was of a kind that had not been manufactured for at least forty years past.' In this world in which '[a]nything old, and for that matter anything beautiful, was always vaguely suspect' (p. 81), Smith's diary is an emblem of a tenuous, soon to be vanquished literate tradition:

> The diary would be reduced to ashes and himself to vapor. Only the Thought Police would read what he had written, before they wiped it out of existence and out of memory. How could you make appeal to the future when not a trace of you, not even an anonymous word scribbled on a piece of paper, could physically survive? (p. 26).

What is finally destroyed by the Thought Police is the freedom that George Orwell and Charlotte Brontë believed we are all offered in the resonance of written language, especially in those complex, personal, and often disturbing meanings we routinely hide away in what we write and ferret out of what we read. Perhaps it is only now, as many of the social conditions that have prevailed during print culture are starting to unravel, that we can at last see the historical contingency of such an attachment to the saving power of this kind of reading and writing.

'To much of the planet', writes George Steiner in the essay, 'The End of Bookishness', (1988) 'what I have called the classical act of reading, the private ownership of space, of silence, and of books themselves, never represented a natural or native formula.' For Steiner, changes in our use of space and silence, brought on by changes in electronic technology, all spell the end of a certain book culture, except perhaps as an object of nostalgic yearning. Gone, for example, is the 'circle of silence which enables the reader to concentrate on the text'. And for this Steiner is not entirely sad, for he sees that we have already lost most of the appreciation for the wondrous things contained in books. Book culture, he speculates, may exist in the future as it once existed in a more distant past, as the expression of a coterie, in what he calls '*houses of reading* — a Hebrew phrase — in which those passionate to learn how to read well would find the necessary guidance, silence, and complicity of disciplined companionship'.

For Steiner, as for Orwell and Brontë, privacy and book culture work together to oppose the totalizing impulse of the public realm. Reading and writing are considered as extensions of the privacy that individuals in industrial culture have traditionally found within their own homes; and one way of defining our modern sense of literacy is as the literary expression of the individual's opposition to the rigid systemization, what sociologist Max Weber referred to as the 'iron cage' of public life in industrial culture. It is not industry or technology that is the main threat, but a new public watchfulness they have engendered, the constant vigilance, abetted by new bureaucracies, that endangers privacy itself. It is an enemy that Foucault, among others, has seen represented by the 'inspection principle' of the nineteenth-century British philosopher and social reformer Jeremy Bentham. Bentham's scheme of educational reform pushes the notions of unfettered industrial efficiency and monomaniacal bureaucratic planning to the limit. Schools, factories, and prisons were all to be housed in a new kind of circular building, called a *Panopticon* (Greek for 'all seeing'), constructed with the master in the middle ('minimizing the distance between the situation of the remotest Scholar and that of the Master's eye'), with the floors inclined ('prevent[ing] remoter objects from being eclipsed by nearer ones'), and with a series of screens that would allow the 'Master to see without being seen' (p. 106).

Bentham readily comes across as the villain in a melodrama pitting literacy against totality, but what is not so clear is who is the hero, that is, in what other belief or institution will we find our principal source of resistance to totality? The obvious answer is the response of Orwell and Brontë and industrial culture as a whole, to rely on literacy itself, yet for increasing numbers of people the sides have suddenly shifted. The traditional practice of literacy, with its authors and readers sharing texts in isolation, is now often aligned with totality, while hope rests with radically new conceptions of the old enemies — the group, public discourse, and technology itself. As elaborated in new college-level writing pedagogies, totality is still the villain, but it is a totality envisioned as rigidly hierarchical in its formulation and distribution of knowledge, a top-down system that guarantees the dependence and isolation of individuals.

The countering force of literacy is thus no longer located in the individual writer and the letters he or she may dare to open only in the privacy of the heart, away from all forms of prying technology. As Patricia Greenfield writes, 'The screen makes an individual's thought processes public, open to others who can observe the screen' — a sentence which, if taken in isolation, can be read in the foreboding spirit of *1984*, as a warning that every classroom in America may soon have its own Madame Beck to force all private thoughts into the public realm. Greenfield's next sentence seems to sustain such a reading: 'It makes writing into an easily observable physical object, which can be manipulated in various ways by other people'. Is not manipulating text pejorative, as compared with creating or exploring it? Yet by the third sentence, the writer's new orientation is clear: 'Thus, the computer makes the private activity of writing into a potentially public and social one' (1984, p. 139). The public realm that threatened

Lucy Snow with exposure is now identified as a source of emotional support. 'Politics, Ideology, and the Strange, Slow Death of the Isolated Composer' begins a two-part title of a recent essay on computer-based writing instruction (Handa, 1990b), again hinting at an older critical tradition, only to make clear in the second half of the title just how much things have changed: 'Why We Need Community in the Writing Classroom'. The resistance of the 'isolated' individual rather than being the primary locus of literacy is now seen as the unfortunate, albeit at the time, maybe necessary response to a hostile, nonsupportive social order. In a new and better world, the primary locus of literacy will be the individual's collaboration with the community, facilitated by the latest computer technology.

Literacy still exists in opposition to totality, but it is a totality defined in terms of the entire authoritarian apparatus established to produce and disseminate what Richard Lanham calls the codex book (1989b). Totality is located not in the social forces depicted in *Villette* and *1984* but in what is perceived as essentially undemocratic institutions, like the traditional upper-division literature class with its lecture format and reverential attitude toward a fixed canon, that have been established over the last hundred years to foster the study of such works. In typically irreverent fashion, for example, Lanham derogates the printed book for being 'definitive, unchangeable' (1989b, pp. 31–32), the very qualities Orwell finds so critical:

> This definitive text has stood at the center of humanism, of liberal arts education, since the Renaissance. It defines the Great Books curriculum, and its passively adoring audience. The definitive great text communicates directly, in Arnold's words, 'what is excellent in itself, and the absolute beauty and fitness of things'. It works, that is, as a cultural communion wafer. We have only to receive to be saved (1989b, p. 32).

With the electronic text, Lanham continues, the entire hierarchical structure of book culture 'collapses'. The text is transformed from a fixed entity to something constantly shifting. For one thing, what Lanham calls the 'transparent surface' of the book, the basis for the 'identity and stability' is transformed into something dynamic. 'The pixeled word vaporizes Arnold's touchstones and the whole conception of the liberal arts as a museum of eternal masterpieces and verities — our conception — which is built upon it.' Or as Greg Ulmer adds with less enthusiasm but no more regret, the novel and the essay,

> the two principal forms of high literacy, invented to exploit fully the specific virtues of the print apparatus ... are disintegrating in the culture of electronics, creating a reservoir of simple forms available for new combinations reflecting the capabilities of the new apparatus (1989, p. 45).

And this change in the text itself mirrors an equally significant change in the reader: 'The electronic reader, unlike the passive reader whom Arnold took over from the newly silent Victorian public audience, need no longer be content with breathless admiration' (1989b, p. 32). Is not the silence of the concert hall that Lanham mocks the auditory equivalent of the spatial privacy required for traditional readers to be able to respond to intimate and probing writing, the kind of material that later in this same essay Lanham debunks as 'transparent expression of pure, apolitical, extrahuman truth' (p. 43)? The reader of the computer text, '[i]nstead of sifting a dubious classic as Arnold recommends, ... can fix it up' (p. 32). What is clear in Lanham is the conviction that it is not computer technology but book culture itself — what he calls '[o]ur whole critical apparatus, built as it is on final cuts, on beginnings, middles, endings, and the structures which depend therefrom' (p. 33) — that has to be re-examined:

> Codex books limit the wisdom of the Great Books to students who are Great Readers.... Electronic text blows that limitation wide open. It offers new ways to democratize the arts, of just the sort society is asking us to provide.

'Let us wage a war on totality', cries postmodern theorist Jean-François Lyotard (1984, p. 82), and few concerned with the present and future status of literacy would disagree. Everywhere we are impelled to oppose those cultural forces that suppress individual initiative in favor of a uniform, collective response, one usually determined by the needs of technology in support of the established power structure. It is as if modern culture is a vast morality play with the creative forces of the individual, or of regional and ethnic diversity, pitted against the relentless drive toward worldwide conformity in response to the demands of ever greater technological efficiency. The enemy here, like Satan himself, can take many forms, including that of a social reformer like Jeremy Bentham or, of perhaps of greater importance for this century, Frederick Winslow Taylor. In extending Henry Ford's model of greater industrial production and technical efficiency to management, Taylor formulated a distinctly American idea whose influence in its own quiet way has rivaled the theories of Marx. Taylorism revealed how the rationality of increased productivity could penetrate what had until then been thought of as a sphere of personal human relations, like the nuclear family itself, where values such as loyalty and trust counted more than statistical measurements of cost per unit.

Before Taylorism, the primary responsibility of management involved choosing the right person for the job, in much the same way we might select a carpenter to install a new patio door in our house. We try to select someone whose demeanor, responses to our inquiries, and references indicate that he or she indeed possesses the necessary skills. With Taylorism things change ominously. Now the first goal of management becomes acquiring the worker's knowledge, abstracting it, as it were, from the worker, so that the managers themselves could develop a rational system for installing patio doors, detail it in a company operating procedures, and then hire other, lower paid, less skilled workers to follow the step-by-step installation procedure that management has established. Or, as Taylor himself writes, the role of management is to collect

> all of the great mass of traditional knowledge, which in the past has been in the heads of the workmen ... then recording it, tabulating it, and, in many cases, finally reducing it to laws, rules, and even to mathematical formulae (1974, p. 40).

13

What had previously been a worker's personal experience is here transformed into public, scientific knowledge for the purpose of increasing production of goods.

Totality is at work here in replacing the unique experiences and diverse inner lives of countless workers with a single company protocol, the ubiquitous standard operating procedure:

> The chief objective of Scientific Management was to annex and control knowledge — both the *savoir-faire* of the workers and also the more systematic knowledge being produced by an increasingly organized research and development — because the possession of knowledge and skill represented the possession of control and power.... The idea of a planning department and a knowledge elite came to appeal to those concerned with the management, not of an individual enterprise, but of society at large (Webster and Robbins, 1986, p. 309).

What had been many is now one — and all for an abstraction, increased efficiency and productivity, that is unrelated (if not detrimental) to deeper, more spiritual human needs. The totality of Taylorism, and of modern life generally, can be expressed in the triumph of what French philosopher Jacques Ellul (1964) nearly thirty years ago referred to as technique: '[T]he totality of methods rationally arrived at and having absolute efficiency ... in every view of human activity' (p. xxv). In the modern age, explains Ellul, '[t]echnique has become autonomous; it has fashioned an omnivorous world which obeys its own laws and which has renounced all tradition' (p. 14).

Just where, we need to ask, does literacy fit into this world without tradition? What is the role of reading and writing in a social world seemingly under the sway of such a totalizing technique? And, more to the point, how is literacy likely to be affected by the introduction into the very processes of reading and writing of new computer-based technologies for manipulating texts? Does it make more sense to see the computer as an extension of Benthamism and Taylorism into what we had previously tended to think of as the largely private realm of reading and writing texts, or does the computer represent an historical opportunity to escape social control in all its forms? It is one thing to consider the nature of reading and writing in a modern, industrial society, one where the principal mode of economic production is manufacturing and the principal mode of literate exchange the book. It may be a different matter entirely to understand reading and writing in what Daniel Bell first labeled a *post-industrial society*, a world where increasingly the principal mode of economic production is information management and the principal mode of literate exchange is the evanescent video display terminal.

What will be the role of literacy, or its nature, in a world where economic expansion will be propelled forward by teams of workers collaborating through computer networks, not as it was in the last century, by amateur tinkerers working in isolation — by bicycle mechanics like the Wright brothers inventing aircraft, by an elocution teacher like Alexander Graham Bell inventing the telephone, and by a mathematical illiterate like Thomas Edison inventing practically everything else? What happens if idiosyncratic and anomalous thinking becomes seen as leading, not to scientific (and humanistic) discovery and material (and spiritual) progress, but reckless adventurism or environmental exploitation? How should we organize language instruction in light of Daniel Bell's prediction that such expansion in the future will be the result of a huge amount of complex and theoretical knowledge being developed and shared by millions of people across immense communication networks? What happens to the value of one's private experience with language in a new century that may be even more dependent than the last on the rationalizing and systematizing of knowledge, the totality of technique, that lay at the core of Taylorism, a future world where in Bell's words, 'information and theoretical knowledge are the strategic resources ... just as the combination of energy, resources, and machine technology were the transforming agencies of the industrial society' (1975, p. 206)? It is easy to agree with Lyotard that

> the proliferation of information-processing machines is having, and will continue to have, as much of an effect on the circulation of learning as did advancements in human circulation (transportation systems) and later, in the circulation of sounds and visual images (the media) (1964, p. 4).

What remains difficult is to know what specific changes in the practice or the nature of literacy to expect, and, perhaps more importantly, to decide how we are to feel about them. So many discussions in this area lead in the direction of gauging the impact of computers on standards of literacy: Will they make us more or less literate? But, as we have seen, our sense of what it means to be literate is likely to shift in the very process of analysis, with the result of our arguing at cross purposes. The only solution here is to problematize literacy, to look more carefully at precisely what it is we have achieved through the technology of print and how such achievements may be affected by emerging electronic technologies. We should recast the question about changing standards of literacy in terms of totalizing forces within society: Are computers likely to decrease or increase totalizing pressures in society? Is the ability to collect, organize, and access vast amounts of information likely to increase or decrease the ability of individuals to make their own way in the world, and just how is this sense of freedom specifically related to 'standards of literacy'? Such questions point to the central concern of this chapter, and of the book as a whole — the complex relationship between technology, the world it creates, and whatever we have meant (and, in the future, will mean) by literacy.

At the center of book culture is the book itself — now often seen, as will be examined in Chapter 3, not as a safe haven from sinister forms of social control, but as the embodiment of new forms of authorial tyranny. Those nostalgic for the book, however, like most of the contributors to the ironically titled collection *Beyond Literacy*, still find it possible to praise its technology and its ideology. It is cheap, portable, flexible, and private: 'If just one person in a room switches on a hi-fi or a TV set', writes Martyn Goff, 'everyone's aural attention is trespassed. But dozens of people in a room can be reading a different book at the same moment without disturbing anyone else' (Howell, 1989, p. 80). It is also, Goff notes, a bulwark against totality: 'New technologies [like 'transmitted programmes'] can be controlled in a way that is impossible via the book' (p. 81); and to strengthen his point he quotes from Barbara Tuchman's lecture at the Center for the Book at the Library of Congress: 'Books by their heterogeneity can never represent a managed culture.' Finally, as another contributor concludes, books are most important as 'channels of transformation', in getting us 'outside of ourselves'. Books here 'are like soldiers on the front lines of consciousness in the war against meaninglessness in life' (Howell, 1989, p. 44).

How different the attitude is in Jay Bolter's discussion of how a printed copy, compared to a manuscript or a typescript, 'because of its visual simplicity, regularity, and reproducibility' enhances the authority of the writer. 'As the author in print became more distant, less accessible to the reader, the author's words became harder to dismiss' (1991, p. 149). The ascendancy of New Criticism in the first half of this century, Bolter notes, 'made explicit ... [an] assumption of all writing in the age of printing. Through the technology of printing, the author and the editor exercise absolute control over the text: nothing they do can be undone after publication' (1991, p. 149). Compare this passivity (indirectly that of a model citizen in a totalitarian state) with the energized, almost frenetic control that Lanham sees student readers of computerized texts exercising even (or especially) over our most prized (entombed?) literary classics. Here he imagines such a student discarding a printed copy of *Paradise Lost* for a computerized version on CD-ROM.

> Wouldn't you begin to play games with it? A weapon in your hands after 2500 years of pompous pedantry about the Great Books, and you not to use it? Hey man, how about some music with this stuff? Let's *voice* this rascal and see what happens. Add some graphics and graffiti! Print it out in San Francisco [the kooky face I used above] for Lucifer, and 𝕲𝖔𝖙𝖍𝖎𝖈 𝖋𝖔𝖗 𝕲𝖔𝖉. Electronic media will change not only future literary texts but past ones as well (1989a, p. 269).

As Lanham comments elsewhere, students today do not possess, nor should they, the capacity for silence and reverence before the printed page (akin to the quiet of a concert hall or museum); they possess, instead, skills honed by a new electronic technology that, in the long run, are more important for real democratic participation — namely, 'volatility, interactivity, easy scaling changes, a self-conscious typography, collage techniques of invention and arrangement, a new kind of self-consciousness about the "publication" and the "publicity" that lies at the end of expression' (1990, pp. xiv–xv).

The codex book may be an inefficient technology for managing information, but, we must ask, what about the traditional role of the book as the embodiment of experience? Books take up too much space, require the destruction of forests, and eventually deteriorate, but we have often turned to them, at least in the past, less for the information they contain — the discrete items which can be extracted, indexed in a giant concordance, and compressed to a few bytes in an electronic database — than for other, more literary values having to do with the wholeness of vision, the expressive power, and the empathetic imagination they embody. And yet are not these literary or 'romantic' qualities in texts, what some may see as the saving power of literacy in the struggle against totality, the same qualities that Lyotard sees as limiting human development over the last two centuries? 'It is the great age of book culture,' he writes, 'the nineteenth and twentieth centuries [that] have given us as much terror as we can take'. He continues in words that clearly connect his sense of the war on totality as a war on an older, deadening literate culture: 'We have paid a high enough price for the nostalgia of the whole and the one, for the reconciliation of the concept and the sensible, of the transparent and the communicable experience' (1984, pp. 81–82).

That the culture of the book and nightmarish attacks on humanity are both products of the last two centuries can hardly be denied. What obviously remains in question, despite Lyotard's assertion, is the connection between the two, so sweepingly claimed by Lyotard and, as is apparent in the following passage, by other postmodernists as well.

> We do not know what 'lines of escape' the pathology of our present discursive practices may reveal; even so the reactive path which claims to (re-)construct meaning and (re-)establish community is all too well known. After the experience of the twentieth Century, the unpresentable cannot hold more terror for us than the known; the unpresentable has become the salvational, if only through default. (Horne, 1989, p. 300)

It has become fashionable for both the right and the left to attack what German social critic Jürgen Habermas labels the 'rational content of cultural modernity that was captured in bourgeois ideals', what he sees as the three great achievements of modern Western society: historically new attitudes (1) about the expanding nature of truth ('the specific theoretical dynamic that continually pushes the sciences, and even the self-reflection of the sciences, *beyond* merely engendering technically useful knowledge'); (2) about the value of democratic institutions for self-government ('the universalistic foundations of law and morality that have *also* been incorporated (in however distorted and incomplete a fashion) into the institutions of constitutional government, into the forms of democratic will formation, and into individualistic patterns of identity formation'); and (3) about the unsettling but creative value of art and, one might add, literacy ('the productivity and explosive power of basic aesthetic experiences that a subjectivity liberated from the imperatives of purposive activity and from conventions of quotidian perception gains from its own decentering') (Habermas, 1987, p. 113).

The assumption in critiques such as Lyotard's and Horne's is either that such accomplishments are not worth protecting or that they are not actually a part of the modernist world that is to be disassembled; that such accomplishments, as it were, reflect universalistic values that can be readily detached from their historical roots. That the future must be better than the past may be only a rash prediction; that what will make the future better is our overthrowing the discourse practices of book culture involves a truly revolutionary change in our understanding of the nature and value of literacy. While some sort of change in our thinking about reading and writing may prove necessary, especially in light of the connections we will attempt to establish between literacy and industrial technology in Chapter 2, it seems reckless to do so lightly, in the spirit of Lyotard and Horne, without a full understanding of, perhaps even a certain nostalgia for, what it exactly is we are about to lose.

'The better we understand society', states the French sociologist Émile Durkheim, 'the better shall we be able to account for all that happens in that social microcosm that the school is' (1956, p. 131). The origins of pedagogy, what

Durkheim calls the 'construction of a technique', lies 'not in the individual, but in the collectivity' (p. 132), that is, in our ability to provide historical, not psychological, insight into the educational process. Where we need to look to understand the evolution of literacy, Durkheim implies, is in the larger connections between schools and society and between pedagogy and production. Behind the contemporary controversy over the impact of computers on literacy lie contrasting attitudes about the most basic questions relating to the material conditions of modern life: Are conditions improving or deteriorating? And what kinds of human activities generally and reading and writing activities specifically will be important in promoting whatever one means by human progress? What we need to examine, in Richard Lanham's words, is the 'computer as fulfillment of social thought' (1992). The introduction of printing in the sixteenth century may have led to a marked decline in literacy, at least of a literacy that defines reading as the ability to recite from memory long passages of important texts and writing, and as the ability to produce beautiful and accurate manuscript copy. With the onslaught of industrialization, the reading and writing skills of manuscript culture were no longer economically important for material progress, and so the loss of these skills was not widely seen as decline. Rather, new reading and writing skills, with more direct links to material progress, emerged and, by the industrial age, led to the rise of a new standard of literacy, which defined writing as the ability to embody a new or personal understanding of the world in a whole text, and reading as the ability to comprehend that new or personal understanding embodied in the texts of others.

In the twilight of that industrial age, the process may well be repeating itself, with the emergence of new notions of reading and writing based on new technologies necessary for continued material progress. The economic foundation of Daniel Bell's information age consists of wealth generated from the efficient 'storage, retrieval, and processing of data' (1975, p. 168). For Bell, the almanacs, atlases, encyclopedias, and other reference works that have been efficient purveyors of information for the last five hundred years, may all prove inadequate for an age when wealth depends upon the rapid exchange of information. At one level, there seems to be a fairly limited range in the rate at which individuals can process information: speaking, 150 wpm (words per minute); listening, 250 wpm; typing, 60 wpm; and reading, 360 wpm (Lucky, 1989, p. 148) — all numbers with which as consumers and producers of texts we are vaguely familiar. At another level altogether, however, there is the rate at which we as a society can process information; here the problem is not, as with individuals, rates at which words can be processed, but rates at which words can be physically transmitted between computer terminals and various storage media.

The notion of literacy as the engagement with content tends to trivialize problems involving the storage and retrieval of materials. Even if we admit they are important problems (and they are), we are unlikely to consider them as problems involving the nature of literacy. Nor, as noted earlier, have we often defined college-level research skills as central to literacy, even while making them part of the regular curriculum for first-year composition classes. We have for hundreds of years depended upon lower-level functionaries in the chain of literacy — librarians and, to a lesser extent, bookstore clerks — to have the material ready for us when we want it. But consider how the problem of comprehending a text changes when the text one wants to 'read' is a needle in an information haystack.

It would take, for example, some 200,000 pages to print authors and titles of worldwide articles in chemistry in just the past decade. According to Louie and Rubeck (1989), there are 7000 journals in science each producing more than 142 articles per year, for a total of over one million articles in a single year! By the year 2040, Bell (1975) speculates, the Yale University Library would need a staff of 6000 just to catalogue and store the books and reports that would come in each year, a situation analogous to the number of telephone operators that would be needed today (the equivalent of the entire female work-force) to handle the current volume of calls using the older operator-assisted technology (p. 191). Or maybe more troubling are the 100,000 mathematical theorems that are published each year in journals. '"If the number of theorems is larger than one can possibly learn", Stanislau Ulam mused during a talk, "who can be trusted to judge what is 'important?'" One cannot have survival of the fittest if there is no interaction' (Louie and Rubeck, 1989, p. 20).

Given such numbers, the problem of filing and retrieving — of finding what one wants — all of a sudden moves out of the background of literacy, and the whole field of information technology, with its new terminology, takes on a new importance. The entire encyclopedia, for example, which traditionally requires so many feet of shelf space, can now fit on 180 floppy disks or, more miraculously, on a single compact disk. In fact, according to Robert Lucky (1989, p. 101), we need only 18,000 such disks to store the entire contents of the Library of Congress — and while it would take some 1900 years to transmit the contents of those 18,000 disks over conventional phone lines, such a transfer can be accomplished in less than twenty-four hours with the latest fiber optic technology (p. 102), the kind being considered for a proposed information super highway system, the National Research and Education Network (NREN). To the extent that we want or need immediate access to vast amounts of materials (the subject of Chapter 3), such technological innovations are liable to revolutionize both our practice and concept of literacy.

But what happens, we may ask, to the private thoughts of individuals transmitted through writing, so highly valued by Brontë and Orwell, in a world characterized by radically more efficient means of storing and retrieving information? For Bell, and, as we shall see, for most enthusiasts of new computer-based technologies of reading and writing, such a question seems misguided, for the greater danger to literacy is the continuance, not the disappearance, of an established literate tradition that they would define as inhibiting truly individual response by sanctioning only hegemonic texts. 'The nature of modern technology', concludes Bell (1975), 'frees location from resource site', that is, in the case of literacy, frees texts from the weight of authorizing institutions, thus 'open [ing] the way to alternative modes of achieving individuality and variety within a vastly increased output of goods' (p. 207), or again, in the case of literacy, the output of texts. Simply stated, computer technology has the potential to open up the entire process of reading and writing, undermining a stolid, entrenched literary tradition of 'classic' authors and in turn allowing everyone to read and write, to exchange texts, on an equal basis. 'Like Orwell's Ministry of Truth', writes Robert Lucky of Bell Labs, 'word processors have done away with the idea of permanency. And what a burden it was!' (p. 164)

We have come full circle, with two warring factions — those championing computer-based literacy and those championing print — seemingly joined only by their common rejection of totality. On one hand, there is the literacy of Lucy Snow and Winston Smith that believes that only when we are alone with written language are we most deeply free and most deeply human; on the other, there is the literacy of Lanham and Lyotard that sees us most under the sway of totalizing forces when as isolated supplicants we approach texts as traditional readers, and most liberated from such forces when working at a computer terminal. The former, grounded in print technology (hence the term *print literacy*), is intricately connected to the ascendancy of modern industrial culture of the last 200 years; the latter, grounded in computer technology (hence the term *online literacy*), is equally connected to various contemporary attempts to move away from industrial culture, to define a new, postindustrial, postmodern sensibility.

On one level, this book is a study of the clash of these two literate traditions, but more than that it is an attempt to historicize that clash, to reveal the common ground, in economic production itself, that connects what seem to be opposite positions. It is an attempt to understand this impasse — two sides fighting against the same enemy, totality, only locating it in the other's camp — by connecting dominant modes of communication and expression, particularly evident in the most passionate programs for education reform, to major transformations in economic production. The governing thesis here is that the most visible and most successful educational reformers are borne aloft, not by their own, occasionally inflated rhetoric, but by a rising tide of profound technological change in how we as a society generate wealth.

What such a thesis suggests is the existence of a more pervasive, largely hidden affiliation between members of opposing camps, for example, between educational reformers seemingly as diverse as Richard Lanham, now writing at the start of a new postindustrial age, and Jeremy Bentham, who wrote at the equally momentous dawn of the industrial age. The differences are clear enough: one seemed intent on basing educational practice on the total control of the student by the school administration, a principle adapted from industrial technology; the other seems to want to give students almost complete control of their education by utilizing the techniques of computer technology. But what is easily lost in this contrast is the fact that both Bentham and Lanham are first and foremost reformers whose schemes for educational reorganization gain power by paralleling fundamental changes in technology. What connects Lanham to someone like Bentham, the embodiment of the bureaucratic efficiency that Lanham and so many others oppose, is the recognition in each that the truly important changes in pedagogy and other patterns of cultural reproduction are in accord with underlying, more basic changes in economic production.

Lanham, for example, is eloquent in recounting how English emerged over the last hundred years as a discipline well suited to educate its original 'white, literate, and at least middle class' audience. 'English studies', he writes, 'now provides a superb instrument to educate such a society. That society, alas, no longer exists.' Students in college English classes nationwide are increasingly non-white, while what is left of the original white middle class is no longer 'reliably literate'. 'English studies', Lanham concludes, 'like so many armies in the past, now stands superbly equipped to fight the last war' (1984, p. 16). It is into this vacuum that Lanham pushes what he calls digital rhetoric, the kind of creative computer-based manipulation and delivery of text and images already briefly discussed. Here is the voice of a reformer, the true believer:

If groups of people newly come to the world of liberal learning cannot unpack the Silenus box of wisdom with the tools they bring, maybe we can redesign the box electronically, so the tools they have, the talents they already possess, will suffice (1989b, p. 33).

While Lanham sees English studies prepared to fight the last war, Bentham confronted the desperate educational needs of an emerging industrial, urban society with practically no army, no organized system of education, at hand. The local, small-scale, paternalistic educational and charitable organizations that had served isolated rural populations in England for hundreds of years were totally inadequate for the newly mobile, largely anonymous population that congregated around new manufacturing centers. The first state grant for elementary education, for example, was not made until 1833, and that was for only £20,000, while even by mid-century there were still only 681 certified teachers with over two million students attending day schools. In education and social services generally, Bentham was attempting to lay the groundwork for the modern welfare state by designing efficient, somewhat austere government services, the kind that are continually attacked across the entire political spectrum. Is it any wonder, then, that he should turn for his model to the organizing principles of control and efficiency that were transforming the physical world?

Lanham's enthusiasm for a new computer technology pales in comparison to that of the utilitarian for the classroom based on the efficient, mutually beneficial pedagogic structure of industrial production. Here, from a letter of 1813 reprinted by Bentham in *Chrestomathia*, his plan for education reform, a fellow reformer rhapsodizes on the advantages of the new system which ensures that 'every boy [out of a class of one hundred] is employed every minute of the time he is in school, either in the acquisition or the communication of knowledge':

> The fifteen highest boys are monitors. The first thing to be done after the meeting of the class, is to see that they have their lessons distinctly. When this is ascertained, the whole class goes into divisions. In this way fifteen times as much work can be done in the same space, and, I can say with confidence, fifteen times better. From this contrivance, instead of the languor and restlessness that too frequently prevails, all is activity and energy. More noise, indeed, is heard; but the sounds are sweet, for they are the sounds of labour. Everyone studies, because by the exertion of his talents, he finds himself equal to every task; and his ignorance is more shameful, where the account is to be rendered to one of his own years, than to a man (p. 137).

Can one imagine a fairer, more harmonious picture of the self-regulation of society, a happier picture of *laissez-faire* economy where the natural expression of competing interests leads to the common good?

It is easy to dismiss the self-serving naiveté of utilitarian reformers who could boast that 'the principle in schools and manufactories is the same' (Adamson, 1964, p. 24). But just how different is the enthusiasm for computer-based literacy? Is it not also based on a re-alignment of pedagogy with technologies and practices of a new workplace, one based on computer-mediated collaboration? As James Berlin, critic of traditional writing pedagogy, notes, 'In teaching writing we are tacitly teaching a version of reality and the student's place and mode of operation in it' (1982, p. 766). Berlin's point here is that students need to assume the same independence from a central authority and the same willingness to work with their colleagues that characterize the best contemporary model of work:

> In our writing classrooms we continue to offer a view of composing that insists on a version of reality that is sure to place students at a disadvantage in addressing the problems that will confront them in both their professional and private experience (Berlin, 1982, p. 777).

Is not the goal here, as with the utilitarians, to found school and work on the same liberating principles? As Carolyn Handa notes, in disparaging traditional educational practice, 'The world we learned to write in is not the world they will be living and writing in' (1990b, p. 182).

The remaining four chapters represent an attempt to provide a fuller historical context for evaluating the role of the two literacies, one print-based, one online, in preparing us to change the world or possibly just to fit into it. Chapter 2 provides an historical overview of print literacy, making explicit how the strengths and weaknesses of the high-level practice of literacy embedded in college-level English studies for the last century is intimately tied to the rise and seeming fall of industrial culture. The final three chapters consider different ways in which online literacy is connected to fundamental changes in that culture — with Chapter 3 looking at new ways of reading and organizing knowledge represented by hypertext, Chapter 4 at new ways of writing and communicating via computer networks, and Chapter 5 at the impact of graphics and multimedia on shaping a new form of online literacy, one better able to meet traditional human needs in a highly non-traditional, post-print age.

As what we mean by *literacy* changes (as it will), specific arguments about progress and decline will prove less instructive than an historical understanding of the process itself — an understanding of where our notions of being literate, of reading, and of writing come from, and how and why they are likely to evolve. Only such an understanding can provide an adequate basis for discussing the larger issues of language and public policy. To argue about the impact of computers on literacy otherwise is akin to designing buildings and bridges without a concern for the geological forces actively reshaping the earth's crust. As educators and citizens, we may not be able to alter the course of history by our own efforts, but like prudent architects and engineers we can survey the terrain, locating the bedrock that can provide the foundation of sound pedagogic practices and social structures.

Chapter 2

The Technology of Print

Were we required to characterise this age of ours by any single epithet, we should be tempted to call it not an Historical, Devotional, Philosophical, or Moral Age, but, above all others, the Mechanical Age. It is the Age of Machinery, in every outward and inward sense of that word; the age which, with its undivided might, forwards, teaches and practises the great art of adapting means to ends.

Thomas Carlyle, 'Signs of the Times'

In his widely noted 1987 book, *Cultural Literacy*, E.D. Hirsch uncovered what seemed to him, and to many others, two obvious weaknesses in our educational system: students neither read with much understanding nor did they have much general knowledge about notable historical or current events. Surely, he reasoned, the two must be connected: the more people know in general about what they are about to read, the more likely it is that they will understand it. Modern educators have been wrong, he concludes, in considering literacy solely as a technical skill — the ability to gain a new understanding of anything based solely on the act of reading. We cannot understand new information, he argued, without a proper frame of reference, one that is based upon at least a passing knowledge of our common cultural experience.

Hirsch was hardly prepared for the numbers and intensity of his critics. He has said on countless occasions that his goal is to help all Americans, not just a select few, to become fully literate. Attacked for having a hidden conservative agenda — one that defines cultural literacy in terms of a fixed set of establishment ideas and figures — Hirsch fired back that any list of basic information should grow as needed and that it should include all sorts of revolutionary ideas and figures, Karl Marx as well as Adam Smith. Too often this is how the debate proceeded, and ended: can cultural literacy be reduced to a list? What should be on it? What happens with whatever is excluded, and what is involved in teaching or mastering such a list? This often rancorous debate has much to tell us about the subject of this chapter — the largely hidden, historical basis of print literacy. In this sense, both Hirsch and his critics were right in sensing, if not fully articulating, how our conception of literacy goes beyond questions of classroom practices (for example, the longstanding debate over whether initial reading instruction should be based on whole words or phonics) to reflect a great deal about our sense of ourselves, who we are as a people and, through our educational system, who we want to become.

At one level, Hirsch is concerned with pedagogy. He is adamant in opposing what he sees as the trend of progressive education, over much of this century, to emphasize a scientific, valueless technique over rich historical content. But his concern with content masks a larger ideological interest that becomes evident if we look more closely at his attitude about electronic technology. Consider, for example, how readily computers could be adapted to address what Hirsch sees as the main problem of student readers, the lack of background information. What better use of computers, Victor Raskin (1992) suggests, than for the construction of a large database that in only a keystroke or two would provide novice readers working at a terminal with such information. Stumbling upon a reference to the Magna Carta, such a reader need only place the cursor somewhere on the phrase and press a designated key, or click with a mouse, and a small box would appear on the screen with information about how this document, signed in 1215, guaranteed certain English rights. The technology exists, moreover, for including graphics, even sounds and animation, with such explanatory text. Although Hirsch's notion of cultural literacy requires only minimal knowledge, this technique of moving from a specific reference to a database with information about that reference can be continued indefinitely so that the reader could request more information once inside the first explanation, for example, about the location and geography of Runnymede, about what else was happening in the year 1215, about other significant events in the history of English civil liberties. What is important here are not all the exciting possibilities that such computer-based reading offers (the subject of Chapter 3) but Hirsch's lack of interest in computers, indeed, his peremptory dismissal of them as a possible solution for what he sees as the main obstacle to Americans' achieving a higher standard of literacy.

One might be tempted to explain Hirsch's lack of interest by noting that his ideas germinated in the years preceding the spread of personal computers. He just does not know enough about computers to consider them as a serious solution. Yet the one direct reference to computers in Hirsch's book suggests there is more at stake here: 'The more computers we have', he argues, 'the more we need shared fairy tales, Greek myths, historical images, and so on' (p. 31). Rather than representing a potential cure for our reading and writing ills, computers are seen as part of the more general movement in culture toward increased specialization, and hence are for Hirsch part of the disease for which the 'antidote ... is to reinvigorate the unspecialized domain of literate discourse'.

Literacy and technological change, as characterized by Hirsch in *Cultural Literacy*, are opposing cultural forces: 'Advancing technology, with its constant need for fast and complex communications, has made literacy more essential to commerce and domestic life' (p. 3). Yet is it not possible, we might ask, to postulate an entirely different relationship between literacy and technology, one in which computers are seen as a technology for extending literacy by making all sorts of stored materials, pictures as well as texts, more accessible? Such an approach, if adopted, would reverse Hirsch's position, causing us to re-word his sentence as follows: 'Advancing technology, with its increasing ability to provide for the fast and natural communication of text, voice, and graphics, has simplified the literacy skills essential for commerce and domestic life.' Consider, for example, how much easier computers have made communicating by voice over long distances — it takes little technical skill to complete a telephone call to almost any place in the world, and with the simple installation of a FAX machine to send printed material as well. Can we not imagine working backward from this high technology present to a switchboard, operator-controlled telephone system where users and operators had to be able to give and receive verbal instructions, referring to a wealth of local places and practices, in many different languages?

Might we not be able to expect comparable breakthroughs in other forms of communication? Are we not looking at a future where advances in computer scanning of text, voice recognition, and voice synthesis may allow people who cannot write (that is, cannot encode speech) to produce written documents, perhaps controlling margins, fonts, and a variety of other graphic features using oral commands — and people who cannot read (that is, cannot decode text) to listen to a computer 'read' (recite) any written text. Rather than heightening the demands of literacy, such computer-based technologies may well wind up relieving us of many of the traditional burdens entailed in transcribing and decoding texts.

It may be this possibility of literacy becoming too easy, somehow degraded by technology, that most concerns not just Hirsch but some of his most ardent opponents as well. A readily identifiable collection of such opponents is the sixty elementary, secondary, and college teachers who met for three weeks during the summer of 1987 to chart the future of American language education. It is noteworthy that this group, representing eight professional organizations and known as the English Coalition, achieved consensus initially through its unanimous rejection of Hirsch's views, as presented to them, first by an official of the Department of Education and then by Hirsch himself. Admittedly, the English Coalition report is in a number of places more open to computers and video than Hirsch, noting at one point how 'electronic technologies supplement and alter literacy as it has been traditionally defined' (p. 37), and specifically endorsing the pedagogic potential for computer-based electronic mail and bulletin boards. Instead of rigorously pursuing this notion of a new, technologically enhanced literacy, the report at key places basically re-states Hirsch's position that technology is making literacy both more necessary and more difficult:

> The information explosion makes learning how to read and write absolutely vital for living, because without these abilities students will not be able to assimilate, evaluate, and control the immense amount of knowledge and the great number of messages which are produced every day. The development of new media similarly requires of citizens an enhanced ability to use different ways of reading and writing (p. 86).

Behind this widespread distrust of computers is a common defining image, one of a glut of information overwhelming the critical and synthesizing powers of the individual, making the mastery of literacy more important and more difficult. Computers can facilitate the movement of information, from one database to another, and eventually to our individual terminal and from there into our own work. But what is truly learned in this process of moving bits and bytes around the world at close to the speed of light? Can literacy be defined as the exchange of information — in which case greater processing power necessarily leads to higher levels of literacy? Or does our increased facility with manipulating electronic information threaten to diminish rather than enhance our greater understanding, our more powerful critical knowledge of the world? As T.S. Eliot asks in 'Choruses from *The Rock*', 'Where is the knowledge we have lost in information?'

Those who would sympathize with Eliot's misgivings about a new information age are well arrayed across the political spectrum, from Hirsch on the right to the English Coalition on the left; all share the same suspicion growing out of the need to distinguish between the manipulation of information and real thought, a distinction often present in the titles of the critiques themselves: Joseph Weizenbaum's *Computers and Human Reason: From Judgment to Calculation*; Theodore Roszak's *The Cult of Information: The Folklore of Computers and the True Art of Thinking*; Langdon Winner's *Autonomous Technology: Technics-out-of-Control as a Theme in Political Thought* (1977); and Hubert Dreyfus's *What Computers Can't Do: The Limits of Artificial Intelligence*. The 'what computers can't do' in Dreyfus's title is quite simply to think, and to the extent that all the razzle-dazzle power of computers to manipulate text and information lulls us into thinking otherwise, they represent a dangerous force. As Roszak writes, 'The powers of reason and imagination which the schools exist to celebrate and strengthen are in danger of being diluted with low-grade mechanical counterfeits' (1986, p. xi). Or in the stronger language of Michael Shallis, author of *The Silicon Idol* (1984), information technology in all its forms is 'the invention of the devil ... born destructive ...', a force that 'enchants people into false belief in a false god' (p. 176). Shallis's conclusion: 'We need to be informed about the machines that "think" but we should be ashamed to use them' (p. 178).

Radical educational critic Michael Apple sums up the concerns of many regarding the dangers involved in increasing the use of computers in our schools. For Apple, the fundamental conflict is between, on the one hand, 'economic and ideological pressures' to make 'the "needs" of business and industry the primary goals of the school system' and, on the other, 'concerns for a democratic curriculum, teacher autonomy, and class, gender, and race equality' (1986, pp. 153–54). Of particular concern to Apple is the tendency of high technology to impoverish the lives both of most workers, creating 'enhanced jobs for a relative minority and deskilled and boring work for the majority' (p. 159), and most teachers, replacing direct pedagogic intervention with prepackaged software. Once again, unabated technology results in questions of 'how to' replacing questions of 'why':

> At root, my claim will be that the debate about the role of the new technology in society and in schools is not and must not be just about the technical correctness of what computers can and cannot do. These may be the least important kinds of questions, in fact. Instead, at the very core of the debate, are the ideological and ethical issues concerning what schools should be about and whose interests they should serve (Apple, 1986, p. 153).

Once again there is a basic dichotomy between technique, what is on the surface, and insight, what is arrived at only by analysis. Apple concludes,

> computers involve ways of thinking that are primarily *technical*. The more the new technology transforms the classroom in its own image, the

more a technical logic will replace critical political and ethical understanding. The discourse of the classroom will center on technique, and
less on substance (p. 171).

It is worth noting that Apple, normally considered an educational radical,
is here reiterating a widely held belief, one that he shares with the nominally
conservative Hirsch as well as with the mainstream English Coalition report: that
substance is more valuable than technique, that insight is more valuable than
manipulation, that the speed and mechanical efficiency of word processing stands
in opposition to what Roszak calls 'the art of thinking'. Even radical critics like
C. Paul Olson who are less suspicious of technology than Apple do not so much
oppose this view as avoid it by redirecting attention to other matters, for
example, assuring greater access to computers for minority students. That the
underlying distinctions between thinking and manipulating has such wide
currency is itself a sign of its centrality to our modern notion of print literacy and
to the broad cultural values upon which that notion is based. The belief that
computers are a threat that needs to be countered by a re-invigorated literacy
seems to be part of the landscape of contemporary language education, its ideological foundation lying far beneath the kinds of political considerations that
would ordinarily separate such politically diverse writers as Hirsch, Apple, and
the drafters of the English Coalition.

Yet where, we might ask, does *this* idea come from, this pervasive, largely
unexamined belief in the opposition of literacy and technology? What do we
really mean by related phrases that we so often use unreflectively: to have *insight*,
to think *deeply*, not superficially, and, possibly most important of all, to think
critically? Why is remaining on the surface, where we spend almost all our lives
interacting with friends and family, bad, and burrowing ourselves deep beneath
the surface in a dark and lonely spot far from all other human beings, good?
Despite all the heated public discussions of literacy, we still lack an adequate
understanding of its historical basis. In particular, we fail to understand how our
current notion of literacy — seemingly in staunch opposition to industrial technology — is itself largely shaped by that technology. As literate offspring of
industrialism, we are too quick to assert the independence of our critical apparatus, in no small way, as in an Oedipal melodrama, by projecting and then
attacking a tyrannical parent. We are forced to critique print culture with the
same critical apparatus we want to examine. The solution to this dilemma is not
merely to be critical but to be critical about critique, to historicize this most basic
concept of print literacy, to see how it evolved in the nineteenth century and how
it may be playing itself out in the twentieth. What such an effort will produce is
the recognition that our current model of print literacy tends to be concerned less
with reading and writing skills or with a specific technology for producing texts
than with the creation of the mental disposition that would allow an individual to
prosper in a given historical moment, one largely shaped by a dominant (albeit
unacknowledged) technology of production as well as communication.

Just what this underlying technology is for Hirsch is hardly a mystery. *Cultural
Literacy* from beginning to end is imbued with the spirit of an earlier, pre-modern
manifestation of print literacy, one which developed out of a pre-industrial,
Jeffersonian world of independent yeomen, farmers and merchants who as self-

sufficient economic units contained within themselves the full knowledge necessary to engage in politics (a point Hirsch makes repeatedly) and to carry on the economic life of the community (a point that Hirsch only implies). To be literate, for Hirsch, is to be capable of fulfilling the role of free citizen and independent producer in this largely agrarian, pre-industrial, mercantile world; it is to be an active participant in what Hirsch calls a 'good and harmonious democracy' (p. 100), a world united by the implicit, self-evident assumptions of natural philosophy (in Hirsch's words, 'nonsectarian civil "religion"') and the explicit world knowledge collected by the Enlightenment encyclopedists — a project which Hirsch is only too happy to try to duplicate for the rest of us over two centuries later.

As noted earlier, Hirsch seemed to have been unprepared for the sustained attacks his work received — after all, there was no reason to question his sincerity in wanting all Americans, not just a privileged few, to have that sense of personal control and civic empowerment that comes from being both an independent economic producer and an informed, engaged citizen. Hirsch felt that his idea represented progressive public policy, and so it did when first articulated by Enlightenment thinkers in the eighteenth century. What John Stuart Mill said of his father, the model of an eighteenth-century thinker, applies as well to Hirsch. He believed that

> all would be gained if the whole population were taught to read, if all sorts of opinions were allowed to be addressed to them by word and in writing, and, if by means of suffrage they could nominate a legislature to give effect to the opinions they adopted (Mill, p. 64).

Such thinking, seemingly commonplace today, was in the eighteenth century enlightened; compare it, for example, with the near-contemporary, unenlightened conservative thought. 'To make the society happy and people easy under the meanest Circumstances,' wrote one such thinker, Bernard Mandeville in 1723, 'it is requisite that great numbers of them should be ignorant as well as Poor. Knowledge both enlarges and multiplies our Desires, and the fewer things a Man wishes for, the more easily his Necessities may be supply'd' (Levine, 1986, p. 82).

Of foremost importance here is the movement from a world view based on scarcity (where only a few can prosper at the expense of the many) to the republican ideal of civic equality based on the assumption of an abundance of natural resources. Literacy in eighteenth-century America, as explained by Soltow and Stevens (1981), was motivated largely by a sense of community sharing equally in this natural abundance:

> Collectively, literacy clearly was considered part of the social cement which helped to guarantee social stability and adherence to cherished social and political norms. The function of literacy was seen as integrative; its value was to be assessed in terms of social cohesion. Individually, literacy was one attribute which helped to make the good man, that is, it was part of being virtuous, and the better man was the man who would improve his skills in reading and writing (p. 85).

What is missing here is any sense of the connection between the explicit call for renewed civic participation and the implicit assumption of economic self-sufficiency. Hirsch leaves us with the impression that all Americans were actively engaged in eighteenth-century public life and that all acted out of disinterested civic duty. The impression he creates is that civic involvement of eighteenth-century Americans was somehow the result (and not the source) of their world knowledge, that their engagement with politics was somehow the result of their having learned their ninth-grade civics lessons much better than we learn ours.

In truth, eighteenth-century American political life was managed, not by citizens who had mastered high school civics, but by a white male governing class, land-owners and merchants who were motivated to get involved by the chance to determine policies that had an immediate and direct effect on their own economic condition and status. Hirsch does not pursue the possibility that we could do more toward reproducing eighteenth-century cultural literacy today by giving all students Jefferson's stake in the American economy than by giving them his education. Alas, it is more comforting — and cheaper — to believe that society can be radically restructured solely through pedagogic practice.

Yet even increased economic participation of all Americans might not be enough to vitalize Hirsch's notion of literacy, based as it is on an eighteenth-century mercantile economic model that defined wealth in terms of the accumulation of pre-existing goods or pre-existing knowledge. Perhaps reading and writing should have made for virtuous individuals, more engaged citizens, but as Kenneth Lockridge points out,

> there is no evidence that literacy ever entailed new attitudes among men,
> in the decades when male literacy was rapidly spreading toward univer-
> sality, and there is positive evidence that the world view of literate New
> Englanders remained as traditional as that of their illiterate neighbors
> (1974, p. 4).

What Lockridge is suggesting is that Hirsch's pre-industrial world was sustained by social bonds that existed largely independent of literacy, and thus could hardly have been undermined, as Hirsch suggests, by changes in the nature of schooling.

Hirsch is finally naive in believing that the destruction (more accurately, 'transformation') of the heavenly city of American democracy was the result of the misguided reforms of educators, the very people who often have a difficult time effecting significant change in their own institutions, and not the immense transformative power of a new industrial technology itself — a force that literally ripped open the earth and re-made the physical landscape. Perhaps it is not surprising for an ideologue, from the right or the left, to believe in the power of the discourse of educational reform; nevertheless, it is difficult to take seriously Hirsch's claim that the 'romantic formalism' of writers like Jean-Jacques Rousseau and John Dewey, in promoting process over content, was responsible for re-shaping the social world — and, conversely, if he can just convince us to change our minds, and hence, our curriculum, we might just as easily reverse the process, restoring a Jeffersonian golden age. As Daniel Calhoun illustrates in *The Education of a People* (1973), what spelled the end of Hirsch's pre-modern model of literacy was not reformers but the entirely new set of technological and cognitive demands of industrial society. Americans in the nineteenth century learned the hard way what happens when an increasingly complex society tries to meet its technical needs using commonsensical, widely-shared, folk practices: bridges collapse!

The reforms that Hirsch sees as the engine of social change amount to little more than a warning flag, raised to signal the approaching gale of industrialism. Such a flag hardly causes a storm, although it does provide people with a sensible plan for surviving the change in weather. Dewey's message, and the message of modern education, has been that the best solutions to real and perplexing problems are not necessarily contained in the storehouse of tradition. The essential historical shift behind Hirsch's analysis was from a mercantile, pre-industrial world where wealth (and, by extension, culture) resulted from the accumulation of land and surplus goods (the economic equivalents of Hirsch's lists of cultural information) to a capitalist, industrial world where wealth (and culture) resulted from the systematic application of technological innovation. At the center of modern educational reform that Hirsch so opposes is the realization that, as industrial production replaced domestic economy in the nineteenth century, it was no longer enough to know what one's parents or one's fellow citizens knew.

The nineteenth century was an age poised to transform all that stood in its way, one with a single message to offer those who wanted to succeed: adjust. Or, as the young Thomas Carlyle states with a flourish, in the prophetic essay, 'Signs of the Times', it was an age 'which, with its undivided might, forwards, teaches and practices the great art of adapting means to ends'. The century and a half since Carlyle penned these words has produced machines that have reshaped not just the technology of composing (with successive improvements in pens and pencils, typewriters, and now word processors) and that of reading with the mass production of books (including paperbacks), magazines, and newspapers, but the shape of thought itself. As Raymond Williams notes in his classic study of the impact of industrialization on language, *Keywords* (1976), it is difficult to overemphasize the magnitude of these changes in shaping our sense of the most basic terms of our cultural and intellectual life. In pre-industrial, craft-based culture, for example, the term *original* referred to something's authenticity, its affinity with what had come first. This is the sense that one of two traditional restaurants with the same name will call itself 'original'. With the cultural revolution occasioned by the new industrial technology, the meaning of this term became essentially reversed, now referring to something's inventiveness, its lack of antecedent. An 'original' restaurant in this new sense would be one whose menu or decor is unique, without precedent, and thus recently created. Modern copyright law, Lanham (1992) contends, like 'literate *homo sapiens*', is based on this new notion of originality as well as the technology of the mass production of exact copies (what he calls 'Romantic Originality' and the 'Fixed Printed Text'). What is of special value in creative work, and what needs legal protection, is not its earliest or 'original' manuscript form but its creative or 'original' insight.

Here, in condensed form in copyright law, is the same dichotomy between surface (and copy) and depth (and originality) at the center of so much contemporary thinking about the threat of technology. Underneath this distinction is the romantic notion of an ever more powerful truth, the Hegelian spirit, that resists all forms of simplification and paraphrase, that is always a step beyond any of our attempts to reduce or capture it. Or, in the more popular form embodied in the words of Ralph Waldo Emerson, 'God offers every mind its choice between truth and repose. Take which you please — you can never have both ... he in whom the love of truth predominates will keep himself aloof from all moorings, and afloat' (1883, pp. 341–42).

Emerson's noble caution applies not just to the workings of philosophers and artists but also at a practical level to the question of organizing literacy instruction. Once Emerson's position is accepted as a serious reflection of the needs of a new technological age, basic changes necessarily follow in the practice of reading and writing — including, for example, a shift away from mechanical correctness (and 'digested systems') in writing and in the direction of organic forms (including notes and journals) and the process of discovery. What follows from Emerson's romantic ideology is the development of a writing curriculum that emphasizes content over form, sincerity over correctness, one that in Ross Winterowd's words always responds to 'semantic intention, not to errors *per se*' (1989, p. 154). The institutionalization of these changes hardly took place overnight, but the cumulative effect of these changes over the last 150 years led to the establishment of an entirely new model of literacy, and an entirely new academic discipline, English, responsive to the demands of modern industrial society.

It is easy to overlook the revolutionary nature of this model since its conceptions of both reading and writing can seem so ordinary today. As detailed in *A Preface to Literacy* (Tuman, 1987, pp. 34–63), reading in pre-industrial America (as in most of the pre-industrial world today) was defined largely in terms of the ability to recite socially important, often religious or nationalist, texts, and writing, when it was taught at all, was defined in terms of the ability to transcribe texts (hence the emphasis on penmanship and spelling). It is only with the great tide of industrialism that the now pervasive notions of reading and writing as the ability to comprehend and to create new material were established. At the heart of this new model is the ability of readers to arrive at and writers, in turn, to express a new understanding based solely on the silent, solitary contemplation of written language. Is it any wonder that language educators motivated by this new, progressive model of print literacy have long placed such emphasis on the processes of reading and writing, the steps that lead beyond the given? It makes little sense to focus on a fixed product when what is valued most is the insight contained in the text that has yet to be read or yet to be written.

This fundamental shift in language practice can be traced in the pedagogical writings of numerous critics. Knoblauch and Brannon's *Rhetorical Traditions and the Teaching of Writing* (1984) is one such work that is especially committed to the need for restructuring writing instruction to meet the cognitive demands of the modern age. Writing in the pre-modern age, they argue, consisted largely of assembling and displaying important ideas of the past (called 'commonplaces') using a wide array of rhetorical strategies; in the modern world things are different:

> Unlike the ancient intellectual world, which it has permanently displaced, this new world features a perpetual search for knowledge, where learning is an endless adventure in making sense of experience, an explanatory effort in which all human beings are both teachers and students, making and sharing meanings through the natural capacities for symbolic representation that define their humanity. It is a world founded

on this perpetual search, not on authoritarian premises and unassailable dogmas of antiquity, not on the passive veneration of conventional wisdom or the declaration of privileged ministers of the truth (pp. 51–2).

It is difficult to imagine a more impassioned, more resounding affirmation of the larger cultural value of the modern literate's responsibility to search for truth.

The imperative of print literacy here lies not in social solidarity, respect for authority, or mastery of tradition, but in the solitary pursuit of truth:

[A]n important implication of modern rhetoric is that what is true of composing on the most sublime cultural heights has relevance down in the valleys as well. *All* human beings share in the creative ingenuity which is supremely articulated by Shakespeare, Kant, or Einstein.... The most mundane revision effort of an inexperienced student writer shares in the spirit of the progress of knowledge provided its emphasis is on the making of meaning, the achieving of richer coherence, the deeper penetration of a subject (Knoblauch and Brannon, 1984, p. 73).

Even more important than process in this new model of literacy, the 'perpetual search' mentioned in the previous quotation, is the crucial role afforded the notion of an ever higher (or deeper) level of understanding, an understanding most often defined by the adjective *critical*. Like the opening discordant notes of Beethoven's Ninth Symphony that seem only slowly to move from chaos to insight, all reading and writing is compelled to begin on the surface with discrete facts and then only through the critical individual effort move to a deeper level of understanding. Or, as described by the author Henry Miller (1941):

I began in absolute chaos and darkness, in a bog or swamp of ideas and emotions and experiences.... I never hope to embrace the whole, but merely to give in each separate fragment, each work, the feeling of the whole as I go on, because I am digging deeper and deeper into life, deeper and deeper into past and future (pp. 19–20).

The English Coalition, as a consensus report of current thinking in English studies, reveals the rugged persistence of this attachment to the belief that the overriding goal of print literacy is to afford students the power that comes from (or, at least, is expressed in) a critical understanding of our world. While there are constant references throughout the English Coalition report to the need to recognize different ways and purposes for reading and writing, as with Hirsch, all are based on the notion of our exerting critical control over information: 'In an information age, citizens need to make meaning — rather than merely consume information — in informal, formal, imaginative, and analytic ways and in many settings' (*English Coalition*, p. 27). Making meaning with language, consequently, becomes a crucial step for individuals exerting control over experience generally; or as Booth notes in his Foreword to the Coalition report, there was wide agreement among the sixty participants in '"teaching English" as the best way we know of "enfranchising", "liberating", "enabling", "empowering", those who will make our future' (1989, p. x).

The English Coalition report remains closely wedded to the demand that individuals reject what is given (what is usually described as trite, hackneyed) to search for new, more powerful explanations or expressions. The goal of print literacy is not greater efficiency in manipulating text (hence, the widespread disparagement among leaders in composition of the teaching of mechanics or of computers and other forms of technology) but a heightened sensitivity to the new ideas of others and, just as importantly, new ideas we generate ourselves. The assertion that writing is a form of discovery is today little more than a cliché, even as it appears in the English Coalition report:

> Assignments [in general education courses] should encourage students to use writing as a means of discovery — a way to experiment with the ideas of the course, to explore their implications, and to find out what they themselves think (p. 30).

Yet behind the cliché resides the historical imperative of industrial culture for greater understanding and ultimately greater control of both the outer world and the inner self, an imperative that is expressed collectively as the technological control of nature and individually as the critical understanding of experience. What has been consistently obscured in this equation, however, has been the role of technology. Although the changes in educational practice are consistently visible on a wide-scale basis only with the spread of industrialism in the United States and Western European countries in the late-nineteenth and early-twentieth centuries, Knoblauch and Brannon would have us locate the source of this change in the shift in an earlier, largely philosophical movement:

> [T]he epistemological crisis in the seventeenth century, when ancient faith in the probity and completeness of traditional lore about the world gave way before a newly skeptical habit of mind, a preference for empirical, 'scientific' investigations of experience, a recognition of the open-ended, but always ultimately limited, character of human know-ledge (p. 51).

This change is important in creating a culture of trade and technological development that would lead to industrialism. But two factors must be noted. First, the shifts in seventeenth-century philosophy were themselves in part responses to changes in production, specifically the increasing reliance of certain Western European areas on commerce and world trade — new thinking tended to be found in areas that were finding new ways to accumulate wealth. Second, the impact of these changes on pedagogy and cultural values was minimal. Most forms of education remained traditional, with an emphasis on mastering a fixed body of material in classics and formal rhetoric, at least until the mid-nineteenth century, and at places of learning that were shielded from industrialism, like Oxford and Cambridge Universities, even longer.

Reforms in thinking and educational practice came about slowly before large-scale industrialization and were to be found mainly in the various dissenters, radicals, and amateur inventors who provided the early impetus for industrialization, first in England and later in the United States. Henry Adams was right in seeing the driving force of the modern age, not in original editions of Descartes and Kant on display at the 1900 Paris exhibition, but in the exhibits of the immense steam-generated electric dynamos, that were collectively a new 'symbol of infinity', he exclaimed, that made 'the planet itself [seem] less impressive' (p. 380). It is only in the last decades of the nineteenth century and the first of the twentieth century that a new model of education (and of literacy) became prevalent, one designed to enhance individual initiative and complex, interdependent specialization — leading among other things to the dual (and, to some, seemingly contradictory) emphasis in college composition courses on both inner and outer experience, the self as explored in the personal essay and the world as explored in the research paper.

'Challenged to establish the validity of his interpretation and judgment of the work', writes Louise Rosenblatt in *Literature As Exploration*, her classic study of the psychological basis for advanced literacy education, the reader 'will be stimulated both to examine the text more closely and to scrutinize the adequacy of his own past experience and basic assumptions.... From this kind of literary study should flow, too, enhanced understanding of himself and the life about him' (p. 124). For the nearly four decades between the first edition of Rosenblatt's book in 1938 and the third edition in 1976, the discipline of English, with its credo of deep reading and writing, was for better or worse at the center of American education. Critics of modern literacy have been correct in pointing out that this discipline supported an overly narrow (too white and too male) definition of the literary canon and, in turn, that its overriding cultural values were oppressively patriarchal. As developed in Chapters 3 and 4, educational methods and goals are changing to reflect new, perhaps less patriarchal and less critical models of literacy, and as elaborated in Chapter 5, print literacy has serious flaws it is never likely to overcome. Nevertheless, one must recognize the continuing role that critique, itself a product of print literacy, continues to play in broadening the literary canon and redefining literacy itself. Not all revisionist critiques of the print model of literacy, in other words, reject the basic premise of that model: that the goal of literacy is to produce, not Hirsch's pre-modern, eighteenth-century autonomous producer and informed citizen, but that social type designed for the modern, industrial age — namely, self-motivated, self-governing workers and reflective, critical thinkers, student-citizens whose liberal education makes them capable of thinking for themselves in a world whose knowledge base is constantly expanding.

The modern literate has the depth of personality, what E.M. Forster, in a series of lectures given in 1927 (not coincidentally an era of great industrial expansion), called 'roundness' of character, found in the great realistic novels of the late-industrial age. Like the complex characters in the probing psychological studies of Virginia Woolf, Marcel Proust, and Thomas Mann, the modern literate is committed to probing his or her own psychological depths. Lying beneath all the writing activities of an effective composition curriculum, Knoblauch and Brannon write, 'is the writer's own growing awareness of intent: his desire, not merely to complete an assignment, or realize some formal absolute, or imitate a teacher's notion of verbal decorum, but to make valuable statements about the meaning of his own experience' (p. 12). As modern literates, we are all characters in our own introspective psychological novels. Or, as Walter Ong writes, 'It would appear that the development of modern depth psychology parallels the development of the character in drama and the novel, both depending on the

inward turning of the psyche produced by writing and intensified by print'
(p. 154). In *Teletheory*, Greg Ulmer fully summarizes the psychological dimension of print literacy.

> In terms of the academic apparatus, we would relate the technology
> of print and alphabetic literacy with the ideology of the individual,
> autonomous subject of knowledge, self-conscious, capable of rational
> decisions free from influences of prejudice and emotion; and to the prac-
> tice of criticism, manifested in the treatise, and even the essay, assuming
> the articulation of subject/object, objective distance, seriousness and
> rigor, and a clear and simple style. The 'originality' that we require from
> students engaged in making such works as well as the copyright with
> which we protect intellectual property are features of this apparatus
> (1989, p. 4).

What Ulmer only mentions indirectly, and what Ong ignores altogether, however, is the source of the connection between this modern literate and the industrial world that he or she inhabits. It must be the culture of print, we feel, and
finally the culture of industrial technology, and not just the technology of printing (as Ong suggests) that shapes the modern literate sketched by Ulmer. The
two ironies about the development of the novel, in other words, cited by Watt in
Chapter 1 — that the novel grounded in print should prove more intimate than
more traditionally oral forms of literature and that people living in an increasingly
crowded world should relish increasingly more private, personalized forms of
expression — are not really ironies at all: they are both grounded in the imperative of industrial culture for people to understand and to control themselves as a
means of controlling the world. The issues here go beyond the scope of pedagogic practice to the questions about the kind of world we have spent the last few
centuries trying to build and the kind of human beings we have tried to become.
It is not possible to assess the prospects for online literacy without an understanding of the interconnectedness of our physical, mental, and emotional efforts in
this regard, and no work has gone further in exposing these connections than that
of the social theorist Alvin Gouldner.

'A bourgeois', writes Winner, 'is above all else someone who has mastered technique' (1977, p. 125), that is, someone who has forsaken traditional, local
practices (something common to all people) for a new, single way of proceeding
that, in accordance with the latest technology, guarantees the most efficient
results. 'The bourgeoisie first developed financial and commercial techniques and
went on to originate the factory system, the rational administration of the state,
technical schools, and so forth.' Winner is here describing the special class of
intellectual activity that Gouldner calls ideology and we would more likely label
critique. Unlike Gouldner, however, Winner fails to connect ideology and technology, condemning 'technological society' for its lack of commitment to
'self-reflection, self-criticism, or the study of its own history' (p. 128) represented
perhaps by his own work. Gouldner overcomes this dichotomy in Winner, and in
most of the other writers discussed so far, by seeing ideology and technology
as emanating from a single source — Western culture's continual project of
remaking the world in accord with its own image. Drawing upon the work of

Jürgen Habermas and Max Weber, Gouldner grounds both ideology and technology in the fact that traditional, largely religious explanations of the world lost
'their power and validity as myth, as public religion, as customary ritual, as justifying metaphysics, as unquestionable tradition' (1976, p. 31). And what led to
this collapse, for Gouldner as for Weber, is the linking, as first expressed through
Protestantism, of 'control of the environment to the conduct of disciplined,
routine work': 'Science and technology arise when the will to know is grounded
in an impulse to *control*, and when this control is felt to be possible through
routine *work*' (1976, p. 28). What is at stake here is the realization on an historical
scale of the real possibility of remaking the natural world via technology (and
disciplined work), and, as a result, the need for a grand plan of what that new
world should be, a plan that Gouldner calls *ideology*. Humanity may always have
had a dream of what the world should be, but before achieving a certain level of
technical competence such images tended to be expressed retrospectively, as
visions of a golden age, what the world once was and which we could perhaps
recover through faith, not work:

> [A]ll ideologies reject the world as it is; they find the world as it is,
> defective. This implies that, at some level, they must distinguish
> between what is and what should be, between the real and the ideal,
> contrasting the former invidiously with the latter. Ideologies as an ideal-
> ism suppose that what is real can and should be brought under the
> control or influence of the ideal.... (1976, p. 85)

For Gouldner, all ideologies embody a utopian projection of a better world; they
are critiques that implicitly compare what is with what can be.

   Here then is the clearest statement of the pervasive irony of Western culture
that lies at the core of Gouldner's work — the insight that the critical spirit of
print literacy, poised as it always is at offering alternative ways of looking at the
world (ways that often involve radical changes in technology) is itself the product
of our power to control nature technologically:

> Both science and ideology are grounded in a culture of careful discourse,
> one of whose main rules calls for *self-groundedness*, requiring, as it does —
> as a regulative ideal — that the speaker be able to state articulately all the
> premises required by his argument, and to show that his conclusions do
> not require premises other than those he has articulated (1976, p. 42).

For Gouldner, both ideology (or 'critique') and science are finally based on the
same rigorously self-conscious mode of intellectual discourse, the same critical
pattern of articulation and exploration we have for most of this century placed at
the center of higher-level literacy instruction, ironically often in the seemingly
anti-scientific liberal arts curricula.

   Our commitment to the notion that print literacy is capable of reshaping our
world is itself the product of our deep cultural experience of the tangible power
of industrial technology in controlling and reshaping the world for our better-
ment. We have believed so fervently in the power of reading and writing to transform individuals and, in so doing, transform society (what Harvey Graff [1979]
debunks as the 'literacy myth') largely because of our longstanding immersion in

an industrial culture whose immense and, at times, broad-based wealth has been built upon the real, not ludic, power to transform nature. It is Gouldner's thesis that ideology as a critique of industrial culture is a manifestation of the same transformative powers that in the form of technology continue to reshape the material world. Harvey Graff's critique of the limited ability of literacy to remake the entire social world, accordingly derives much of its power from an objectifying, rational discourse that exists as a direct counterpart to the material power of technology. And, Gouldner might argue, Graff's critique really is not that print literacy lacks real transformative force (a position that would undermine the persuasive thrust of his own highly literate work — 'Why bother writing?') but that the transformation it offers is not evenly distributed across society, that, in other words, there are winners and losers — and the winners are, to use Winner's (1977) phrase, those who have 'mastered technique'.

Gouldner's model of cultural change thus works in two directions simultaneously — outward in terms of the collective power of society to reshape the natural world, and inward in terms of the individual's power to remake himself or herself:

> [O]ne toward the *world* itself and one toward the *self*, as it faces the world. In the first case, the rationality of the ideological implies a declining hold in traditional and in sacred definitions of social reality, thus allowing them to be made *problematic....* In the second case, the rationality of the ideological predicates a self that feels self-confident and potent enough to pit itself against familiar versions of reality and to question, prod, and probe them (1976, p. 87).

And it is this dual movement that most clearly provides the grounds for connecting technology and print literacy, for it is the function of a specific form of language, what Gouldner calls the 'culture of critical discourse', that in the end connects the outward control of the world and the inward control of the self.

'How the world is to be changed,' Gouldner writes, 'finally comes down to the linguistic relation between the ideological believer and nonbeliever.... Their relationship is nothing less than the core paradigm of modern world transformation' (1976, p. 83). Writing in this sense is possessing the technical power to organize a discourse capable of addressing the 'nonbeliever', the unpersuaded, that group of people capable of being enjoined through the power of discourse itself to reshape their own understanding of the world and join, either imaginatively and literally, in some larger social project. Gouldner refers to ideology as a 'discourse on behalf of public projects of social reconstruction' (1976, p. 79). But the implications of this paradigm apply to more than limited political discourse:

> [T]he ideological believer teaches the nonbeliever *a new language* and, through this, he develops (in the latter) *a new self — emancipated from the old language*: a self poised more instrumentally toward the old and distanced from the old social world it had embodied, constituted, and protected. *Ideological change is a linguistic conversion that carries with it a reorganization of the self*, on the one hand, and an alienation from old

social conventions, on the other; that permits the *new* self to act *against* the old world. It is this conversion from an older, unreflexive and restricted linguistic variant to a more elaborate and reflexive variant ... which is always involved in learning an ideology, and that unifies social and personal change (1976, p. 84).

Ideology thus subsumes the entire project of using written language to situate oneself in a dynamic social world; as used here, it is no less than our modern notion of print literacy.

While privacy, as noted in Chapter 1, is a defining characteristic of our modern experience of print, it is a privacy that exists in close and continual contact with the social realm. It is the place into which one retires to contemplate and, with the help of books, to imagine alternative ways of acting in the world. The thrust of print literacy, therefore, does not entirely reject the concern with a universal public discourse in Hirsch and pre-industrial Enlightenment culture. The goal of reading and writing is still participation in the world — what is new in print literacy, as developed by Gouldner, is the sense in which the world and the self each undergoes a process of transformation, first the world through technological intervention, and then the self through reorganization of the personality in an effort to direct such changes. Whereas in Hirsch all citizens had access through literacy to full participation in public discourse, in Gouldner such participation is available only to that special class of citizens who have mastered critical discourse, that is, only to intellectuals.

Intellectuals, for Gouldner, are those individuals who have mastered critical discourse, a discourse that he defines in terms of universal characteristics common to college composition for much of this century. The primary characteristic of intellectuals as a class, even for nominally conservative intellectuals Gouldner points out, is a consistently critical stance with regard to the *status quo*, what (borrowing from sociologist Edward Shils) he refers to as the '*alienative* disposition of intellectuals' (1979, p. 32). Being an intellectual, Shils writes, necessitates 'a partial rejection of the prevailing system of cultural values' (1972, p. 7). The culture of critical discourse becomes universal not just in this common critical attitude but also in its adherence to common practices of style and expression. 'The culture of critical discourse', Gouldner writes, 'de-authorizes all speech grounded in traditional societal authority, while it authorizes itself, the elaborated speech variant of the culture of critical discourse, as the standard of *all* "serious" speech' (1979, p. 29). There is in Gouldner, as there is in the social theorist Habermas and in the conservative Hirsch, the belief that intellectuals can be elevated into a universal class, one that rises above immediate parochial issues, by their mastery of a common critical discourse. Hence the belief at the center of modern literacy education for the last century (although increasingly under attack now, along with modernism generally), that a universalist discourse instructed in the schools will allow all students, and eventually everyone exposed to education, to rise

above the conflict of different sections of the society with their differing regional dialects and class sociolects.... An elaborated speech variant thus serves in some part as a *unifying* culture of discourse, permitting the collaboration of different social sectors and speakers of different language variants, of various restricted variants, without manifestly siding with or speaking the speech of any one of them (1976, p. 64).

Much of the contemporary debate over literacy policy can be seen as a discussion of the status of this unnamed class of intellectuals. As those who have mastered the technique of critical discourse, intellectuals possess a tangible advantage in modern society. So much of the controversy in contemporary literacy theory arises when the term 'literate' is loosely applied to refer alternately to this high level of technical expertise necessary to master critical discourse and to the most minimal achievements in reading and writing that would qualify one as no longer illiterate. Matters are hardly made less confusing by the fact that critiques of the misplaced importance of 'literacy' (as minimal skills) are themselves such powerful examples of 'literacy' (as critical discourse). What may be most ironic of all is that the notion of *literacy*, related as it is to the art of clear thinking, should be the center of so much discourse at cross purposes. Hence, Hirsch, coming from the right, can base his critique of modern education on the misguided notion that the mastery of critical discourse can be equated with a superficial knowledge of cultural facts; and Harvey Graff, coming from the left, can suggest that literacy (as the mastery of technique) is merely a form of hegemonic control since literacy (as the attainment of minimal years of elementary schooling) does little to change one's position in the world.

What is too easily lost in such debates is the broad consensus that, despite Hirsch's nostalgia for a more stable world of farmers and merchants, has underlain the status of print literacy. In the pre-industrial age, the major school test of reading was oral recitation. Students were required to recite aloud passages memorable for their rhetorical, ethical, or patriotic fervor. The various McGuffey's Readers that dominated American education in the nineteenth century all contained such selections along with instructions on oral recitation. Beginning in the late-nineteenth century, reading instruction and testing changed markedly. Now for the first time in history, reading was considered a silent activity, and testing in reading, as in college-entrance exams, began to be based on answering a series of comprehension questions based upon the silent reading of short prose passages on topics that were deliberately chosen to ensure that students knew as little about their content as possible. At a minimum, we expected students who could read to be able to arrive at the new understanding of the new worlds embodied in those texts. For the higher levels of reading in our literature courses we expected even more — namely, that students working independently would each try to go beyond all existing readings of a text, even those of professional critics, in the process of pursuing ever more powerful readings.

In the industrial age there has been wide agreement that writing and reading are acts whereby individuals create and comprehend ever-deeper understandings of the world. The goal of the modern reading, therefore, has been to produce divergent interpretations, not just to encourage either individual expression or collective tolerance of individual differences, but to increase the likelihood of producing the one truly powerful interpretation that will deepen our collective understanding. This ideal of critical discourse in the form of ever more powerful understanding of experience had its corollary, as Jay Bolter demonstrates in *Turing's Man* (1984), in industrial culture's quest for ever more powerful forms of energy. The spiritual quest for understanding, as Bolter notes, so clearly manifested in Goethe's *Faust*, parallels what he calls our pursuit of 'the politics and economics of infinity' (1984, p. 227):

> [I]f nature could never be completely dominated, completely transformed into capital, that too was the glory of the entrepreneur — his work was never done. Mechanisms must always be made more exact, metals converted into stronger alloys, new sources of power exploited on a grander scale.

Or, to paraphrase in language that exposes the industrial basis of print literacy: if human experience could never be completely reconstructed, completely transformed into understanding, that too was the glory of critics — then work was never done. Observations must always be made more exact, information connected to more powerful explanations, new techniques of criticism exploited on a grander scale.

Whereas pre-industrial cultures have based education largely on what seems the most natural pattern, having children master the ways of their parents, the established practices and traditions of the group, modern industrial culture embarked on what has been a radical enterprise, basing education on preparing students to comprehend as readers and to create, as writers in texts, and as scientists and engineers in the world itself, entirely new ways of organizing experience. John Stuart Mill's classic tract of industrial culture, 'On Liberty', opens with an epigraph from German idealist Wilhelm von Humboldt. 'The grand, leading principle, towards which every argument unfolded in these pages directly converges, is the absolute and essential importance of human development in its richest diversity.' How extraordinary, we should exclaim, that a culture (a group ordinarily concerned with preserving its collective identity) would place such importance on individual development — and finally, for what purpose? Artists in the United States have recently been concerned over possible restrictions on their freedom of expression tied to government funding, for the moment a clear political attack from the right; in the long run, however, we should ask for what purpose a people acting collectively would want to promote a modern tradition of art that regularly defines itself in terms of promoting visions of individuals (those we label 'artists') that are best defined as extending, going beyond, or somehow challenging traditional, hence widely shared conceptions of the world.

In supplying an answer, Gouldner turns to the mandate of industrial culture, sometimes explicit, always implicit, to innovate, to seek out an 'unending perfection'. '[T]he particular set of assumptions at any given moment — the cultural *status quo* — is always subject to challenge. Inherent in this structure of rationality, then, is the potential revolution in permanence, the "permanent revolution"' (1976, p. 49). Behind the industrial basis of print literacy, and behind industrial culture itself, is the image of the restless, solitary being. In its negative form such an individual is subject to what Gouldner refers to as an 'unceasing restlessness and lawlessness ... first called *anomos* and later, *anomie*' (1976, p. 49); in its positive form such an individual is the representative romantic artist, whether a poet like Wordsworth recollecting experiences in tranquility, a philosopher like Nietzsche alone in the Alps, or a self-educated inventor like Edison — someone whose importance to the world at large resides in the widespread distribution of his or her highly individual work, akin to the universal, beneficial application of one person's discovery of an oral vaccine for polio. Propelling both industrial culture and print literacy has been an overriding belief that progress, material as well as artistic, grows directly out of the unfettered creative insights of exceptional individuals — be they eccentric tinkerers, brooding theoreticians, or temperamental artists.

How different things are as we approach the end of the twentieth century, with practically all aspects of print literacy, and, in turn, the industrial culture on which it is based, under attack. Verticality now loses its spiritual dimension, its association with the sublime, and knowledge is instead associated with hierarchical forms of governance, what Harlan Cleveland calls 'vertical structures of command and control' (p. 61). Truth is still above the masses, but it is now conceived, not as something rarefied or spiritual but as a trade secret at the top of a corporate pyramid — what separates holders of 'truth' from the people below is not knowledge but institutional greed and power. Meanwhile, instead of Faustian man, committed to an endless, solitary quest for knowledge, the new age, Bolter speculates, is marked by the programmer, someone whose work at every step makes him or her aware of the physical limits of electronic time and space. The programmer, Bolter contends, does not make bold new discoveries but instead subtly manipulates finite parts within a finite world: 'He remains in the confined logical universe of his machine, rearranging the elements of that universe to suit the current problem' (1984, p. 223). This programmer, this student of a new online literacy, is exempt from Knoblauch and Brannon's imperative 'to make valuable statements about the meaning of his own experience' (p. 12), to probe the unexplored territory of his own psyche:

> The programmer reworks his logical world to make it more efficacious or more comfortable, and he proceeds until he comes up against the ultimate electronic limitations of time, space, or logic. In the process, he learns nothing more than what he put there himself, for he does not discover his world, so much as invent it (Bolter, 1984, p. 224).

With such changes the old values of print culture — originality, sincerity, and depth — are replaced by a new set of 'online' values — inventiveness, frugality, and technical dexterity.

For Bolter it is as if this movement is directed by the calmer, more focused personality of the computer itself:

> The computer does not strive; it proceeds to a predetermined goal. The striving after infinity or self-knowledge or God, so important in the previous age, is especially foreign to electronic thought. And if the Western mind has often dreamed of overcoming its mortal limitations, its finiteness, in one way or another, the programmer has no such ambitions. The very structure of the CPU and of the languages used to program it reminds him that he must proceed a step at a time and in a finite number of steps to produce a useful result (1984, p. 79).

The new world of online literacy replaces the search for psychological depth of print literacy with a rediscovery of the creative power of craft and manipulation.

With the ascendancy of online literacy we can expect specific changes in literacy education as well as broad changes in cultural values. No longer will it be possible, for example, to continue to define reading in terms of the traditional comprehension questions based on short readings found on college-entrance examinations when the paradigmatic text becomes the associated collections of screens that an individual user links together while working at a computer terminal (that is, a hypertext discussed at length in Chapter 3). There is no pre-existing text, with its own special vision of the world, that we as readers are required to grasp; instead, the text comes into existence through our own manipulations and decisions as we sit at the terminal. Likewise, in accord with the declarations of postmodern critics (to be discussed in Chapter 4) such 'readings' signal the literal end of the author — it is now the reader who is charged with creating the text. It is the reader who, in combining pre-existing materials to meet some special purpose, writes.

Computers do have the potential to revolutionize our understanding of literacy, in the process changing the three basic terms *text*, *reader*, and *writer*. Yet just as it is not the industrial technology of printing but industrial culture in its entirety that is responsible for the shape of print literacy, so it is the totality of post-industrial culture, and not computer-based techniques for manipulating text, that will determine the future of online literacy. Signs that we are moving into a post-industrial world should be apparent everywhere. The figures in Chapter 1 concerning the amounts of information we are collecting and the limits on storing, accessing, and transmitting such information represent one indication. The actual changes in the US work force (Cleveland, p. 57) represents another: in 1920 over half the work force was involved with manufacturing, commerce, and industry, less than ten per cent in information services; by 2000 it will be less than a fourth in industry, and nearly two-thirds in information services. Such changes in the work force, along with the geometric explosion in information noted in Chapter 1, suggest that future standards of living will be increasingly tied to the information-handling power of computers.

But the numbers themselves tell only a small part of the story of the end of industrial culture. What they do not capture is the now pervasive sense that the age of continual industrial expansion and limitless growth is over — everywhere today we live with signs of the limits to our power to remake the world. While technological optimists like Daniel Bell and Harlan Cleveland, themselves products of the unprecedented industrial economy following World War II, see the information age as freeing us from the material scarcity of earlier economies (where 'the few had access to resources and the many did not'; Cleveland, p. 60), the spirit of the age is generally less sanguine. It is less than a century ago that, in the robust adolescence of industrialism, Henry Adams could describe the steam turbine as an awe-inspiring, benign force, a 'huge wheel, revolving within arm's length at some vertiginous speed, and barely murmuring — scarcely humming an audible warning to stand a hair's breadth further for respect of power — while it would not wake the baby lying close against its frame' (p. 380). Are there any parents today — especially from the professional classes that shape educational reform — who would not associate proximity to such powerful machines with various forms of cancer and other long-term, largely hidden health risks? While industrial culture in part could be defined by its hosts of vaccines and cures it discovered for illnesses that had plagued humanity throughout history, we now confront today's dreaded diseases, cancer and AIDS, with less optimism that a lone scientist or even a team of scientists, will discover a single miracle vaccine or a single miracle cure for them. For all that ails industrial culture today, energy shortages as well as incurable diseases, our attention more and more seems to be turning away from the prospects of miraculous discoveries (involving still more powerful transformations of nature) and in the direction of altering our own behaviors. While reports of room-temperature fusion may make headlines — offering us the illusion that there still may be miraculous, industrial solutions to our post-industrial problems — we are all becoming more aware of the need for conserving energy, for changing our lifestyles, and especially for finding more cooperative patterns of existence. Developers and entrepreneurs of all sorts, all proponents of industrial culture, are right to see in the moral fervor of environmentalists a direct challenge to the foundation of industrial culture. And, to the extent that the thesis of this chapter is valid — that print literacy is based on that same foundation — then it too stands ready to topple.

It is hardly surprising that industrial culture, a world that Knoblauch and Brannon see as 'founded on this perpetual search, not on authoritarian premises and unassailable dogmas of antiquity' (p. 52), should continually produce critiques of its own assumptions. Yet the ever-growing attack on print literacy, the rejection of the symbolic, transformative power of the literate text, as articulated in the writings of Eric Havelock, Jack Goody, David Olson, and Walter Ong, among others, is more than perpetual revisionism. Instead it is a clear symptom of the emergence of a new post-industrial sensibility, one that rejects the status of texts as higher or more logical expressions of symbolic knowledge, texts as the embodiment of history, philosophy, literature, science, and other ways of understanding the world not immediately supported by the traditions, often the prejudices, of the group. For industrial culture, it was precisely the ideal, innovative, anomalous component of this symbolic content that was responsible for the immense value afforded literacy. While educators may have discussed literacy in terms of transcription skills, it was always the power of the text, as an extension of the transformative power of technology, to change both the individual and the world that was at issue.

The widespread critique of print literacy can be traced back at least to the late 1960s when higher literacy standards and the entire academic tradition were associated first with the gross misuse of technology in American military expansion in Southeast Asia and eventually with the growing sense that Western civilization in its entirety, driven by technique in the direction of relentless expansion, was out of control. Whatever symbolic truths its texts contained were no more than recipes for cultural domination, and the tradition of valuing such truths at the expense of local knowledge and practices (how critics often defined Western education) only guaranteed the hegemonic practice of justifying the failures of those least equipped for reading and writing such texts. Everywhere, from William Labov's 1969 essay, 'The Logic of Non-Standard English' to Deborah Brandt's 1990 book, *Literacy as Involvement*, the attack on print literacy has been in the ascendent, promoting all forms of local language practices, from the signifying of black urban youths to the composing practices of professional writers, at the expense of what has become the lowly autonomous text.

Brian Street's *Literacy in Theory and Practice* is just one of many attacks on what he calls the 'autonomous' model of literacy:

> The model tends, I claim, to be based on the 'essay-text' form of literacy and to generalise broadly from what is in fact a narrow, culture-specific literacy practice.... The model assumes a single direction in which literacy development can be traced, and associates it with 'progress', 'civilization', individual liberty, and social mobility.... It isolates literacy as an independent variable and then claims to be able to study its consequences. These consequences are classically represented in terms of economic 'take-off' or in terms of cognitive skills (pp. 1–2).

Street would have us instead adopt what he calls an 'ideological' model, one based on the notion that 'what the particular practices and concepts of reading and writing are for a given society depends upon the context':

> What practices are taught and how they are imparted depends upon the nature of the social formation. The skills and concepts that accompany literacy acquisition, in whatever form, do not stem in some automatic way from the inherent qualities of literacy, as some authors would have us believe, but are aspects of a specific ideology (p. 1).

As expressed by linguist Michael Stubbs, the attack on print literacy seems to attain the status of a platitude, something so obviously true that it is difficult to imagine how or for what legitimate reason anyone could oppose it:

> People speak, listen, read and write in different social situations for different purposes ... If a coherent theory of literacy is to be developed, it will have to account for the place of written language, both in relation to the forms of spoken language and also in relation to the communicative functions served by different types of language in different social settings (pp. 15–16).

Such self-assuredness about the superiority of a new model of literacy at the end of the twentieth century parallels attitudes that accompanied the triumph of print literacy at the end of the nineteenth century. It was just a hundred years ago that educators were first stating what all of a sudden seemed obvious — that reading was largely a silent activity to be measured by written tests of comprehension. Such a sense of certainty in the correctness of what historically is a novel idea is a clear sign of a major shift in cultural orientation, one triggered today by a technological change as profound as the triumph of industrialism a century ago.

Among the many who have heralded the revisionist orientation in literacy over the last two decades, few have received wider acceptance and praise than Shirley Brice Heath. In *Ways with Words* (1983) and a series of related articles, Heath recounts the reading and writing experiences at home and at school for children of two Carolina Piedmont working-class communities, one white and one black. Two aspects of Heath's treatment of language use in Trackton, the black community, place her work in opposition to the model of print literacy. First, she is keenly appreciative of the rich linguistic and cultural diversity of black family life in the rural South, especially the story-telling tradition known as 'talkin' junk,' a method of embellishment involving hyperbolic compliments and unexpected comparisons. Her purpose here is to counter the assumptions built into the modern model that only the family life of professionals provides the proper setting for the acquisition of literacy:

> Any baby born into Trackton is born not to a family, but to the community.... Integration of the infant as a social member of the community is taken over by all; older siblings or children in the neighborhood carry the baby about and introduce the infant to their games and other social interactions. Immersed in a constant stream of multi-party communications, the child comes to define himself as a speaker. Nicknames, plaza-center roles, playsongs, and frequent teasing help each child learn how to act to enlist the greatest number of supporters in the crowd and thus to insure emotional and social support (1983, p. 146).

The black child growing up in Trackton is literally surrounded by the words and love of a highly supportive community.

Unfortunately, as Heath admits, the actual kinds of support offered in Trackton does not seem to prepare students well for the demands of school. And here is the second important aspect of her work — her criticism, not of the community for failing the school, but of the school for failing the community:

> Trackton parents believe that when their children go to school, they will continue to learn the same way, the only way they have known how — by watching, listening, and trying. For the children, however, the school is a sudden flood of discontinuities in the ways people talk, the values they hold, and the consistency with which the rewards go to some and not others (1983, p. 348).

Heath, as an educator herself, rightly senses that for the school to be effective it must reach out to the children being educated, and she cites case histories of teachers who incorporated ethnographic techniques (Heath's own specialty) 'as an approach to *learning* to move to new ways of *doing* in their classrooms':

> Their interactive approach to incorporating these communities' ways of talking, knowing, and expressing knowledge with those of the school enabled some Roadville and Trackton children to understand how to make choices among uses of language and to link these choices to life chances (1983, p. 343).

What is somewhat unclear in this summation is the extent to which effective teachers are merely using a new strategy to reconstruct the established model of print literacy, a model which located in the acts of reading and writing texts the opportunity to gain critical distance on and hence reach a deeper understanding of one's own place in the world. Elsewhere, for example, Heath is totally open in noting the limits of the literate practices in Roadville and Trackton:

> Written materials are not a major source of new information for either community, and neither community writes to distribute ideas beyond

their own primary group. In neither community does literacy bear any direct relationship to job status or chances for upward mobility (1986a, p. 225).

Reading in the black community, Heath notes, was a decidedly social activity, with solitary reading, like women's reading of romances and men's reading of 'girlie' magazines interpreted 'as an indication that one had not succeeded socially' (1986b, p. 21). Indeed the following seven uses of reading that Heath lists for Trackton exclude reading either for critical insight or pleasure: instrumental (reading street signs), social interactional (reading posters or recipes), news related (reading newspapers), memory supportive (reading calendars), as substitutes for oral messages (reading notes from school), reading permanent records (such as tax forms), and reading to confirm understanding (as with directions or the Bible); (1986b, p. 21).

One is tempted to respond here that there are many possible uses for reading and writing of great interest to an ethnographer that do not in themselves directly support literacy, and let the matter rest. The problem with such a response is that revisionist critiques of print literacy, in defining reading and writing in terms of the actual language practice of different peoples, are increasingly vitiating any such distinctions:

> If 'standard' literacy is to be achieved among all students, then the scope of the 'standard' must broaden. If standard skills are to be achieved by all, then what counts as standard skills also has to broaden. Pluralism not only requires that many voices be heard but that the differences in those voices be understood. (Brandt, 1990, p. 124)

The specific broadening that Deborah Brandt here has in mind is our moving beyond what she calls the 'strong-text model of literacy', one that characterized literacy in terms of a limited notion of texts as 'abstract objects, conceptual, logical, literal, and detached' (p. 25). Texts for Brandt are not repositories of symbolic truth but instructions for maintaining the processes of reading and writing:

> [T]exts are the way they are because they facilitate the work of writing and reading. They are not merely the objects of outcome for writers nor the objects of consumption for readers. They are the means by which present-tense literate acts are carried out (p. 99).

While the exact distinction Brandt may be making may be somewhat obscure, the thrust of her analysis is not: reading and writing — literacy itself — are acts of involvement, ways of doing things in this world, or as she might say, ways to keep communication going between different individuals.

What is crucial to Brandt's critique of print literacy and that of others is the insistence that it is no longer texts that sustain literacy: everything is a text — informal notes, casual conversation, even gestures — and consequently nothing is a text as previously defined in print literacy, nothing privileged as a place where special, symbolic kinds of verbal meanings are created and comprehended. Brandt, like Heath and many others, calls for a new model of literacy largely on ethical grounds — the countless compelling uses of language by disenfranchised groups have been sacrificed too long in favor of the practices of a single, albeit dominant, social group. There is no shortage of moral fervor in this critique, but one must look elsewhere to explain the ever-growing appeal of this new model. After all, Hirsch's attack on modern literacy practice, which has had almost no support among language educators, also makes a strong ethical appeal — he too wants to achieve a more democratic society. What distinguishes the work of Brandt and other dismantlers of texts is the consonance of their critique of print literacy with the general transformation of industrial culture on which that model of literacy is based. Of what special good are reading and writing if they are just two other ways for people to relate to each other through language? Of what special good are texts if we no longer believe that they contain new, more powerful ways of being in the world?

With cracks in our collective faith in progress apparent everywhere, it is hardly surprising that even in the consensus report of the English Coalition (a work whose subtitle, *Democracy through Language*, proudly announces its connection to the founding figure of modernist education, John Dewey) key components of the now aging print model of literacy are repeatedly merged with, and subsumed by, a newer, post-industrial sensibility — one that implicitly recognizes the limits of growth and, one suspects, is more in accord with the post-industrial lifestyles of the educators themselves and their own families. It is hardly surprising that goals of literacy in an age that increasingly generates its wealth by transmitting information would be expressed, not in terms of the universal application of individual insight (one idea benefiting and somehow transforming everyone), but in terms of the need of different groups of people to learn to live together, accepting each other's differences and, by implication, accepting our limited ability to remake the world:

> Language arts instruction is especially important in a heterogeneous, post-industrial society.... The increased heterogeneity of our society also gives new urgency to enhancing students' ability to appreciate cultural diversity and multiple ways of reading and writing (*English Coalition Conference*, 1989, pp. 85–86).

The drafters note that 'because students no longer conform to a single type' (p. 85), pedagogic practice needs to be both more individualized and more interactive. That modern educational practice, grounded in the image of the melting pot, never saw students as belonging to a single type is not the point. Modern pedagogy still saw the 'single type', the student adjusted to the demands of industrial culture, as the desired outcome of all education; the new, postmodern policy creates the virtue of diversity out of our new awareness of the real limits of technological change.

The critical reading and writing skills that for a century have defined the goal of higher literacy education are now seen as representing the language needs of a particular, not a universal, group — a change reflected in the increasing practice of referring to such language use as *academic discourse*, a mode of communication presumably necessary only for those with aspirations of working in a university-like setting. The language of academics is no longer seen as a universal discourse. Implicit in this shift of focus is the belief that the key to becoming literate is not learning the language forms of any one group — not even the academic discourse of teachers — but learning the general system by which different groups use language for their own advantage (and often for the disadvantage of others). One attains literacy either by mastering one or more of these discourse practices (hence the common use of the plural form, *literacies*) or by grasping the general social process of domination and control that underlies all language use. Whereas the modern model of print literacy emphasizes transformation and transcendence (getting beyond the limits of one's present state and one's own group), the postmodern model emphasizes negotiation and social construction, or, as expressed in the college strand of the English Coalition, 'that the arts of language (reading, writing, speaking, and listening) are social and interactive and that meaning is negotiated and constructed' (p. 25). The report itself refers to this new, postmodern sensibility as the 'collaborative model', and describes it as one where 'the teacher acts as an informed and challenging coach, offering multiple perspectives, while students practise and experience the kind of cooperation all citizens increasingly need' (p. 28). As with Hirsch's agrarian model and Dewey's industrial one, the goal of a new literacy education is still expressed, not in terms of reading and writing skills, but in the creation of a new economic type — here that person best able to flourish in a zero-sum world: the sensitive, supportive team player, the person with both the technical skill to do his or her own job and the interpersonal skill to help others do their jobs as part of a collective effort, whether that effort is an individual school or work-related project or the collective project of managing our precarious human existence.

The haunted narrator of Robert Pirsig's meandering autobiographical, philosophical novel, *Zen and the Art of Motorcycle Maintenance* (1974), is a man determined to overcome the dichotomy inherent in Carlyle's Mechanical Age and, in turn, the world of print literacy and the industrial culture on which it is based — the split between means and ends cited by Carlyle and its extension, the split between emotion and reason, between civilization and nature, between scientist and artist and, for our purpose, most importantly, between a technological control of the world and a psychological understanding of the self. All of Western history from Plato and Aristotle onwards is, for Pirsig's alter ego narrator, little more than a brash attempt to use the spirit of inquiry, not to understand and live in harmony with the totality of existence, but alternately to control the natural world and to think about the self. The culprit in such schisms is, for Pirsig, not just the scientists who lack a proper appreciation of the arts but the rest of us, the humanists like his sometime traveling companion John, who lacks any interest in technology whatsoever, and who as a consequence wants all work on his motorcycle, even routine maintenance, performed by experts. Today, Pirsig complains, we have scientists whose lack of knowledge about creativity leads them to 'blind data-gathering', just as we have artists whose lack of knowledge about 'underlying form' leads them to 'a lot of stylishness in the arts — thin art ... and the result is not just bad, it is ghastly' (p. 287).

The solution for Pirsig is for all of us to perform our own maintenance, to stay in touch with the world and our deepest selves by close attention to the ordinary. What he seeks throughout the novel is an honesty and simplicity of expression in dealing directly with the world, an experience he calls Quality which in confronting the essence of things transcends all traditional dichotomies. It is not technology that is evil, for Pirsig, but dualistic thinking based on a false objectivity. Our 'flight from and hatred of technology' is for Pirsig ultimately 'self-defeating'. 'The Buddha, the Godhead, resides quite as comfortably in the circuits of a digital computer or the gears of a cycle transmission as he does at the top of a mountain or in the petals of a flower' (p. 18).

This compelling image of the natural, the technological, and the spiritual all coming together suggests Pirsig's affinity with Brandt, Heath, and other critics of print literacy. Like Pirsig, such critics are concerned with reducing the characteristic tension in modern industrial culture between natural exploitation and psychic exploration. In such a reading, *Zen and the Art of Motorcycle Maintenance* would be seen as calling on us to change our attitudes by becoming more accepting of both the natural world and the variety of people who inhabit it. Pirsig's narrator, one suspects, would have been a less tormented soul if such were the case, if he truly felt the tolerance for difference that characterizes the postmodern critique of print literacy, if as a technical writer he had followed Bolter's directive for becoming a survivor in the computer age — someone whose 'concern with functions, paths, and goals overrides an interest in any deeper kind of understanding' (1984, p. 220).

As it is, he is better characterized as just the opposite — not as Bolter's new literate for the computer age, someone 'destined to lose the Faustian concern with depth' — but as the epitome of the modern literate, as the technical writer consumed by the ideal of the perfectly lucid text. Bolter concludes, 'The rejection of depth for considerations of surface and form, long a feature of modern art, is now spreading throughout intellectual life' (1984, p. 220). Yet Pirsig's narrator is relentless in his commitment to resolving the schism between appearance and underlying form, between what he labels a romantic and a classical understanding, between the solitary self and the all-encompassing world at the foundation of modern literacy — all by using the ultimate tool of print literacy, an ever more powerful critique.

'Essential to this ideal of rationality,' observes Gouldner, 'is the standard of self-awareness' (1976, p. 48). Like Bolter's archetypal Faustian man of letters, Pirsig's narrator is a loner, an intellectual rebel, a Nietzschean Zarathustra attracted to wandering in the mountains. 'People spend their entire lives at those lower altitudes,' he muses, 'without any awareness that this high country exists' (p. 119). Like the timber wolf he associates with his own alter ego, Phaedrus, the narrator is a traveler of abandoned roads:

> The main skill is to keep from getting lost. Since the roads are used only by local people who know them by sight nobody complains if the junctions aren't posted. And they often aren't. When they are it's usually a small sign hiding unobtrusively in the weeds and that's all. Country-road-sign makers seldom tell you twice (p. 6).

And like all such wanderers what he is seeking is that most mysterious commodity of the industrial age, an ever-more powerful level of understanding, expressed in Emerson-like fashion in the metaphorical language of depth. 'In this Chautauqua I would like not to cut any new channels of consciousness but simply dig deeper into the old ones that have become silted in with the debris of thoughts grown stale and platitudes too often repeated' (p. 8). There is no goal to this journey, no real destination for this ever deepened channel; there is only, as in motorcycle maintenance itself, the task of continual renewal and struggle in mastering both the outer world, here the motorcycle, and the inner self:

> The real cycle you're working on is a cycle called yourself. The machine that appears to be 'out there' and the person that appears to be 'in here' are not two separate things. They grow toward Quality or fall away from Quality together (p. 319).

But what is this Quality but that higher (or deeper) form of experience available to the perceptive individual, the critical as compared to the mythos, the collective misrepresentations of the group:

> There is only one kind of person, Phaedrus said, who accepts or rejects the mythos in which he lives. And the definition of that person, when he has rejected the mythos, Phaedrus said, is 'insane'. To go outside the mythos is to become insane....' (p. 344).

But what choice do we have than to become insane if the higher truth of Quality lies, not in mythos, but in the *terra incognita* beyond mythos? 'The mythos that says the forms of this world are real but the Quality of this world is unreal, that is insane!' (p. 346).

'Pioneers', the narrator at one point concedes, 'are invariably, by their nature, mess-makers' (p. 249), but it is not just the world they leave behind that is broken but their own lives as well:

> I think present-day reason is an analogue of the flat earth of the medieval period. If you go far beyond it you're presumed to fall off into insanity. And people are very much afraid of that. I think this fear of insanity is comparable to the fear people once had of falling off the edge of the world. Or the fear of heretics. There's a very close analogue there (pp. 164–65).

Zen and the Art of Motorcycle Maintenance is a philosophical reverie on the nature of truth, but it is also a painful narrative account of the narrator's severe mental crisis and the resulting breakup of his family. It is, in this sense, a cautionary tale about the psychopathology of print literacy, a morality play about the romantic mythology of industrial culture that leads us to expect poets and philosophers will, in the pursuit of truth, sacrifice all bourgeois comforts, risking their professional standing and their own family's well-being.

What is becoming less clear as we begin to extricate ourselves from the ravages, environmental and psychological, of that culture is just what it is we had hoped to gain in the bargain:

> Phaedrus remembered a line from Thoreau: 'You never gain something but that you lose something.' And now he began to see for the first time the unbelievable magnitude of what man, when he gained power to understand and rule the world in terms of dialectic truths, had lost. He

had built empires of scientific capability to manipulate the phenomena of nature into enormous manifestations of his own dreams of power and wealth — but for this he had exchanged an empire of understanding of equal magnitude: an understanding of what it is to be a part of the world, and not an enemy of it (p. 372).

The relentless critical spirit of print literacy is willing to risk all the riches of material success in exchange for the truth, while failing to recognize that it is only the riches, only the continual search for greater control of nature, that empowers the spiritual quest in the first place. What Pirsig's narrator fails to grasp here, and what so often eludes most critiques of technology, is that there can be no empire of understanding without an empire of wealth, no critique of the self without an equally profound mastery of the world. That so simple and so basic a truth can prove so elusive says much about the prospects and limits of critical discourse. If, as critics of modernism contend, we cannot fully control the world, what chance do we have of fully understanding ourselves?

The new modes of computer-based reading and writing discussed in the next chapter are as a group more attuned to sharing information and less attuned to probing the secrets of ourselves or of the universe. When in Chapter 5 we come back to a consideration of the future of critical discourse in the computer age, we may be saved from being overly nostalgic about whatever it is we may be losing by the thought of Pirsig's solitary technical writer — a man whose passion for some deeper, purer form of truth, what he called the Church of Reason, led to his successive isolation from his fellow composition instructors at a Montana college, from fellow graduate students and the professors at the University of Chicago, and finally, after acts of psychic desperation, from his wife and son. What we are left with is a terrifying image of the solitary traveler, cut off from that son by the soundless glass door of a mental hospital:

> *'CHRIS!' I shout through the door. 'I'LL SEE YOU!' The dark figure moves toward me threateningly, but I hear Chris's voice, 'Where?' faint and distant. He heard me! And the dark figure, enraged, draws a curtain over the door.*
>
> *Not the mountain, I think. The mountain is gone. 'AT THE BOTTOM OF THE OCEAN!!' I shout.*
>
> *And now I am standing in the deserted ruins of a city all alone. The ruins are all around me endlessly in every direction and I must walk them alone* (p. 267).

Here is the psychic isolation and eventual paranoia, the 'mess', that can accompany the relentless explorer of *terra incognita*. For whatever rewards print literacy has had to offer — and they have been many — there has also been a price to pay: much of our landscape, like Pirsig's, has already been destroyed.

Chapter 3

The New Reading

> The birth of the reader must be requited by the death of the Author.
> Roland Barthes 'The Death of The Author'

On April 7, 1817, three enterprising young publishers called upon the great English poet and scholar, Samuel Taylor Coleridge, hoping to convince him to accept the position of editor of a new encyclopedia project, one designed to challenge the continuing prominence and commercial success of the *Britannica*, then already in its fifth edition. Their plan for this encyclopedia, the *Metropolitanna*, was based on a new answer to an old and perplexing question: what is the best way to arrange information so that it may be easily retrieved by future users with their own individual needs and perspective?

The easiest solution, and the one chosen by the original editors of the *Britannica* some half-century before, is to opt for simple, but random, alphabetic order. In such a reference work the entry for 'Pickett's Charge' presumably comes between 'piccolo' and 'Pickford, Mary', maybe under the entry for 'Pickett, General George E.', a handy arrangement when one wants only a quick identification, but not especially useful if one wants to learn more about the Battle of Gettysburg. Even a cross-reference from 'Pickett' to 'Gettysburg, Battle of', surrounded as it is by 'Gethsemane' and 'geysers', may not tell us what we need to know about Lee or Lincoln; for that, we need the major entry on the American Civil War, and perhaps on American history. To overcome these problems, encyclopedias organized by alphabetic systems have utilized what has become known as 'line-and-blister' method — a series of short entries interspersed with considerably longer, bulging (or 'blistering') entries. Using an alphabetic encyclopedia like the *Britannica* often involves a gallop through a series of cross-references and, beginning with the seventh edition, completed in 1842, an index as well, in search of the full context of what began as a single entry.

Coleridge, the model of the absent-minded professor intent upon reorganizing the world, not surprisingly had an intense dislike of the workable, although philosophically naive system of alphabetic ordering, and had so expressed himself in a letter fourteen years earlier. 'To call a huge unconnected miscellany of the *omne scibile*, in an arrangement determined by the accident of initial letters, an encyclopedia, is the impudent ignorance of your Presbyterian bookmakers' (Collison, 1966, p. 231). Thus it was with some expectations of success that Rest Fenner and his associates, Thomas and Samuel Curtis, approached the great author with a plan for publishing a new encyclopedia that would be based upon an idealistic philosophical tradition, one that sought a higher, unifying truth behind the vagaries of the particular. While neither his health nor his temperament proved suitable for such a project, Coleridge did agree to write a 'Treatise on Method', to be used as the Introduction to the encyclopedia, in which he outlined the principles for organizing all human knowledge, a problem of increasing interest today given the huge database capacity of modern computers and, as noted in Chapter 1, the seemingly geometrical increases in information, although at the time, one that did not seem to have much to do with literacy.

For the literate mind prior to the advent of computers, the central problem of human knowledge had to do, not with finding one's way through a forest of information, but with achieving genuine insight, usually expressed in terms of vertical movement. The original thinker gains a deeper (or higher) understanding, mainly through undertaking a more intense analysis of a single given situation or creative work — in literary study, for example, a reader undertakes successively more intense readings of a poem or short story, just as a writer in turn works more intensely at producing poems and short stories that reward such readings. In such a world the most valuable knowledge is not some huge concordance of ideas but the searing thought of a single philosophical or poetical mind, a thinker whose *magnum opus* (if only a single mathematical theorem) may lie unpublished, even undiscovered, for generations but, due to its brilliance, will eventually come to light, exerting its influence on readers, without public fanfare or the hype of publishers. It is the intensity of the writing experience — literally its distance (up or down) from a common baseline — that assures that a truly exceptional work will be found by any reader capable of climbing the necessary heights (or plummeting the depths). In true romantic spirit, the great work should remain hidden until the reader, as if on a quest, is spiritually ready to find it.

Best known as a Romantic poet and literary critic, Coleridge was also a product of an older rationalist tradition that was preoccupied by the larger question of the general structure of all human knowledge: how does one move from one experience or piece of information to the next? How does one structure the totality of knowledge so that individuals can use it for their own distinct purposes? Here, for example, in the speculations of H.G. Wells at the end of a long career marked by extended writing about the possibility of human progress, we can see such questions being raised:

> An immense and ever-increasing wealth of knowledge is scattered about the world today, a wealth of knowledge and suggestion that — systematically ordered and generally disseminated — would probably suffice to solve all the mighty difficulties of our age, but that knowledge is still dispersed, unorganized, impotent (p. 67).

Wells's solution, like Coleridge's, is to call for a more powerful means of organizing knowledge, specifically, for 'a new world organ for the collection, indexing, summarising and release of knowledge' (p. 85). What we need, finally, is not more original thought but 'the creation of an efficient index to *all* human knowledge, ideas and achievements ... the creation, that is, of a complete planetary memory of all mankind' (p. 60), what Wells calls 'a permanent world encyclopedia'. Here is an approach to knowledge that falls largely outside the modern literate tradition: we already know enough — we don't have to continue climbing higher, or digging deeper — what we have to do instead is to come up with an easy way of finding what we already know.

Just how far computers have come today in providing such planetary memory is a matter of some debate. Through the technology of storing an entire encyclopedia on a single laser disk, for example, computers do seem to have solved, at least for the moment, the problem of how to arrange individual entries. With computer-based access to information, the problem that entries must be in physical proximity to one another and therefore either arbitrarily or thematically juxtaposed simply disappears. The user of this new technology, the computer-based reader, is free, given the indexing apparatus built into the laser disk encyclopedia, to move through the text using either simple or compound searches (those involving *and*, *or*, and *not*) to retrieve any combination of information. In addition, certain important words and phrases can be premarked so that when an indicated key is pressed, for example, either a small window pops up with a detailed definition (and disappears with another keystroke) or one is moved to an entirely new but related entry (presumably with some means of returning to one's starting place). Yet the CD-ROM technology now used to distribute electronic encyclopedias (basically the same one now used to distribute up to seventy minutes of music), besides providing relatively slow access times, also suffers from a large but fixed capacity. As computer pioneer Ted Nelson notes, 'The good news [about CD-ROM] is that you can have 400MB on your disk; the bad news is that you can have *only* 400MB. What good are 400MB? I want everything' (Ditlea, 1990, p. 204).

Vannevar Bush's epochal 1945 *Atlantic Monthly* essay, 'As We May Think', is today widely recognized as the first serious attempt to lay out the principles and functions of a machine capable of meeting Nelson's demand, a true memory machine (what Bush calls a *memex*) that radically transforms the storage and retrieval limitations of print technology. 'The summation of human experience', Bush wrote nearly a half century ago, 'is being expanded at a prodigious rate, and the means we use for threading through the consequent maze to the momentarily important item is the same as was used in the days of square-rigged ships' (p. 102). Just as Coleridge in the 'Treatise on Method' decries the limitation of alphabetic ordering, what he called the 'dead and arbitrary arrangement, containing in itself no principle of progression' (p. 240), so Bush attacks 'the artificiality of [existing] systems of indexing':

> When data of any sort are placed in storage, they are filed alphabetically or numerically, and information is found (when it is) by tracing it down from subclass to subclass. It can be in only one place, unless duplicates are used; one has to have rules as to which path will locate it, and the rules are cumbersome. Having found one item, moreover, one has to emerge from the system and re-enter on a new path (p. 106).

What Bush envisions instead is a computerized workstation that would allow an individual to access and search massive amounts of information, retrieving and annotating whatever one would find important, what he calls 'a future device for individual use, which is a sort of mechanized private file and library' (p. 106).

For computer pioneer Ted Nelson, developer and promoter of perhaps the most ambitious and most widely publicized attempt to realize Bush's memex, the principal problem with traditional texts is that they provide readers with only one path, the author's, through a given body of information. What we need instead, Nelson argues, extending Bush's argument, is not a collection of books, like a metaphorical encyclopedia consisting of a series of individual articles placed one after the other, but a system that gives any user full and complete access to the total world of human knowledge, what he calls the *docuverse*. What we need is not a series of different interpretations of the world — not the insights of hundreds of Zarathustras — but all thoughts and ideas arranged in such a way that we can readily use this information for our own purpose. Or, as Bush suggests in an extended illustration, let us imagine a scholar interested in the general properties of the bow and arrow, specifically, in investigating why the Turkish short bows seemed to have an advantage over the English long bows during the Crusades:

> He has dozens of possibly pertinent books and articles in his memex. First he runs through an encyclopedia, finds an interesting but sketchy article, leaves it projected. Next, in a history, he finds another pertinent item, and ties the two together. Thus he goes, building a trail of many items. Occasionally he inserts a comment of his own, either linking it into the main trail or joining it by a side trail to a particular item. When it becomes evident that the elastic properties of available materials had a great deal to do with the bow, he branches off on a side trail which takes him through textbooks on elasticity and tables of physical constants. He inserts a page of longhand analysis of his own. Thus he builds a trail of his interest through the maze of materials available to him. (p. 107)

The organization of written materials in such a format, one that readers can move through in non-sequential fashion, in pursuit of their own ends (as opposed to the author's) Nelson has labeled, likely for all time, as *hypertext*. For Nelson, hypertext is more than a new mode of communication:

> Imagine a new libertarian literature with alternative explanations so anyone can choose the pathway or approach that best suits him or her; with ideas accessible and interesting to everyone, so that a new richness and freedom can come to the human experience; imagine a rebirth of literacy (1987, p. 1/4).

It is appropriate that Nelson has named the universal hypertext system he has developed and promoted over the last thirty years Project Xanadu, after Coleridge's own brilliantly hypertextual, poetical union of images, 'Kubla Khan'. Nelson's goal in Project Xanadu, like Bush's in 'As We May Think' from the mid-twentieth century and like Coleridge's 'Treatise on Method' from the early nineteenth century, is to break away from the arbitrary and isolated nature of individual writings by creating a single system that provides all of us with complete access to the endlessly expansive world of texts (the documentary equivalent of Coleridge's 'caverns measureless to man'). What is needed for such access, as noted by Coleridge, is a system based on a true understanding of

'Method', a term Coleridge traces back to its literal Greek meaning of *'a way, or path, of transit....* [T]he first idea of Method is *a progressive transition* from one step in any course to another; and where the word Method is applied with reference to many such transitions in continuity, it necessarily implies a principle of UNITY WITH PROGRESSION' (p. 239). Here then more than a century and a half ago is language that anticipates the 'trails' and 'pathways' that form the metaphoric language of hypertext:

> All things, in us, and about us, are a chaos without Method; as long
> as the mind is entirely passive, so long as there is an habitual submission
> of the understanding to mere events and images, as such, without
> any attempt to classify and arrange them, so long the chaos must
> continue.... But as soon as the mind becomes accustomed to contem-
> plate, not *things* only, but likewise *relations* of things, there is immediate
> need of some path or way of transit from one to the other of things
> related.... We may, therefore, assert that the *relations of things* form the
> prime objects, or so to speak, the *materials of Method*: and that the
> contemplation of those relations is the indispensable condition of think-
> ing methodically (p. 240).

Or as Vannevar Bush was to write, the mind works 'by association', not by filing and retrieving one item at a time:

> With one item in its grasp, it snaps instantly to the next that is suggested
> by the association of thoughts, in accordance with some intricate web of
> trails.... [T]he speed of action, the intricacy of trails, the detail of mental
> pictures, is awe-inspiring beyond all else in nature (p. 106).

Bush, like Coleridge before him and Nelson since, is seeking a new way to move through a text, a way that reflects the deeply held belief that, in the words of another hypertext enthusiast, Michael Joyce, 'habits of mind are naturally associative' (1988, p. 41) — that the basis of creative thought lies in our ability to make connections and, as a consequence, that the inestimable value of hypertext, or any earlier system of organizing writing, rests on its ability to represent information in the same infinitely fluid way we use it in the course of ordinary and extra-ordinary thinking. All three thinkers would fit in that group who see hypertext trails leading in Joyce's words, 'to a kind of shining electronic village upon a hill — an integrated, personalized, machine-enhanced, universally accessible, associative, new, yet familiar, world platted upon the patterns of synapses, deeded to each according to her or his needs.'

The promise of distant hillside cities undoubtedly has a certain appeal, especially for teachers who often feel as if their students are trapped in smog-covered lowlands of print technology. 'Imagine', Nelson challenges us, 'a new accessibility and excitement that can unseat the video narcosis that sits on our land like a fog' (1987, p. 1/4). There is an unmistakably visionary aspect of hypertext — and Ted Nelson is, if nothing else, a prophet. Before rushing off to join a new exodus to this virtual promised land, however, we do need to subject the promises of hypertext to more careful scrutiny. After all, many of us can still remember the time before 'video narcosis' when the world was filled with exaggerated expectations for the educational possibilities of that other electronic technology, television. We have all witnessed the triumph of the video revolution, but not all of us are comforted by the fact that our students learn more today from watching television than from reading books.

There are many old uses for a new technology. A typical use for a parent with a new video camera is the filming of a child's school play, usually with one continuous fixed shot. Likewise, we can read an ordinary piece of writing on a computer, using the 'page down' key (itself a metaphor) to move through this text *as if* it were part of a book, that is, as if the screens were physically linked together like the pages in a printed volume. And in either case, the new technology serves as only a limited substitute for the original — the book is easier to read and manipulate in printed form just as the play is more enjoyable in person. Indeed, the original form is so superior that in both cases we have tended to see the new technology merely as a means of aiding in the production of the older form. Video cameras, for example, were first widely used in schools, not in new experimental film-making classes, but in traditional drama classes for taping rehearsals. And so computers have been seen as enhancements to the existing writing curriculum, as CAI ('computer-aided instruction') replacing the ubiquitous ditto worksheets in less progressive classes and as word processors facilitating revision in more progressive ones.

It may seem odd that a book dealing with computers and the future of literacy will have so little to say about the impact of word processing, a technology that for the 1980s was almost synonymous with the use of personal computers in writing programs. Yet Michael Heim's *Electric Language: A Philosophical Study of Word Processing* (1987) demonstrates the difficulty in discussing the wider cultural implications of this technology. Computer-based writing, like computer-based reading, the subject of this chapter, is based on a simple technological breakthrough — the ability to insert new material anywhere in a piece of writing and, as it were, automatically and instantly push over all the remaining text. With such an ability — a common feature of all word processing programs — it becomes almost as easy for a writer to change, or revise, a text as to leave it alone. Whether or not students, or writers generally, are inclined to take advantage of this technological facility for revising, and just what classroom practices might better equip them to do so, continue to be major areas of investigation in writing research. It is in some ways an important discussion but in the end one not unlike a consideration of the impact of using videotaped rehearsals to improve dramatic performance. In each case the emphasis is on using a new technology to facilitate a pre-existing product, either a class play or a student essay.

The really interesting philosophical questions about word processing that Heim attempts to raise in his study begin only when the technology works to undermine, or deconstruct, the traditional literate text in one of two ways: either by enhancing its printed form, what happens when we gain the power to produce what looks like a 'published' document, or (what interests Heim more) by enhancing its screen form, what happens when because of our editing skills the text begins to seem completely malleable, almost fluid on the screen, becomes a virtual text, what Diane Balestri (1988) calls *softcopy*. Word processing, in other words, begins to exert a significant impact upon the future of literacy only when we become either more or less interested in the traditional printed (literally, typed) version of what we are writing.

Increasing the emphasis on print moves word processing in the direction of desktop publishing, a practice already well-established in the word processing market because of the intense competition among software developers to enhance their programs with more of the complex tools required to design and print documents with multiple fonts, columns, and graphics, tools that were formerly the exclusive province of professional typesetters. We have hardly begun to ask, for example, how giving all writers the ability to produce published forms of their own texts will affect our notion of authorship or how giving them the ability to integrate graphics into their documents will affect our notion of writing. Such questions concerning the changing authority of authors and the impact of graphics deal in a related but opposite way with the main focus of this chapter; they ask about the effect of moving word processing in the direction of *hard* rather than *soft* copy. The two, however, may not be entirely the opposites they seem, since what eventually is to be printed must first exist on the screen in soft, malleable form, and all contact with such a text, even if it is to be printed at some point, moves the experience of word processing in the direction of hypertext. That is, the longer and the more intensely involved we become with a virtual text — the more familiar we become with its inherent flexibility — the less satisfied we are likely to be producing what can only be a mere snapshot of what in its electronic form seems to have a richly multidimensional life of its own.

Yet it is not in the act of writing, but of reading, that online literacy, like the alphabetic and print literacy before it, has its revolutionary impact. The vital role the recently perfected alphabet played in classical Greece, argues Eric Havelock, had less to do with allowing a few people to write (only a few people then, or possibly ever, have had much to say) and more to do with allowing many people to read. And so it was with the invention of mechanized printing in the fifteenth century, and so it seems it will be the case with computers today — that basic changes in literacy are triggered by new technologies of reading. At the core of each of these revolutions rests an extraordinarily simple technological break-through: with the alphabet, the ability to create all possible syllables by combining a limited number of consonants and vowels; with printing, the ability to create a plate for a page of text by using individual letters; and with the computer, the ability to move via the computer screen from one place in one text, depending on the system used, to practically any place in any text.

Where one can move in any one jump is an important element, and constraint, in any hypertext system, yet the main idea behind hypertext is largely independent of any particular system. Word processing programs with search commands, for example, already allow us to move forward and backward to the next occurrence of any term, or possibly combination of terms, in any one document, and there are simple retrieval programs that extend this capacity to all data files on one's hard disk. The newer storage medium of CD-ROM contains the equivalent of roughly 200,000 typed pages, usually with a built-in indexing procedure for moving directly from one screen to another. Even as we search across a single file, hard disk, or CD-ROM, our activities take on the two defining characteristics of hypertext. First, the individual works lose their distinctive boundaries (their former clearly marked beginnings and endings) as part of a larger database, and second, the searching and eventual reading activity are themselves largely driven by the user or 'reader'. The author, when there is one (reference databases often being anonymous), has the task of providing the general context, not a single specific track, within which a reader moves.

When we read a loosely structured literary work like Whitman's *Leaves of Grass*, for example, we are given a path to follow — image by image, line by line, stanza by stanza, poem by poem — throughout the entire text. When we work with this same volume online, searching backward and forward following the trail of images and illusions that interest us (even using nothing more powerful than a simple word processing program), the entire nature of the reading process is transformed. *Leaves of Grass* changes from a set of poems with an extended linear sequence established by the author to a computer database, a collection of information stored in one form by the author (or compiler) but accessed by the reader in another. Traditional readers have always had the option of browsing through a text, especially reading poems in a collection, in whatever order they chose. What is special about hypertext is the possibility that, given the needs of specific users, the boundaries of the individual poems will disappear, as it occurs regularly without computers, it should be noted, in a critical analysis of poetic images in Whitman or in any work of literary criticism that treats themes and other topics as they appear in a number of different works.

Hypertexts obviously have more powerful designs than the simple search procedures of word processors or retrieval programs, although their immediate, stated goal may be quite traditional. For George Landow of Brown University, a fully developed hypertext system is less a means of dissolving Whitman's poems into a shapeless database than it is a system for providing all readers with access to the full range of historical, literary, textual, and biographical materials that might enrich their reading of the poems. His specific concern is notably conservative, to provide college students in an introductory survey of English literature with access to the same full range of references and allusions that characterizes the informed readings of experts. The professor and the student, in Landow's view, ordinarily read different versions of *Paradise Lost*, although each is using the same text:

> Whereas Professor Jones experiences the great seventeenth-century epic situated with a field of relations and connections, her student encounters a far barer, less connected, reduced poem, most of whose allusions go unrecognized and almost all of whose challenges pass unperceived (1988, p. 1).

Hypertext for Landow is a technology for allowing 'Mr Smith, the student, to experience some of the connections obvious to Professor Jones.'

Here is Landow's account of how Jane Lee, another imaginary student, actually uses the Brown University hypertext system to 'read' Charles Dickens' classic novel, *Great Expectations*.

> Jane sits down at a computer console with a large screen on which she encounters three-dimensional images of folders lying on a desk top. Touching the folder labeled 'Literature' with her finger tip, she thereby opens it, finds another series of folders bearing names of various languages and nations, and chooses 'English'. Upon opening the English

folder, she encounters others inside bearing names of authors (Dickens, Lessing), movements or periods (aestheticism, Victorian), and concepts or approaches (literary techniques, feminism). Touching that for Charles Dickens, she opens it and finds a series of documents and additional folders that include several graphics documents some of whose titles include the word *overview*. Choosing 'Dickens overview', she finds a familiar graphic directory in which the name of the novelist appears together with his portrait and dates within a rectangle at the center. Surrounding this rectangle are a number of others bearing various texts, including 'Biography', 'Literary Relations', 'Cultural Context: Victorianism', 'Literary Techniques: Imagery', 'Political and Economic Context', 'Religion', and 'Works'. Choosing 'Works', she opens a list of the novelist's complete works, which appears on the lower left of her computer screen, and then opens *Great Expectations*, which appears in the center of her screen, to the page at which she had last been reading the paperback copy she left in her room. (Approximately thirty seconds have elapsed since Jane first sat down to work.) (1992).

The electronic version of the novel is enmeshed in a world of choices that does not end once the student has begun reading. Information that in a richly annotated student edition might be physically placed on all sides of the primary reading — before it in a preface, under it as footnotes, alongside it as marginalia, above it as picture, and after it as an afterword — is now electronically linked to the text itself. One can effortlessly re-create the formerly arduous task of physically searching a library to locate a series of secondary sources on *Great Expectations* merely by pressing the indicated key whenever a change in the cursor indicates that the current text is connected to other material.

Such a hypertext system may seem to be only a vastly more efficient means of providing students with a wealth of ancillary materials — a high-powered footnoting system in the same sense that a word processor can be seen as a high-powered typewriter. It is this capacity of computers to intensify the basic pattern of print literacy that Landow sees in the work of Walter Ong. '[T]he sequential processing and spatializing of the word, initiated by writing and raised to a new order of intensity by print, is further intensified by the computer, which ... optimizes analytic sequentiality by making it virtually instantaneous' (Ong, 1982, p. 136). Yet such an analogy is only partially accurate. Landow's students are not just reading works in the modern sense (striving for an ever richer personal experience) but 'reading up' on those works in a post-print sense, striving to place the work in a universal context. These students move from screen to screen when working with text on a computer as a means of establishing what Landow calls 'a web of relations' (1988, p. 11). The key to hypertext, for Landow and for others, is a fundamentally new way of thinking, a mode of thought based on a specific belief:

[that] one proceeds in understanding any particular literary or other phenomenon by relating it to other phenomena, and that one begins this process by asking about the possible existence of relations to other such phenomena, at which point one investigates them and tries to perceive relations among them all (1988, p. 6).

Here is the new spatial world of online literacy, one where the metaphorical journey through text, formerly linear and hierarchical in the age of print, now becomes nonsequential and multidimensional, and in so doing radically alters the connection between reader, author and text at the center of print literacy.

'Can technology', asks Landow rhetorically, 'so challenge established notions of writing, authorship, and authorial property?' (1990, p. 427) Can hypertext erode the notion of the self-contained text that forms the basis of print literacy, alter the belief that a unique piece of writing, created by an author, protected by copyright, and systematically consumed by a reader is the product of a particular historical period? Have there not been equally momentous changes in the past? Before the alphabet there was only utterance, some more complex and protracted than others; before printing, only a multitude of copies. As Landow reasons:

> Since the technology of printing and book production clearly created current notions of grammar, fixed orthography, national languages, copyright, and so on, one should expect that a technology that again shifts the relation of author, reader, and work would again have equally powerful effects' (1990, p. 427).

Technology does powerfully affect literacy, but Landow seems only interested in those technologies that enhance (deepen) our experience with print. The more we know about a literary work, or presumably a painting or musical composition, he suggests, the deeper our experience of it. Landow rejects the tension, explicit in New Criticism, and implicit in print literacy generally, between gathering information about the text and having a private, intensely personal experience of it — hypertext, the ultimate information-gathering tool, thus becomes the ultimate reading environment. His imaginary scenario, however, only masks this tension between conflicting models of reading. While Landow does describe a student reading *Great Expectations* at a computer terminal — the opening hypertext screen coinciding with the title-page of the novel, each successive screen representing the next printed page — using an elaborate hypertext system for such a purpose is a clear example of the retrograde application of a new technology, analogous to early use of the alphabet to write out speeches so that they could be memorized, or to the early use of print to reproduce the florid manuscript style. The practice of reading self-contained printed texts is hardly going to disappear overnight, or any time in the foreseeable future. Memorizing remained a principal component of education well into the twentieth century (over 2000 years after writing made it technologically obsolete for many purposes), and some people still recite stories using structuring devices from an oral tradition just as others still practise calligraphy — although both now frequently at craft shows where they are clearly marked as productive activities of an earlier economic age.

The reading and writing of individual texts may also become crafts in the world of online literacy. There the object of exchange will not be the individual text but literature itself, defined as the full extension of the connective and storage capacity inherent in hypertext, what Nelson defines as 'a connected system of documents' (1992). Thus there is for Nelson the *literature* of Dickens, and the *literature* of English literature, and even the *literature* of literature, which is to individual literatures (of Dickens, for instance) as the universe is to the galaxies, hence his term, the *docuverse*. Reading a Dickens novel on a hypertext system that gives one access to the wider (complete?) literature of Victorian England naturally encourages wider-ranging questions, in a process that reaches far beyond the scope of any one class. There is only one future, Nelson argues, and that is 'open hypertext publishing', a 'unifying system' capable of merging 'many different hypertextual and hypermedia objects[,] ... created under different rules, with different graphics, with different styles of interaction, into a unified literature ... that we may all access through whatever machine we use' (1992).

In a world defined by a single literature rather than a multitude of texts, reading becomes essentially a means of finding one's way — one moves, not ever deeper into a single text in quest of some world-altering hermeneutic understanding, but playfully between texts, from side to side as it were. As Landow quotes Thaïs Morgan, it is a matter of a new 'intertextuality', one concerned with a 'structural or synchronic model of literature as a sign system' replacing an older 'evolutionary model of literary history'. 'The most salient effect of this strategic change is to free the literary text from psychological, sociological, and historical determinisms, opening it up to an apparently infinite play of relationships' (Landow, 1988, p. 9). Hypertext thus supports the wider contemporary movement away from a serious, introspective, relentlessly psychological (and often Germanic) hermeneutic tradition of interpretation — one often associated with modernism, despite its unmistakable nineteenth-century romantic origins — and toward a decidedly more ludic (and often Gallic) postmodern concern with defining reading, and cultural criticism generally, as the play of signs. In the sections below, we will consider how this shift alters our primary understanding of the central terms of *text*, *author*, and *reader*.

The Text

Roland Barthes' 1971 essay, 'From Work to Text', although nominally about the changing status of the literary work, can also be read as prolegomenon for a new computer-based, hypertextual notion of text. For Barthes, the *work* is the literary object with which we are accustomed: the product of a more stable Newtonian world, it is something real, something that can be 'held in the hand'; even if it is only 'a fragment of substance', it is nonetheless something that can be seen 'in bookstores, in card catalogues, on examination syllabuses' (Barthes, 1986, p. 57). The *text*, on the other hand, represents less a new object than a new attitude, a view of the goal of reading as a locus of activity, a place where the experience of reading a traditional work causes one to reach out in many directions, to link to (in a hypertextual sense) an ever-expansive world of meanings: '*The Text is experienced only in an activity, in a production*. It follows that the Text cannot stop (for example, at a library shelf); its constitutive moment is *transversal* (notably, it can transverse the work, several works)' (1986, p. 58). Whereas the work is often in need of interpretation ('Marxist, psychoanalytic, thematic, etc.'), an understanding of the Text is 'not achieved by some organic process of maturation, or a hermeneutic process of 'delving deeper', but rather by a serial movement of dislocation, overlappings, variations; the logic governing the Text is not comprehensive (trying to define what the work 'means') but 'metonymic', a term Barthes describes as 'the activity of associations, contiguities, cross-references'

(1986, p. 59). Or, as Ted Nelson says less obliquely, 'In any ongoing literature, there is perpetual interpretation and reinterpretation, and links between documents that follow up the connections' (1987, p. 2/10).

Barthes' 'Text' is thus a precursor of the hypertextual notion of all writing as part of a single universal literature.

> The Text is not coexistence of meaning, but passage, transversal; hence, it depends not on interpretation, however liberal, but on an explosion, on dissemination. The plurality of the Text depends, as a matter of fact, not on the ambiguity of its contents, but on what we might call the stereographic plurality of the signifiers which weave it (etymologically, the text is a fabric) (1986, pp. 59–60).

For Barthes, the defining metaphor of the work, like writing before hypertext, is that of an organism, something that 'grows by vital expansion, by "development"', as if a single lifelike entity: the defining metaphor of the Text, most appropriately, is that of the '*network*' (1986, p. 61). This networked Text embodies what Barthes calls 'a paradoxical idea of structure', an idea that as well as any defines hypertext, 'a system without end or center' (1986, p. 59).

A text without end or center is in our normal usage not a text at all but literature itself, or conversely, as Barthes says in *S/Z*, 'literature itself is never anything but a single text: the one text is not an (inductive) access to a Model, but entrance into a network with a thousand entrances' (1974, p. 12). To read this text is, in Barthes' words, to take 'aim', not at an object, but at a 'perspective (of fragments, of voices from other texts, other codes)'. The object of our reading, this 'perspective', is obviously a text only in some new and, in terms of print technology, seemingly paradoxical sense. Only in the electronic world of hypertexts does the enigmatic aphorism of Marxist philosopher Theodore Adorno make sense literally: 'Today the only works which really count are those which are no longer works at all' (1973, p. 30).

The Author

At the conclusion of 'From Work to Text', Barthes suggests how this open-ended notion of text will affect our traditional understanding of what it means to be an author by considering parallels with changes in the social function of music. Once, Barthes notes, thinking of the role of the piano in the bourgeois family, playing and listening to music 'constituted a virtually undifferentiated activity' (1986, p. 63), at least among a certain class. Here is a world without clear demarcation between creating and performing, and, by extension, between writing and reading. While a text in such a world may be generated by an individual, the life of that text is defined less by that individual than by those active participants — players or readers who freely interact with and transform whatever authorial intent has been implanted in the text. As Barthes writes, the modern notion of text 'requires an attempt to abolish (or at least to diminish) the distance between writing and reading, not by intensifying the reader's projection into the work, but by linking the two together into one and the same signifying practice' (1986, p. 62). This text, like the music of an earlier age, is designed as the basis of collaboration. Against such free play of the text, the formal concertizing tradition, like the modern tradition of print literacy, has tended to render the listener (reader) passive, exalting first the performer and later the composer. With the advent of recorded music (now of increasingly high quality), the modern listener has become more passive and more isolated. Serious music in the age of print, like serious writing, is organized in the service of the dominating author/composer — it is his wishes (and such a god-like figure was normally marked as male), as expressed in the score, or literary work, that listeners, readers, and critics are supposed to serve.

As Barthes describes in another seminal essay, 'The Death of the Author', the text is similar to hypertext and the soft copy of online literacy:

> [It] consists not of a line of words, releasing a single 'theological' meaning (the 'message' of the Author-God), but of a multidimensional space in which are married and contested several writings, none of which is original: the text is a fabric of quotations, resulting from a thousand sources of culture (1986, pp. 52–53).

In exposing the popular notion of a unified text as the expression of unified psyche, Barthes provides a systematic literary analysis of the founding notion of online literacy, that computer-based writing is essentially authorless.

> [S]ucceeding the Author, the *scriptor* no longer contains passions, moods, sentiments, impressions, but that immense dictionary from which he draws a writing which will be incessant: life merely imitates the book, and this book is itself but a tissue of signs, endless imitation, infinitely postponed' (1986, p. 53).

If any text is, like a hypertext, no more than a collection of fragments, the author becomes no more than that personage charged with collecting and arranging that material. Behind our traditional notion of the author as the unifying force responsible for creating the text — what Italian author Italo Calvino satirically refers to as 'that anachronistic personage, the bearer of messages, the director of consciences, the giver of lecturers to cultural bodies' (1986, p. 16) — is not a human being but an historical construct. The future of authorship may have less to do with a single vision of writing defined in terms of invention, creativity, and copyright than with earlier, multiple visions. In the thirteenth century, for example, Saint Bonaventura spoke not of one type of producer of books but four: *scriptor*, one who 'might write the works of others, adding and changing nothing'; *compilator*, one who 'writes the work of others with additions which are not his own'; *commentator*, one who 'writes both others' work and his own, but with others' work in principal place, adding his own for purposes of explanation'; and, finally, *auctor*, one who 'writes both his own work and others' but with his own work in principal place adding others' for purpose of confirmation' (Eisenstein, 1983, p. 84).

All forms of computer-based writing seem to be returning us to a world of multiple notions of authorship, based on multiple notions of texts. The concept of the author, Foucault argues, since the eighteenth century tied it to bourgeois notions of 'individualism and private property' (1984, p. 119) and embodied it in the image of 'a necessary or constraining figure', is in the process of changing like society itself, loosing all connection to an identifiable human form, disappearing as it were into a vast system of writing, the rules that govern what is considered writing. What can change — including our sense of what it means to be an author — likely will change, not just as some may have first interpreted Foucault, in some metaphorical sense but in real and practical ways. As with Nelson's docuverse, or the totality of messages on an e-mail system, there are many individual writers, players of the game, but no authors, no one who has written the interconnected set of writings that now constitute the text. At that point, Foucault concludes, 'All discourses, whatever their status, form, value, and whatever the treatment to which they will be subjected, would then develop in the anonymity of a murmur' (1984, p. 119).

The Reader

The deaths of the author and the text so boldly announced by postmodern critics and so clearly visible in the conditions of online literacy itself are offset by the renewed life of the reader. The online reader is a new form of Barthes' amateur musician, the person who as readily makes music as listens to it — or, to phrase matters more exactly, the person for whom the seemingly separate acts of creating and reproducing are inextricably interwoven. As a team of actual hypertext developers writes,

> Ideally authors and readers should have the same set of integrated tools that allow them to browse through other material during the document preparation process and to add annotations and original links as they progress through an information web. In effect the boundary between author and reader should largely disappear' (Yankelovich, *et al.*, 1985, p. 21).

It is in the new role of the reader that Barthes locates the entire movement of a new, postmodern literacy.

> Here we discern the total being of writing: a text consists of multiple writings, proceeding from several cultures and entering into dialogue, into parody, into contestation; but there is a site where this multiplicity is collected, and this site is not the author, as has hitherto been claimed, but the reader: the reader is the very space in which are inscribed, without any of them being lost, all the citations out of which a writing is made; the unity of a text is not in its origin but in its destination (1986, p. 54).

The online text is nothing but a database out of which new readers construct paths to meet their specific and individual needs — it is akin to a board game, a place where many individual pieces are connected by the rules for play. Meanwhile the author of the online text is nothing but the source (often corporate rather than personal) responsible for establishing and maintaining the rules for operating that database. There is no longer any basis for the central notion of print literacy, that literate exchange involves the comprehension of the unity of knowledge or vision represented by structures in either the distant author or the present (and seemingly stable) text.

What there is, instead, is the new notion of the fully engaged reader — the performer as well as the listener. For its advocates, hypertext is a medium for literate exchange that truly engages students, lifting them out of the passivity and lethargy associated with being only the receivers of other people's prepackaged ideas. It stands in opposition to traditional patterns of learning, even ordinary computer-assisted instruction — what George Landow refers to as 'a McDonald's of education whose products they can engorge in passivity' (1988, p. 3). Landow's students in his hypertext-based literature course, Context 32, are asked to do more than follow predetermined links. They are encouraged to add their own comments and their own links to this ever-expanding web of information about English literature. And in wandering through and connecting the links in such a web his students are engaging in the central activity of education — the development of independent critical thinking. Such thinking, Landow argues, 'centers on the notion that an educated intelligence perceives any particular phenomenon as potentially multi-determined and subject to multi-causation'. Immersing students in hypertext 'encourages the habit of approaching any literary (or other) fact from multiple directions' (1988, p. 3) — that same associative model of understanding at the heart of Coleridge's notion of method.

What remains unclear in all such discussions of hypertext is the connection between the associative thinking of this 'new' literacy and the critical thinking of print literacy. This question, in turn, raises the larger one about the connection between print and online literacy, and here the most obvious and most immediately appealing argument is to see computers as adding to, not reversing, the best that has come before. For example, one of the most vocal advocates of computer-based writing programs, Cynthia Selfe, uses the metaphor of 'a multi-layered literacy' to express the sense of how students trained in print will adjust to online literacy. For Selfe, print literacy is likely to remain our first language for some time, with teachers having to offer students direct instruction in using the grammar of the screen, not just how to move quickly from one place in the text as readers but also how to use specific screen characteristics such as color to indicate levels of importance in creating texts. Rather than confront an entirely new pedagogic future, one totally liberated from print, Selfe prefers to see the associative powers of online literacy as an enhancement to existing literate practice. One teaches hypertext, as Joyce here suggests Balestri does, as a means of extending critical thinking. '[She] points to the need for training hypertext audiences in these new habits of thought necessary to perceive coherence in patterns and links, and to generate patterns and links of their own' (1988, p. 13). The new expands the powers of the old, or as Ron Fortune states,

> By developing visual abilities in conjunction with verbal, we may be providing students with a special means of extending their critical thinking and writing abilities more efficiently and more effectively than is possible if we restrict writing instruction to verbal expression alone' (1989, p. 160).

Fortune's position articulated here, that the computer technology most evident in hypertext enhances, not subverts, the critical aim of print literacy, is expanded upon by Michael Joyce and Jay Bolter, collaborators on the hypertext program *Storyspace*. Joyce's thought-provoking speculations, contained in his article 'Siren Shapes: Exploratory and Constructive Hypertexts' (1988), reflecting his practical experience as a writing instructor at a community college, provides an extended gloss on the connections between online literacy and critical thinking. For Joyce the key to both critical thinking and hypertext is the same active 'transformation of knowledge', one based on the recognition that 'understanding, plotting, navigating, and recreating knowledge structures is the essence of learning' (p. 12).

Joyce sees the mainstream hypertext system (is it already possible to talk of 'traditional' hypertext?) as a technology for exploration, what he calls 'a delivery or presentational technology', one that allows 'an audience (users or readers are inadequate terms here) to control the transformation of a body of information to meet its needs and interests' (p. 11). An exploratory hypertext system allows users 'to view and test alternate organizational structures of their own and, perhaps, compare their own structures of thought with hypertext and traditional ones.' Constructive hypertexts, on the other hand, Joyce defines as 'an invention or analytic tool' like outlining programs and personal information managers (programs designed for what Joyce, borrowing Jane Douglas' term, calls 'scriptors'). 'More so than with exploratory hypertexts, constructive hypertexts require a capability to act: to create, to change, and to recover particular encounters within the developing body of knowledge' (p. 11). The 'trails, paths, webs, notebooks' we ordinarily create with exploratory hypertexts now reflect something truly different and more creative, what Joyce calls 'versions of what they are becoming, a structure for what does not yet exist.' A constructive hypertext affords users a new technology, not to map what we already know, but instead to create 'visual representations of the knowledge they develop.' In their activity here, the computer has truly become 'a tool for inventing, discovering, viewing, and testing multiple, alternative, organizational structures, as well as a tool for comparing these structures of thought with more traditional ones, and transforming the one into the other' (p. 12).

Print literacy compels us to adjust the fullness of experience to the linear demands of writing. 'To make someone write', explains Harry Berger, 'is to make him reduce the multi-dimensionality of all his experiences, squeeze them through the typewriter as through a wringer, and turn them out as black print' (Farrell, 1977, p. 451). The text that we produce using the conventional tools of print, unlike Joyce's constructive hypertext, is necessarily the result of this compromise, or, as Bolter suggests, a constant struggle between the principles of hierarchy, the order we impose upon our writing, for example, by outlining — and association — all the connections that work to 'subvert that order' (1991, p. 22). Associative relations, 'subversive texts-behind-the-text' are always present working against the order that we announce in our headings and structural divisions. While the table of contents of a traditional book represents an abstract of its actual linear structure, the index represents its associative potential, defining 'other books that could be constructed from the materials at hand'. With a tool for constructive hypertext, such either/or choices can be avoided; what is possible, instead, is the attainment of what Bolter calls 'topographic writing', writing that not only discusses different topics but in an electronic sense actually occupies different places. 'In the world of hypertext', Bolter states, 'to write is to make connections' (1992); to make what Joyce calls, in an admittedly bad pun, 'missing links, i.e., novel structures of thought and new rhetorical forms', forms that will replace 'structures we have come to believe are more god-given than Gutenbergian' (p. 14).

The replacement of Gutenbergian structures in practice proves to be more problematic. It is easier to praise the postmodern aesthetics of hypertext, it turns out, than to demonstrate it in any compelling fashion. Embedded in Joyce's article, for example, is the anecdote of Les, the basic writing student who used the hypertext program *Storyspace* to organize an essay about various cars he had driven. In a class discussion of the paper, Les finally made it clear that he actually saw the parts of the paper as existing synchronically, as parts of a map in space. 'On the computer', he said, 'that stuff about the car belongs next to the Lynx, and I moved the box but forgot to put it back. It makes sense in the right place' (p. 41). Here for Joyce was joyous confirmation that *Storyspace* was not just an outlining tool but a tool for a new kind of spatial thinking. 'The verbal formulation of the paper led, topographically, from the visual representation of it. O brave new world, he was saying.'

Joyce himself, in his hypertext fiction, notably in his interactive story, 'Afternoon', is an explorer of this new world, just as Jay Bolter is his main champion. For Bolter, Joyce's endlessly shifting literary construction is the embodiment of the postmodern aesthetic — 'An electronic text like "Afternoon" . . . not meant to be read, but always reread' (1992). It is a story embedded in hypertext form allowing readers to choose an individual path each time they encounter the screen — 'An electronic fiction [that] is not only a fictional universe, but a universe of possible fictions' (1992). In response to charges that the element of play dominates the reader's involvement with hypertext fiction, Bolter replies that it is instead 'the antithesis of escapist literature: there would be no escaping the text as a structure of elements.' Reading a hypertext, in other words, is 'in the tradition of good critical reading in all of the previous technologies of writing', requiring as it does 'the constant engagement of the reader with the text as texture' (1992).

One can hardly question Bolter's sense of the intensity required of a reading of a single hypertext fiction, but consider as well the different sort of problems confronting another hypertext reader — Landow's imaginary student, Jane, sitting at the computer console preparing to read *Great Expectations*. It is impossible to deny that many students in George Landow's English literature survey at Brown University profited from using the extensive hypertext system as a means of preparing for classes. Discussions were livelier — and why shouldn't they be when students had quick and easy access to a range of secondary sources about the texts under consideration? Anyone who has taught literature knows that students are frequently baffled by the complexity and at times stylistic impenetrability of the literary texts themselves, and, consequently, relish all sorts of classroom aids into the materials. One might argue we live in an age that routinely discusses many cultural icons — from Marx and Freud to Allan Bloom and Alice Walker — not by reading their works but by reading and, more frequently now, viewing popular discussions about their works. But Jane, faced with the task of actually reading Dickens' novel, must nevertheless plow through approximately 180,000 words of text, some eight and a half hours of intensive labor (at the rate of 360 words a minute), with no guarantee of attaining a satisfactory level of understanding unless her comprehension skills are above average.

Students in Jane's situation, in much larger numbers than any of us care to admit, have long turned to literary guides, simulacra of the texts — the most visible being the boldly striped *Cliff's Notes* — to provide them an easier path through (and, at least as often, around) complex and long literary texts. What Bolter does not consider in his discussion of the experience of reading Joyce's 'Afternoon' is what happens when the story is not a self-contained fictional universe, read by someone interested in having a rich aesthetic experience, but only a tiny part of a vast hypertext network. One where harried and information-driven readers, instead of spending a few hours exploring Joyce's constantly shifting story, can find out the least they need to know more readily by clicking on screens containing background information about Joyce, interactive fiction, and the story itself. The point at issue here is not whether the hypertext environment can support the level of aesthetic reading associated with print literacy, especially for those fully acculturated into the world of print — but how different the experience of reading the most aesthetically complex hypertext may be for 'readers' in the future who will be fully acculturated into an electronic world, possibly ordinary students of the next century who have no sustained experience of print. Just how likely is it that people for whom reading has become an act defined largely in terms of using the computer either to access needed information on demand or to be entertained by the slam-bang integration of 3-D graphics and CD sound will be willing — or able — to sit before a terminal patiently selecting the paths in a single author-designed hypertext in order to have something akin to a traditional literary experience?

We seem to have little idea of just how dynamic (hyperactive?) the computer screen is likely to become once the hardware and software are in place to support real-time video and the wizardry of multimedia. Richard Kearney cites a relevant and troubling, albeit undocumented, statistic: 'that since the arrival of multi-channel press-button TV in the US, less than 50 per cent of American children under the age of 15 have ever watched a single programme from start to finish' (1988, p. 1). Some might be tempted to find hope in such numbers, given the dreadful programming on TV, yet 'zapping', as anyone with such a device must realize, has far more to do with pacing than with judgment, more to do, that is, with our exploiting the hypertextual capability of a new online technology in order to assemble a more pleasing (more postmodern?) procession of images. Our ability or willingness to attend closely and for prolonged periods of time to the narrative experiences of others — the basis of nineteenth-century novel reading and until recently twentieth-century television watching — is intimately connected to our broader experience of print culture and the inner consciousness that it both demanded and rewarded. A new cultural landscape, one grounded in computer technology, will affect all of us, professors and students alike. All of us, and not just hyperactive adolescents, will zap. 'When the only tool you have is a hammer', quips Abraham Maslow, 'everything begins to look like a nail' (Burnham, 1983, p. 151).

Liora Alschuler elucidates the knottiness of these problems by distinguishing two kinds of hypertexts: hypertexts where the nodes are identified and the links are made by an 'author' (hypertexts she helpfully labels *hand-crafted*; 1989) and those formed by allowing readers to access any materials with the right kind of computer program, one capable of indexing diverse textual materials and enabling users to jump (and to mark those jumps) from place to place. The difference here is between hypertext as a new kind of document, one with a certain literary potential that demands a new kind of author and a new rhetoric of composition, and hypertext as an information management system, controlled by the users (consumers) of information, people formerly called 'readers.' This second kind of hypertext, based upon what Alschuler calls 'random, intelligent, or automated linking' (p. 344), has few literary pretensions — to be successful, it needs neither new authors nor new rhetoricians, but only programmers capable of indexing and linking ever-increasing amounts of information and users who for practical reasons (for example, managing a stock portfolio) need access to this diverse material. Such automated, information-based hypertext undermines the kind of literary hypertext Bolter works so hard in *Writing Space* to establish as a major new literary genre. It is hypertext without the remnant of an older, print-based literacy theory, hypertext without the romance of authorship.

To highlight the differences between hand-crafted and automated (what might be called literary and nonliterary) hypertext, Alschuler compares three different hand-crafted hypertexts, each representing a hypertextual version of the same six essays on hypertext that were first delivered at Hypertext '87, a conference held at the University of North Carolina, and then later published in the July 1988 issue of *Communications of the ACM* (Association for Computing Machines). In hypertext format they were called, not surprisingly, *Hypertext on Hypertext*, and appeared in separate versions prepared by the top investigators in the field — a HyperCard version for the Apple Macintosh, prepared by the Institute for Research in Information and Scholarship (IRIS) at Brown Universities (the same group who developed George Landow's Intermedia project), an IBM version, using HyperTIES, developed at the University of Maryland, and a version for the SUN-3 workstation, using a third program.

Alschuler's conclusion was that there were enormous differences among the three programs as well as enormous inconsistencies within them, having to do less with 'design decisions' than with 'the subjective nature' of such hypertexts. 'The lack of relationship between different linking schemes, even within the same program, the random order of embedded links and their erratic coverage of the subject matter are all hallmarks of hand-crafted hypertext links' (p. 358). For many of their needs Alschuler suggests that users will be as well, if not better, served by key-word searches that are entirely machine-created. 'Even in hyperspace', Alschuler writes, 'without multiple windows, the user goes to only one place at a time' (p. 359), and with windows, one has only the maddening options of many places one cannot possibly go next. Alschuler concludes, 'It may be that the 'linearity' of print derided in the hypertext literature is less constricting for the reader than the blind loops and directional links of subjective hypertext.' Or a bad situation (a 'tangle of linkages') is made worse, Barrett notes, when the 'hypertext is unmediated by an instructor or experienced guide.' The problem that Barrett is addressing here, as with Alschuler, strikes at the very possibility of hypertext continuing to be seen as a new literary form, one that extends rather than repudiates print literacy. 'A user may just glance over the surface of a body of knowledge without integrating it into a personal knowing. And if pathways are too firmly established, then the point of hypertext is lost' (1988a, pp. xix–xx).

Yet, as we have seen in our analysis of print literacy, what gives depth to writing are the pathways carefully plotted out by Barrett's 'instructor or experienced guide', what we used to call the author, and, as Barrett notes, when the author is constantly present pointing out the way, we no longer have hypertext.

Such scepticism in Barrett, someone working in English composition, is unusual, although he does not push his misgivings to their limit. As a rule, humanists, in their flight from all appearances of authoritarian relationships — and their subsequent embrace of liberated and liberating discourse (a topic to be considered in detail in Chapter 4) — have too often been uncritical in their acceptance of hypertext, seeing it not as a user-driven information management system, but as a new, egalitarian mode of communication. It is only when one turns to computer scientists with experience developing and evaluating large-scale hypertext systems that the structural limitations of such systems are openly addressed. Ben Shneiderman, for example, one of the developers of HyperTIES, debunks much of the mythology of this new medium in his three golden rules for creating hypertext. 'There is a large body of information organized into numerous fragments, the fragments relate to each other, and the user needs only a small fraction at any time' (p. 115). While Shneiderman admits that 'hyper-novels, hyper-poems, hyper-fairy tales, hyper-newspapers, and hyperbooks are possible', provided one rethinks these 'traditional forms so that they satisfy the Golden Rules' (p. 116), the actual uses for hypertext that Shneiderman surveys are more practical and prosaic.

> Museum exhibits, educational course materials, organization orientation, as a tool for diagnostic problem solving, as an environment for creating checklists for complex procedures, in online help, to browse computer programs, as a public information resource, or to explore cross referenced materials such as scientific journal articles or technical documents. (p. 117).

Hypertext, as used in such situations, is an environment for retrieving a few distinct items of information out of a large pool.

One such carefully constructed hypertext system is IBIS (for Issue-Based Information System) or gIBIS (for its graphical version), a program designed to solve complex problems by facilitating a 'conversation among the stakeholders (i.e., designers, customers, and implementers)' (Begeman and Conklin, 1988, p. 255). The program keeps the discussion focused and manageable by restricting participants to three kinds of statements — articulating basic *issues, positions* about those issues, and *arguments* that support or attack positions — and nine kinds of links (such things as responding to arguments, asking questions). Yet even such a highly structured system is fraught with problems, as the researchers Michael Begeman and Jeff Conklin openly admit in the sidebar, 'Problems in Paradise'. '[S]ometimes it's unnatural to break your thoughts into discrete units, particularly if you don't understand the problem well and those thoughts are vague, confused, and shifting' (p. 260). While they recognize the benefit of eventually separating 'elements into Issues, Positions, and Arguments', they concede that 'when you're struggling to solve a problem, the mental effort required to separate it into discrete thoughts, identify their types, label them, and link them can be prohibitive' (p. 260).

While IBIS is admittedly an imperfect tool, one that will be improved, there may be, Begeman and Conklin admit, 'a more subtle issue here', one that goes to the heart of hypertext. As in Shneiderman's first golden rule, that hypertext demands that information be broken into 'numerous fragments', they too recognize that hypertext demands that the author 'express ideas in a fine-grained, separated manner', a practice that easily 'obscures the larger idea being developed'. The inescapable conflict here is between the trees — the multitude of individual points (with links) — and the forest — the larger, unifying vision, what Begeman and Conklin refer to as 'the thread of thoughts as it winds through several dozen nodes'.

> Traditional linear text provides a continuous, unwinding context thread as ideas are proposed and discussed — a context that the writer constructs to guide you to the salient points and away from the irrelevant ones. Indeed, a good writer anticipates questions and confusions that you may encounter and carefully crafts the text to prevent them.
>
> The hypertext (or at least the gIBIS) author, however, is encouraged to make discrete points and separate them from their context. Sometimes, the gIBIS author, in a hurry to capture a design Issue and its analysis, may write only the bare minimum necessary to record the essence of the Issue, Positions, and Arguments. Even the careful author, however, may not anticipate all the routes to a given node, and so may fail to develop the context sufficiently to clarify its contents (p. 260).

As Shneiderman concludes, when hypertext is poorly implemented ('too many links, confusing structure') or used in other, less suitable situations, 'there is a real danger that it can also lead to hyperchaos' (p. 116).

It is difficult to have things both ways, to praise certain traditional literary values in reading hypertext format while at the same time celebrating hypertext as signaling the death of the author and the end of the only thing of note that the author ever gives us — the complex but unified literary text. To the extent that any single literary work is little more than the author's compromise with linearity, an effort to harness together multiple narratives in a single linear format, then it may do little damage to read that work on a technology that allows us to find our own individual way through the text — it is as if we could decide on our own order for reading through the multiple, parallel plots that make up a Dickens novel, rearranging the chapter groupings at will. Yet to the extent that we push this process much further and see the novel as a compromise with linearity at every moment and at every level, then the text as a unified structure and as the basis of a sustained reading experience does disappear. We are left then, not with individual novels that are read one at a time, but with a series of overlapping worlds — the world of Dickens, the world of the nineteenth-century novel, the world of Victorian England. As noted in Chapter 1, reading Dickens in such an environment is akin to studying Dickens in a graduate seminar, a powerful arena for reading, to be certain, but one that regularly assumes that students have already worked through the individual texts in some traditional (aesthetic) fashion. With hypertext, there is neither author nor work, only field — neither Dickens the author nor *Great Expectations*, his work, only the vast and ever-expanding field of Dickens study.

It is as if Ken Burns, the producer of the magnificent television series on the American Civil War, had collected the thousands of photographs and hours of music and spoken dialogue — and then left it all uncompiled on the editor's table. *The Civil War*, as eventually broadcast, can be seen as just one person's version of how all this material might be arranged — a task that doubtless took Burns and his staff hundreds of hours. The producer of the next generation of *The Civil War* will be able to leave all this material unassembled in hypermedia format, so that all of us with access to the right equipment (soon perhaps as common as VCRs) will have the chance to forge our own links, in effect creating our own documentary. Why we should want to do so is another matter. Indeed, placing *The Civil War* in multimedia format changes its nature, in ways that are not all positive. In its original broadcast form it is a product of print literacy, a long, intensely moving narrative, not unlike a traditional novel, that has among its many functions conveying a sense of the wholeness of past experience — it is a work designed to educate the senses as well as to convey information. In hypermedia format, however, *The Civil War* becomes a niche product, an information rich, lifeless database out of which American history students can cut and paste material (as they do today from encyclopedias) for their own use. As hypermedia, it becomes the equivalent of an historian's notecards.

The best analogy here is to the kind of personal anthology building using photocopying that has been an increasingly popular practice in university courses. Instead of ordering someone else's anthology, the professor creates his or her own, picking a dozen or so favorite articles and having them copied and bound by a local service. At first glance it may seem that the course anthology, using the older technology of photocopying, has none of the advantages of hypertext, which allows students access to hundreds of articles, indeed to the whole library, to the sum total of human knowledge. If we are able to resist the notion that more is better, we can discern an important difference between the course anthology and the hypertext. The former uses the technology of photocopying to replace having to store a limited number of materials, often critical essays presenting alternate viewpoints, on a library reserve shelf; the latter uses the technology of computer storage and retrieval to replace the traditional task of finding those materials, or, more accurately, the desired information such materials may contain. The course anthology provides students with a dozen or so essays or chapters, each of which represents the results of an expert's own attempt to integrate a wealth of materials — it is a means of allowing students to compare the understandings of a dozen different thinkers, each represented (or, worked out) in a single linear structure. The anthology and the hypertext thus represent different ways of finding direction when exploring new terrain. The hypertext format represents the maps, atlases, and directories we consult when traveling, most helpfully when we are trying to reach a particular destination. The original essays, meanwhile, represent the equivalent of the guided tours, or tour books with prescribed paths, that we often turn to when we are trying to learn as much as possible about a place in a relatively short time.

With hypertext we can compile a dozen different tours, and a dozen different readings, all in one retrieval system, but with this change comes, as all the most ardent hypertext advocates willingly admit, a shift to a user-driven information management system — and, at least when that user is a naive tourist, the increased possibility of confusion. The totality is of greatest value to us when we have a firm sense of direction, of purpose, when we play the role of information-seeking user rather than print reader; yet for the last half a millennium it has been to books and to the authors of books that we have turned for such guidance. With hypertext, we may be in even greater need of guides (and authors), but, as Bolter admits, as if an afterthought, with this new medium, 'the loss of the great text as a touchstone and of the great author as authority is real and unavoidable' (1992).

Yet we do want to have it both ways — to use hypertext to extend our own reading practices, often of traditional literature (individual works by single authors), and to maximize the advantages of this new electronic medium. For literary critic John Slatin, for example, hypertext represents a more natural, more accurate means of presenting the intertextuality of Marianne Moore's poetry. Using the hypertext program HyperTIES, Slatin demonstrates how links can be provided with important words and phrases in Moore's poem, 'Poetry', and, in turn, with important words and phrases in the notes themselves. By moving the cursor and pressing the Enter key, the reader can move freely between a series of different texts — the poem as it might appear in a traditional book, her notebooks, other poems, and so on, revealing in the process what determined literary critics have long known, that 'the apparent linearity of Moore's text is at best an illusion; like other texts, this one is made up of other texts, of several different types' (Slatin, 1988, p. 120).

On one level Slatin's point is obvious and incontrovertible. No one creates anything out of a vacuum; everything we do — in art, especially — has roots in our experience. And literary and other art critics have long earned their living in part by unearthing those connections and publishing them in their critical and biographical studies. What is less clear is the absolute value in providing all those connections for the general reader, deconstructing the surface unity of the poem in the midst of its presentation. Clearly, writing has always involved choice — and writers consequently have had to leave out materials, changing their minds countless times in generating a published text. While there may be some readers interested in the historical evolution of any work — noting, for example, all the changes made in rehearsing a play for its first performance — there are many readers (and viewers) who have only the time and patience to sit through the finished product, trusting that what is at last presented to them is in the opinion of all the craftspeople involved the best possible product. Most readers of Hemingway are likely satisfied with the single ending of *A Farewell to Arms*, even if they know that Hemingway scholars armed with a hypertext system might be able to provide them with access to all thirty-two versions of those famous last paragraphs.

Hypertext can reveal the rich intertextuality of all writing (the interconnectedness of all human experience), but, as Slatin demonstrates, only at a cost. 'The very capabilities that make hypertext such a useful tool for revealing the intricate intertextuality of Moore's poem, also make negotiating the hypertext document a rather complicated process' (p. 120). For people with such practical concerns the principal difficulty with hypertext, navigation, has grown directly out of its principal virtue, the ability to move instantly between places that in the metaphor of print are far apart. Slatin then proceeds to demonstrate the almost agonizingly complex trade-offs that confront the hypertext 'author', at least one using HyperTIES, version 2.2 where something has to be defined as the leading article and information that is linked (called 'nodes') can be only 10,000 characters. The limitations of the hypertext, however, hardly explain the full range of the complexities that confront Slatin and that he considers in a series of defining questions (p. 124): '(1) what constitutes a node? (2) which nodes should be linked to one another, how should they be linked, and how many nodes and links should there be? (In other words, how does one decide where to stop?)' With only four choices for each screen, there are over a thousand different paths to the fifth screen, over a million to the tenth. The other side of being able to jump anywhere is never quite knowing where one is or how one got there.

Slatin's answer to these questions is that writing, like conversation, is always embedded in a situation, one that places 'the writer and the text at a nodal point in a complex system' (pp. 125–26). The problem here is that a hypertext has no author and exists ultimately beyond, or possibly before, rhetoric. 'What is the problem that is to be solved in and by the creation of the hyperdocument?' asks Slatin. 'Then and only then, will an adequate strategy emerge for determining the boundaries of specific nodes' (p. 126). What continues to mislead Slatin and others into treating hypertexts as 'extended books' is a fallacy of misplaced concreteness. Hypertexts are not really texts at all, not documents prepared by authors to convey a distinct world view to readers; they are systems for storing and retrieving information, in much the same way that an online version of the Library of Congress catalogue is a system for shelving and subsequently locating library materials. It is only future users of this information — readers, not hypertext 'authors' — who can ever answer Slatin's question regarding nodes and links.

What advocates like Slatin are finally reluctant to acknowledge is how hypertext fundamentally alters our primary notion of what it means to read. During the modern age we have read many different kinds of texts, including reference books, for many different reasons, including tracking down information, but at the center of print literacy has been a single notion of reading, that of one's sustained, close involvement with one text. The task of reading has entailed our understanding this text as the projection of the author's imagination; what we understand in reading is the author's projection of a possible world. Central to print reading is the ability (and willingness) of readers to delay fulfilling their own immediate needs (an act that hermeneutic philosopher Paul Ricoeur calls *distanciation*) so that they could participate in (what Ricoeur calls the act of *appropriation*) the imaginary world projected in the text — in reading as in play, we forego the demands of the present to live by some other, imaginary rules. A developmental model of literacy grounds reading, as with other playful activities, in our serious commitment to following a new set of rules, and thus radically curtailing our impulse to continue to transform the world to accord to our own wishes, what Piaget refers to as the process of *assimilation* (Tuman, 1987, pp. 78–83). As readers (or players) we must change ourselves to be in accord with the demands of the world, we must imitate or match a new mode of action, what Piaget refers to as *accommodation*. For Ricoeur, distanciation must be followed by appropriation, the gaining of 'a new *self*-understanding' by following the 'injunction of the text' (pp. 192–93). According to this model of literacy, misreading occurs when readers are unwilling or unable to change their attitudes to conform to the sense of the text, if only temporarily in what Coleridge referred to as 'the willing suspension of disbelief'. The great sense of psychological growth that motivates Louise Rosenblatt's classic *Literature As Exploration* derives largely from this capacity that print literacy affords us of denying the immediate and the practical (a condition of play) in order to understand, somehow to re-live, the experiences of others.

Hypertext denies such an approach to reading by removing the experience of another from the center of the text (which other? which text?) and by giving the reader the real, not just ludic, capacity to change the text. Reading a hypertext, as Bolter argues forcefully in *Writing Space* (1991), can be, for anyone fully indoctrinated into the ideology of print literacy, a dazzling, liberating experience. But Bolter is stacking the deck, applying the reading experience developed from a lifetime's exposure to print to a hybrid or literary hypertext, one that in turn reflects its author's own acculturation into print. Literary hypertext still embeds the experience of an author in a text, but in a more playful, more open-ended experience, one that questions but does not radically undermine the single-minded, probing seriousness of linear texts and, by extension, of print culture. It is a specialized product. For authors and readers who themselves are disillusioned with the limitations of that culture — its endless and, for many, reductionist psychologizing of both author and reader, its outmoded roles of author as concert artist and reader as hushed audience, its association with a tired European (dead, white, male) tradition — literary hypertext has all the exhilaration of the Marx Brothers' *Night at the Opera*. Nor is it surprising that Bolter in looking for print precursors of literary hypertext should turn to such stylistically inventive, iconoclastic writers as Laurence Sterne, James Joyce, and Jorge Luis Borges. For Bolter these writers were creative hypertext authors compelled to work within the limited conventions of print.

Bolter does not see our reading of literary hypertext as representing a complete and radical break with the reading of print literacy. Despite working within a new computer environment that literally removes the need for an author — and with a postmodern aesthetic that seems to demand it — literary hypertexts, it turns out, have authors who in some ways exercise greater power than print authors, both writing the text and through the manipulation of the software controlling the degree of 'freedom' the reader experiences.

> The rhetoric of hypertext — and all of us who work in hypertext are guilty of this exaggeration — tends to be a rhetoric of liberation. We sometimes talk as if the goal of electronic writing were to set the reader free from all the arbitrary fixity and stability of print culture. In fact hypertext simply entangles the reader in nets or networks of a different order. (Bolter, 1992)

The result is a refreshingly different kind of reading, one where the open-endedness of the text and lack of an immediate authorial presence (note that it is the hypertext, and not an author, that 'entangles the reader') seem to reflect a new, less confined (postmodern?) way of living in the world.

Literary hypertext no doubt can be a legitimate form of artistic experience, for both reader and author, one which may well become more popular as we all spend more time at computer terminals. What is not so obvious are two other claims, one explicit and one implicit, Bolter makes: the explicit claim that a great deal of past writing (like Sterne's) is really repressed hypertext, and the implicit claim that literary hypertext will somehow occupy the same central position in online culture as linear literature, for example the nineteenth-century realistic novel, did in print culture. Regarding the former claim, one needs to point out two seemingly conflicting observations: first, that few writers, professional or student, relish the task of organizing their thoughts into a single linear form, and thus at a practical level many authors will welcome a writing system that frees them from this responsibility; and second, that much of what we most admire in human experience entails people pushing against, not transcending, the limits of nature or social conventions. It is not obvious what is to be gained by freeing Baryshnikov from the constraints of gravity, or Shakespeare from the limits of the sonnet, nor what particularly aesthetic advantages we will gain by giving writers the same freedom of random movement that seems to be the curse of serious contemporary composers who, freed from most conventions, now spend so much of their time trying to re-invigorate older musical forms.

The latter claim, that hypertext will be the major literary genre, raises the issue of whether or not readers will actually relish the 'freedom' of piecing together their own text, an organizational task not unlike the one authors are forswearing. The best answer to this question is likely that readers will expend the energy to the extent that they are adequately rewarded. *Open* structures sound more democratic than *closed* ones, although for many there is a special resonance in the experience of closure, a keenly human sense of the loss and possibility (a way of dealing with our own mortality, perhaps) that Frost expresses as our not being able to travel both roads. And here the inherent strengths and weaknesses of the print versus the online format are at issue. Each format can theoretically support multiple kinds of reading — one can write novels with a hypertext just as one can store random data in a bound book. Editors of reference books for the last four hundred years have been ingenuous in reconfiguring the traditional book with tabs, notched pages, and other sorts of mechanical aids to help readers overcome the linearity of print. (Clever bookmakers have even realized that it is possible to configure a book to produce a brief 'movie' by having readers thumb through a sequence of pictures arranged one to a page.) And today, one vendor is attempting to squeeze as many (uncopyrighted) books as possible on CD-ROMs under the series title of *The Library of the Future*. (The first 'volume' has 450 titles.) The fact remains that just as the book, while a spectacular medium for the sustained development of a single, continuous verbal project (literary, historical, or philosophical), is a terrible medium for making movies and (as encyclopedia designers have grappled with for centuries) only an adequate one for collecting random information.

The 'libraries' of CD-ROM books that are now being marketed are likely to appeal, not to traditional readers, those who want to spend a summer month reading *War and Peace*, but to scholars and researchers who need to move at random through the corpus of Tolstoy's works. To extend the analogy, as a home product students are more likely to use hypertext to get biographical information on Virginia Woolf than to read *The Waves*. Here we also need to recognize another shift. While reference books have played an important supporting role in the teaching of print literacy (for example, dictionaries, thesauri, and the ubiquitous handbooks used in teaching college composition this century), print-based literacy instruction itself has offered only incidental instruction in reading such materials (and none in writing them) while focusing almost exclusively on the task of teaching students to read and write linear texts.

The central question for hypertext is not whether it can be manipulated to support a print-based critical and aesthetic reading (especially by readers and writers who themselves are proven masters of print), but whether literacy education in an age fully acculturated into hypertext and online reading will keep such a traditional reading experience at the center of instruction; or put in another way, whether the academic discipline that concentrates on critical and aesthetic reading and writing, instead of information retrieval and report generation, will remain at the center of liberal education. Things have changed dramatically in the past, and there is no reason to assume that they will not do so again in the future. It is easy to forget that a little over a century ago classics, a subject with minimal presence on contemporary American campuses, was the primary subject of higher level literacy education. The issue for the year 2092 (and possibly the year 2002) is the place that aesthetic and critical reading will occupy in the curriculum — and here the dilemma can be simply stated. Not whether or not hypertext can support the aesthetic, critical tradition of print literacy, but will it? Is it possible for the ascendancy of hypertext to do anything but push literacy in the direction of information management? Will literary hypertext ever be more than a diversion in the computer age, a relic or craft from an earlier time, occupying something of the status of calligraphy in the age of print?

The basic problem of hypertext is not the technical limitations revealed by Shneiderman and others — hypertext is a new technology and will overcome certain problems. The problem rather lies in the fervor of its champions, many of whom for all their deconstructive, postmodern rhetoric, seem beguiled by their own nostalgia for print literacy. These are readers and writers who themselves are both deeply trained in print literacy and fervently opposed to its own hierarchical structures. What they seek, therefore, is a new literacy practice, one that will at once destroy all the authoritarian aspects of the old (including the notion of fixed authors and texts) and yet retain the essential parameters and feel of what they have always known (including new kinds of cooperative authors and new kinds of open-ended texts). As a result hypertext is oversold as a new kind of text (although it is not really a text at all) that allows for a new kind of open-ended author (who turns out to be not really an author). The hand-crafted hypertext is thus reified as a a new, liberated literary genre in the same way that, as Jameson suggests, merely talking about a postmodern text is 'to turn it into the work of art it no longer is, to endow it with a permanence and monumentality that it is its vocation to dispel' (Stephanson, 1988, p. 27). It becomes a new kind of book written by a new kind of author, despite the widespread agreement that the genre destroys our notion of text and author.

Beyond this confusion, however, lies a powerful truth: that we will all be using computers more and more in schools and in the workplace to search, to access not just information, but pictures, music, and anything else that can be digitized. What is unlikely is that reading online for most of us will involve anything that resembles current literacy practice. In the midst of all the enthusiasm about hypertext it is too easy to overlook the fact that it is fundamentally a system for retrieving digitized information and, as such, is a technology that has vast economic potential for anyone who has the resources to collect such information and the legal right to distribute it. For centuries, people have been collecting such valuable information in reference books — atlases, encyclopedias, dictionaries, handbooks — and making money out of their efforts by selling such volumes, usually at steep prices, to professionals who need the information and can recover the cost through their practice, to libraries, or to individuals and families who either have a real need for the information or have been pressured into seeing the personal ownership of this material as an upwardly mobile step. Above all else, hypertext will play a central role in an entirely new and seemingly more affordable way of marketing such information, selling it to people as they need it, piece by piece. While hypertexts like online encyclopedias are already being sold to individuals outright in CD-ROM format, the real potential for profits lies in selling the information on an as-needed basis, and more import-antly, convincing millions of people that they should pay a small monthly access fee (like their telephone bill or, more recently, cable TV charge). Our drive to commodify and to privatize information, for private gain rather than public good, may well be reshaping us into what Vincent Mosco (1989) playfully calls a 'pay-per society', although the opportunity that digitized information affords a few multinational corporations for parcelling out 'information transactions with considerable quantitative precision' (p. 26) is, as Mosco warns, hardly a light-hearted issue.

As such online 'reading' continues to become a major form of economic activity, who can doubt that it will also become increasingly important in education as well, possibly our dominant model of reading, with the kind of protracted, critical, often solitary engagement with text — the model of reading for the last two hundred years — consigned to George Steiner's 'houses of read-ing'? Such radical shifts have happened before — with reading before the nine-teenth century defined largely in terms of oral, public declaration. The model of reading that will emerge with the triumph of hypertext in the twenty-first century is likely to be far more radical — shaped more by practical business needs than by literary sensibilities — than what most hypertext advocates are now willing to concede.

At issue here is the difference between hypertext as a universal storage and retrieval system for all texts, what Nelson refers to as universal, open hypertext publishing, and hypertext as an authoring system, a system of branching screens that a lone creative writer like Michael Joyce, for example, uses to author a single recognizable literary work, albeit one in interactive form. What is ironic here — although hardly surprising — is that many of the same hypertext advocates who see the form as leading to the death of the author are also trying to 'author' their own hypertexts and in so doing often still treat hypertext as an extension of the book. What else should we expect of writers, critical and creative, who having assimilated print culture themselves are given the historically unique opportunity to tinker with new computer-based ways of reading and writing? Is it not natural to expect that the principal use of this new technology will be to extend the liter-acy powers for others in the future just as it has done for them? To expect that the future will combine the best of print literacy — its critical, personal, and ex-pressive dimensions — with the best of online literacy — its playfulness and immediacy?

Is it not natural, in other words, for masters of print literacy — and that is what writers such as Richard Lanham, George Landow, and Jay Bolter are — to see hypertext and online literacy generally as doing for others what it has done for them: for Richard Lanham, a brilliant critic of current rhetorical practices, to see students using computers to deconstruct the stodgy discourse strategies of his colleagues, and eventually the fading literary tradition to which they are too fondly and too blindly attached; for George Landow, an acclaimed literary historian, to see students using computers as an infinite reserve shelf to gain the interdisciplinary knowledge of the interconnectedness of British literature, history, and art that many traditional scholars lack; for Jay Bolter, the resourceful innovator of *Storyspace*, to see students using computers to read and write the kinds of playfully associative stories and other texts that can be created only with such a program? Yet in all this enthusiasm for the liberating power of hypertext, one question goes unaddressed: what happens to future generations of students who differ from Lanham, Landow, and Bolter in not having spent the first forty years of their lives mining the vast cognitive and psychological resources of print literacy?

It is too easy for all of us to peer dimly into some distant but reassuringly similar future and ignore the immense cultural transformations that are already happening all around us, closer than some of us realize. As Provenzo (1991) describes, sophisticated multi-media computers — with only a minimal textual component — have already found their way into tens of millions of American homes. Yet just what impact Nintendo video games are having on our children now — and what impact such 'toys' (when marketed to adults possibly in the form of pornography) will have in the future when integrated through cable systems with broadcast television and multimedia databases — are subjects which are rarely raised in the context of the future of literacy. No one believes that the computer revolution that has already affected our understanding of text is even close to complete, that it will not also go on to revolutionize the relation between words and pictures as well (the subject for Chapter 5). Yet too few are willing to consider the radical implications of these changes, not for our own print-based literacy practices and those of our high-achieving children and students, but for generations upon generations of future children who will grow up with only inci-dental contact with print culture. As a group, advocates of hypertext, their own careers energized by the acceptance of technology, seem too eager to make a virtue out of a looming necessity, and as such tend to gloss over the inevitable intellectual and social dislocations (the losses as well as the gains) represented by the radical restructuring, if not the demise, of print literacy. To understand these transformations we need to move beyond the question of the strengths and limitations of hypertext itself to consider the wider social context in which people read and write — namely, the school and the workplace. What will be evident in this survey is that in both situations computers, for better and worse, are furthering the erosion of hierarchical structures not just, as we have seen in this chapter, in the organization of thought, but in the organization of society as well.

Chapter 4

The New Writing

'Centers' exist everywhere.

Marshall McLuhan and Bruce Powers, *Global Village*

In Isaac Asimov's 1957 story 'The Fun They Had', two school-aged children of 2157 reflect upon the distant past 'when all stories were printed on paper', when readers actually 'turned the pages, which were yellow and crinkly', and when the words 'stood still instead of moving the way they were supposed to' (p. 308). It was a time, alas, before hypertext, a time when one 'turned back to the page before, it had the same words on it that it had when they read it the first time'. This slight fancy does not lament the end of the book — the subject of Chapter 3 — so much as it does the end of the traditional school, with its teacher-centered classes — the subject of this chapter. Faced with the relentless demands of her home-based, computer tutor, one of the children reflects wistfully on 'the old schools they had when her grandfather was a little boy'.

All the kids from the whole neighborhood came, laughing and shouting in the schoolyard, sitting together in the schoolroom, going home together at the end of the day. They learned the same things, so they could help one another on the homework and talk about it.

And the teachers were people ... (p. 310).

Here the loss of school signals what we shall see is the central concern of many contemporary language educators, the loss of a real community. What marks Asimov's tale as a product of a receding age — the 1950s — is its nostalgia for the teacher, implicitly the person at the center of this community. Contemporary educational reformers, especially those concerned with the reform of the college writing curriculum, are more likely to reverse this arrangement, casting the teacher as the primary threat to community and the computer as liberator.

The traditional teacher, in Ted Nelson's phrase, dominates the classroom 'as a feudal lord', with 'absolute power to bore, offend, and sever access' (1987, p. 1/20). For Thomas Barker and Fred Kemp, two enthusiasts of a new, computer-based writing curriculum, there is a direct, geographical connection between traditional instruction and that icon of print already discussed, the concert hall. Such instruction, they contend, takes place in a 'proscenium classroom' (p. 10).

with chairs, lighting, instructional aids, even the flag, all focusing attention forward, 'overwhelmingly reinforc[ing] the notion that the instructor is the master of the room, the arbiter of classroom action, and the source of whatever value the room (and the instructional experience) holds' (p. 8). Here the traditional teacher becomes the source of all meaning, the pedagogic equivalent of the concert artist/print author, the key figure around which students gather in their role of passive audience of readers. With the introduction of the third element, text (in the form of the teacher-controlled lesson) the allegory is complete. The traditional classroom becomes another site of educational/social control with student/readers struggling to succeed by attempting to comprehend the lesson/text of teacher/authors.

> The students, quite unconsciously, have learned in their years of school-
> ing to read teachers much more proficiently than to read textbooks, and
> they have learned that success or failure depends much more on that
> reading than on what is assigned. The traditional classroom suggests
> nothing else (Barker and Kemp, 1990, p. 9).

This general criticism is part of a more focused, more sustained attack upon the workings of the teacher-centered composition class. In such an environment, all instruction, including all discourse, is top-down, from the single teacher to the students. Through the selection of topics, the management of written and oral comments, and the assigning of grades, the traditional composition teacher controls the discourse world of the student, deciding what is and is not acceptable written communication. Or, as expressed by Marilyn Cooper and Cynthia Selfe, traditional composition pedagogy — including 'group discussions, lectures, teacher-student conferences, written assignments — generally support[s] a tra-ditional hegemony in which teachers determine appropriate and inappropriate discourse' (p. 847). For them the structure of the class is a barely disguised 'polit-ical arrangement', one that 'encourages intellectual accommodation in students, [and] discourages intellectual resistance'. If students do have the chance to interact with one another, in a group editing session, for example, it is usually only a means to help them meet the teacher's standards, by reducing errors or introducing certain stylistic improvements in transitions or parallel structures prompted by the teacher. The student's grade in such a course is a reflection of his or her ability to meet a single standard of writing embedded in the teacher's grading policy.

In continuing to dominate the writing classroom, the traditional composition teacher is regularly pictured as an agent of control — of students' actions, words, and thoughts — while the computer, contrary to Asimov's fantasy, is pictured as a tool of empowerment. Someone from Asimov's generation may well be surprised by this switch in roles, although educators like C.A. Bowers (1988) and Eugene Provenzo (1992) do continue to warn against the totalizing, panoptic powers of computers to monitor the entire learning process, especially to keep tight control of all student records. Computer-based reforms of the writing curriculum are thus connected to a larger ideological association of the teacher — and not technology- with the same top-down, hierarchical control that leads to the suppression of dissent, diversity, and minorities throughout society. Accordingly, for Cooper and Selfe and other critics of traditional instruction, new forms of computer-based teaching represent a revolutionary breakthrough in this pattern of control; they do for the classroom what hypertext does for reading — removing the author/teacher from the middle, allowing readers/students to pursue their own interests.

The implication here is that teacher-centered instruction, regardless of its content, intention, or skill, extends oppressive social forces, isolating individuals from one another and emphasizing the deficiencies in what they produce (their product), and, in turn, that increased reliance upon the technology of computers will result in a diffusion of power to students and, presumably, to readers and to citizens at large — presumably for everyone's benefit. The computer, not the classroom teacher, is an instrument for the 'increased levels of intellectual divergence and dissent' that Cooper and Selfe argue 'balance our impulse toward the status quo'. 'If we can't eliminate the effect of racism, sexism, and classism in our traditional classrooms because of social inertia,' they conclude, 'we may be able to set aside smaller electronic spaces in which such problems can find expression and be debated' (p. 867).

Why, we might ask, should composition specialists be so eager to reverse traditional roles, to see the computer as a radical alternative instead of a more efficient extension of existing instructional practice? How does it come about that the teacher, long portrayed as a kindly, if somewhat ineffectual, Mr Chips (a descendant of Chaucer's Clerke) or an inspiring, if slightly dotty, Jean Brodie — or, in more contemporary terms, an inspirational math teacher like Jaime Escalante in the film *Stand and Deliver* or the charismatic principal Joe Clark in the film *Lean on Me* — all of a sudden becomes an instrument of oppression, while the computer, the soft-spoken but menacing HAL of the film *2001*, becomes the agent of student empowerment? What has happened, we might ask, to the teacher as sage — the teacher as wise parental figure, a loving, supportive Anne Sullivan or a noble, stoic Zen master who patiently trains the novice in character as well as craft? Such questions are related to another, broader question — why should composition specialists, many of whom are committed feminists, feel more confident with instruction mediated by electrical gadgetry, long associated with male culture, than with that mediated by other teachers, the vast majority of whom, at least in language education, are women? As Sherry Turkle writes:

> Women look at computers and see more than machines. They see a culture that has grown up around them and they ask themselves if they belong.... It is a world, predominantly male, that takes the machine as a partner in an intimate relationship (1988, p. 42).

The advocacy of computer-mediated writing instruction, by feminists and others concerned with radically transforming existing pedagogic practice, seems to represent a reversal of a well established cultural pattern. What has happened, we might ask, to the sentiment expressed by a woman disgruntled with computers: 'I wanted to work in worlds where languages had moods and connected you with people' (Turkle, p. 41)?

The answer to this last question, and indirectly all of the others, is that for an increasing number of composition specialists computers are machines ideally suited for the job of connecting people directly with each other. Despite the feeling, echoed by Turkle, that 'mastery of technology and formal systems can become a way of masking fears about the self and the complexities of the world beyond' (p. 43), there is now a new sense, especially among women, of computers as a wonderful tool for facilitating expanded and enriched interpersonal communication, a means of communicating that at once seems to displace traditional control and to facilitate greater involvement by those on the margins. At the heart of this transformation is a major shift from our notion of the computer as a calculating machine designed to enhance individual productivity. 'PC', Janet Eldred reminds us, 'stands for *personal* computing. It is not until we encounter electronic networking that computers move into the arena of the public' (1989, p. 202). And it is as a networking rather than a calculating tool that computers are transforming composition studies at the levels of practice and theory. Whereas earlier educators may have seen computers as a means of increasing our students' ability to produce better individual documents through the use of word processing, prewriting, revision, spell checking, style checking, and desktop publishing programs (or the exercises in error avoidance that characterized an earlier generation of computer-aided instruction), educators today are increasingly thinking of computers in terms of local and wide-area networks: files servers, modems, and telecommunications networks at the level of hardware; electronic mail, information services, and computer conferencing at the level of software. The new networking technology is important, not in providing us with greater power in composing individual texts, but in providing us with the opportunity to communicate through reading and writing immediately with other people in situations similar to ours, or in providing students with the opportunity to communicate in real-time with each other, rather than with their teachers.

The networked classroom — popularized by a project begun in 1985 by Trent Batson under the acronym ENFI (Electronic Networks for Interaction) — seems to reverse all the negative aspects of teacher-centered education. Developed to help a student population for whom traditional instruction poses particular problems — deaf students at Gallaudet University — the ENFI classroom transforms the traditional roles of teachers, students, and texts. No longer can the teacher command the attention of the class in the midst of group discussions; instead, the teacher's voice is just another voice in the class conversation, a voice easily disguised by the use of pen-names. While the teacher may be at work behind the scenes setting up and maintaining the structure of the class (an important point to be addressed later), the actual discussion that forms the basis of the class proceeds independent of teacher control. To the extent possible, students in networked classrooms are supposed to write directly to each other regarding topics and material under discussion. In such an environment there are no isolated authors, no privileged texts, only actively engaged, co-equal readers and writers. In this regard, the networked classroom in representing a new form of social interaction as well as a new means of organizing instruction appeals to those as interested in transforming social as pedagogic practice. The organization of instruction in the networked classroom, in other words, parallels fundamental and pervasive changes in the organization of society, changes that finally relate to new roles for individuals in generating, first, knowledge and, eventually, wealth.

This transition derives from the ability of computer networks, in a classroom or across the world, to put people in touch with one another seemingly without the mediation of instructors or authorities in general. Students and groups on the margins of power can connect with each other directly in the same way that groups of computer users with more traditional interests — called special interest groups, or SIGs — have been communicating with each other using national information services like CompuServe. What writer Howard Rheingold (1988) describes in an anecdote is no less than the defining moment of online literacy — the transition of the computer from writing to communicating tool and, by extension, the transition from the writer as solitary figure to the writer as someone regularly in touch with people of similar interests.

> Because I'm a writer, I spend a lot of time alone with my words and thoughts. After work, I reenter the human community via my neighborhood, my family, my circle of personal and professional acquaintances. Until recently, I often felt isolated and lonely during the working day, and my work provided few opportunities to expand my circle of friends and colleagues. For the past three years, however, I have participated in a wide-ranging, intellectually stimulating, professionally rewarding, and often intensely emotional exchange with dozens of new friends and hundreds of colleagues. And I still spend my days in an office, physically isolated. My mind, however, is linked with a worldwide collection of like-minded (and not so like-minded) souls: my virtual community (p. 203)

This community, Rheingold goes on to explain, is the electronic combination of a neighborhood gathering place and a national professional meeting — it is a place where one can discuss either specific concerns relating to one's work or general issues about the state of the world, a place where, in Rheingold's words, one 'can participate in a hundred ongoing conversations with people who don't care what I look like or sound like, but who do care how I think and communicate' (p. 204).

For Rheingold, and for many others, virtual communities are 'a harbinger of changes to come in the way people deal with each other on a daily basis' (p. 205), a new form of social organization latent with utopian possibilities, 'a whole new kind of community for this planet' that we may have 'to invent ... if we want to continue to exist' (p. 233). Not only does the interaction of computers and telecommunications, called *telematics*, provide individuals with the ability either to swap messages, using *electronic mail*, or *e-mail*, or to carry on an extended discussion of a single issue, using *electronic conferencing*, it also allows us to find people with similar interests, whether it is someone (as Rheingold notes) 'with a three-year-old daughter or a thirty-year-old Hudson'. With networked computing we can form virtual communities that provide not just isolated individuals but isolated groups — people of all kinds on the margins of society — with a means of building directly upon their common interests. The revolutionary potential of this technology resides largely in its decentralized network structure. As Rheingold triumphantly proclaims, 'A million small computers, linked by ordinary telephone lines, can suddenly wield formidable computing power that is extremely hard to control in a rigidly hierarchical, centralized manner' (p. 233).

It is this lack of hierarchy or, stated positively, this dispersal of authority throughout a horizontal network or web, that seems to explain best the enthusiasm of women social critics in general and composition instructors specifically.

'A feminist design aesthetic', argues Sue Jansen, 'would presumably favor development of decentralized, egalitarian, accessible, process-oriented information technologies' — the opposite of 'the design logic that has fostered development of capital systems which currently facilitate global control systems' (pp. 209–10). Here Jansen is echoing Carol Gilligan's often cited assertion that the thinking of men and women conform to different topographical models, models that indirectly reflect the basic difference between print and online literacy.

> Thus the images of hierarchy and web inform the different modes of assertion and response: the wish to be alone at the top and the consequent fear that others will get too close; the wish to be at the center of connection and the consequent fear of being too far out on the edge (1982, p. 62).

What men in general fear is the same dread of involvement and cooption that seems to haunt Pirsig's peripatetic protagonist.

It is difficult to deny the historical and metaphorical connection between teachers and authors. Seeing themselves as primary sources of knowledge, if not instruments of social control, both have tended to see the imposition of authority, in part through attempts to reformulate the judgment of others, as an essential component of their work. But what may now seem strange to those versed in the romantic ideology of print literacy is the association of author — long envisioned as the ideological rebel, the solitary Zarathustran figure contemplating truth alone in the mountains — with the unthinking, heavy-handed pedant who thoughtlessly imposes conformist dogma. It is as if those who have for so long prided themselves for being independent thinkers are now assigned the role of the Heideggerian 'they', the leveling voice of the masses. In the model of print literacy, teachers would have welcomed the association with authors, seeing themselves as having the personal power to liberate students from parochial and outmoded thoughts just as great writers have the literary power to compel society at large to ponder some new vision of reality. Teachers and authors have been more accustomed, at least since the Enlightenment, to seeing themselves as the great enemies, not the upholders, of superstitions and prejudices of all kinds, and thus accustomed to seeing their exertion of the authority that is vested in their roles as legitimate acts of moral persuasion. 'Authority', writes Hans-Georg Gadamer (1982), 'is something that is "acquired", not "bestowed". It has to do with "knowledge", not "blind obedience to a command"': '[T]he recognition of authority is always connected with the idea that what authority states is not irrational and arbitrary, but can be seen in principle, to be true' (pp. 248–49). In the moral world of print literacy, what is common and widely shared — from the whispered opinions of the citizens of Winesburg, Ohio to the unrestrained comments of callers on talk-radio shows — is more likely to prove untruthful or bigoted.

And yet it is precisely an electronic version of the public forum of talk-radio — not always a bastion of fair play — that in some ways seems to provide a model of the new computer classroom. The teacher's exclusive concern with commenting on texts, whether by students or professional writers, is now replaced by the entirely new environment of the computer network, a technology that ideally allows students to write to each other directly, to share their texts freely, so as to receive the free and open responses of their classmates. A

networked classroom using what Barker and Kemp call 'an egalitarian instructional system' is the antithesis of the proscenium classroom, an environment
where even the most intense discussions between students still lie under the control of the teacher. In the networked classroom, each student station contains a
direct link to all other stations.

> No link is privileged. There is no master control over them. If the
> instructor wishes to participate in the discourse, she must choose a
> workstation and participate at a transactional level equal to that of any
> other person sitting at any other workstation (Barker and Kemp, 1990,
> p. 16).

Behind the widening acceptance, and often advocacy, of the educational value of
networked computing lies the recognition that computer-mediated communication really does have revolutionary potential, that in Sherry Turkle's words,
the computer can become 'a screen for the projection of differences' (p. 57). All
those committed to social change, in or out of the classroom, are encouraged by
the possibility, expressed by Pamela McCorduck, that 'one of the most important
world-wide effects of computing might be its introduction of a new ethos of
cooperation' (p. 65).

Propelling this transformation of the print-based writing classroom are two
interrelated factors: the ideological interest in new, collaborative forms of social
interaction in and out of the classroom, and the ability of students and teachers to
exchange texts easily with each other via a computer network. Just as print-based
writing instruction does not collapse with the introduction of computers, neither
does the presence of a network automatically create a networked classroom.
Without sufficient encouragement, for example, students with access to word
processors often use the machines only to check their spelling and produce clean
final copy, and not to undertake extensive revisions of their work. Computer-
based writing instruction in the short run is not incompatible with print literacy,
nor conversely does the dramatic restructuring of print-based instruction require
students to work at computers. That is, networking and the attack on print-based
writing instruction are today operating independently of each other but often
with the same goal of establishing a new, cooperative model of writing instruction. To understand the full revolutionary impact that computers are having on
this instruction, it is necessary to consider the parallel and interrelated workings
of these two factors: the technology of networking and the ideology of curriculum reform.

The Educational On-line System (EOS), developed at the Massachusetts Institute
of Technology with assistance from Edward Barrett and James Paradis, is
intended to support a more traditional, print-based form of writing instruction.
Lacking revisionist fervor, either against teacher-centered instruction or in support of student-centered cooperation, Barrett and Paradis envision the networked
classroom basically as an extension rather than a transformation of traditional
pedagogy. Their own description reflects this conservative bent; the networked
classroom, they claim, 'will be to the next generation of writing instructors what
word-processing software is to the present' (p. 154). Technology is for them a
neutral force ('transparent' is their word) facilitating the four kinds of activities

that they see as central to all writing instruction: (1) 'the presentation of texts for discussion and peer review', (2) 'the exchange of texts in and out of class', (3) 'text writing and editing in and out of class', and (4) 'the annotation of texts by instructors and, sometimes, students' (1988 p. 158). Writing instruction remains focused on what has been its main concern for most of the last century — texts, written by student-authors and responded to by teacher-readers.

Barrett and Paradis criticize most existing composition software for pedagogical assumptions that are at odds with the current classroom practices. Prewriting software, in particular, they criticize for forcing students to respond to a series of canned prompts about their topic, prompts which, as Helen Schwartz notes, the students then internalize, programming themselves as it were. Instead of altering student behaviors and attitudes so that they are less print-based and better able to interact effectively with the new technology, they suggest that we use the technology to perfect, as it were, the traditional classroom, making the four central components of print-based writing instruction immediately available to all students in the networked classroom. Students still write and swap papers, complete class writing assignments, read and discuss texts (including their own) in class — everything is the same as in a traditional class, except all these transactions are now mediated by the computer in real time. The computer in their classroom, they claim, is a facilitating rather than a transforming agent, what they call (borrowing from Seymour Papert) 'an object to think with' (Barrett and Paradis, p. 157), here with the assumption that the thought process itself remains largely unaffected.

Such a claim obviously raises the difficult question of the relationship between technique and substance, and between quantitative and qualitative differences. While certain technological changes may well facilitate a practice without radically transforming it — engineers, for example, who use calculators may think essentially the same as those who use slide rules — there are clearly limits to how far such thinking can be pushed. At some critical point, the sum of quantitative differences can have immense qualitative effect. A few early car owners may well have seen their new vehicles as little more than carriages without horses, yet as twentieth-century urban development continues to reveal, the immense quantitative advantage of cars has led, for better or worse, to equally immense qualitative changes, remapping the entire social and political landscape. Yet Barrett and Paradis seem only dimly aware of the potential networking has for redefining literacy.

> As is clear from this brief description, the cycle of lecture, in-class exercise, review, and feedback was much more immediate than in a conventional class. More material could be displayed in class, and more examples of student writing could be discussed. Not only was it very easy for students to practice what we had just taught, but it was possible to go through that cycle three times during one class meeting (p. 163).

Only once do they seem at all aware that their high-tech classroom is more than a horseless carriage that students and teachers of the future will use for more than short weekly rides into town, that the 'virtual classroom' they have created really is something radical: 'an invisible, dynamic set of interlocking systems or activities that form the "text" of any class' (p. 160). Such a classroom, they realize, represents 'a deconstruction of the actual classroom' by eliminating the need for students to be in the same place at the same time in order to have class: 'the on-line classroom can exist anywhere at any time for anyone with access to the network.'

What they do not note is the ease and thoroughness with which this 'virtual classroom' will inevitably transform the traditional notion of text, relocating writing from the primary control of a single person (the traditional author) to an 'interlocking system of activities', specifically, the talking back and forth carried on by the participants. Here the basic issue is technical, involving the relative ease with which networking allows texts to be swapped and annotated. With print, there is a clearly marked text, usually a typed manuscript, that must be physically transported, to which comments, usually hand-written, can be attached on the periphery, in the margins (now often with self-adhering notes) or at the end. In any case, the original text remains intact and of primary consideration, partly because of its superior legibility. There is little question here as to what is primary — the typed text that reflects hours of planning and deliberation — and what is secondary — the handwritten commentary, dashed off with little chance for revision. Yet when swapping and annotating are facilitated by a network, the seemingly clear distinction between text and commentary quickly becomes less stable. Texts can be readily moved and copied and, depending on the software used, a multitude of 'typed' comments and responses can be attached, creating a situation where the original text begins to be seen less as the primary focus of concern and more as the occasion for an extended dialogue among interested parties. Barker and Kemp see such 'textual transactions between students' as the defining element of what they call 'network theory': the facility for the rapid exchange of files, they claim, results in '*deneutralizing* of text itself and a greater emphasis and skill on the part of the transactor in rendering such text' (p. 15).

Characterized by a series of intermediate transformations, such changes may not be apparent immediately, but it seems inevitable that over time the means of storing and representing writing in the networked classroom will also have a radical impact on the nature of that writing. Just as people can read and write hypertexts like Michael Joyce's 'Afternoon' as Bolter suggests, much in the spirit of print literacy, so too students, much in the fashion of a newsroom, can circulate text files to student-editors with the final intention of submitting them to the teacher as editor-in-chief. Like the hand-crafted hypertext, the networked classroom also has a traditional mode, a phase where it is represented mainly as an extension of existing practices — here the creation of a networked classroom that facilitates the swapping and annotating of the same kind of texts that have characterized literacy in the age of print. It is doubtful, however, if such an environment can be maintained. As with hypertext, this new environment seems destined to transform, and not merely extend, our notion of text. Or, as Brian Gallagher explains, the fluidity of electronic text gives it 'a status closer to the spoken word than all other kinds of "written" texts, since it can be reconsidered and restructured in much the same way spoken text can (i.e., instantly, on the spot)' (Davis, 1988, p. 351).

The technology driving the networked classroom, just like that driving hypertext, seems to lead inevitably to a redefinition of literacy. In the long run, just as hypertext is ill-suited to support a traditional author, so networking undermines the central status of the teacher. In either case, the primary organizing figure — be it teacher or author — is replaced by individuals (students or readers) who have the task of organizing materials for their own purposes. More immediately, the technology of the networked classroom shifts the primary focus of literacy away from the self-contained text and toward a new kind of interactive discourse akin to conversation, and in so doing complements the broader trend in contemporary criticism of undermining the special status of all texts. Network technology, working independently of any one school of criticism, in other words, reveals one of the founding truths of postmodernism, as articulated by the Russian theorist Mikhail Bakhtin — namely, that even the most carefully wrought literary texts are sites of conflicting forces and voices, tensions that are 'practically impossible to recoup, and therefore impossible to resolve' (p. 428). All discourse, including the seemingly unified, univocal literary text, is for Bakhtin the product of a loud clash of voices, a universal condition he labels *heteroglossia*.

It is in the vibrant crowd, the practices of the people themselves — notably their rowdy carnivals — that Bakhtin locates what he calls *internally persuasive discourse*, language that is:

> denied all privilege, backed by no authority at all ['religious, political, moral; the word of a father, of adults and of teachers, etc.'], and is frequently not even acknowledged in society (not by public opinion, nor by scholarly norms, nor by criticism), not even in the legal code (p. 342).

Such discourse, critics of print literacy claim, has too often been suppressed in the language classroom as well as in society generally. As in society itself, what is most vital and compelling in social discourse has been suppressed by what Bakhtin calls *authoritative discourse*, or language that we are asked to accept because of the status of those who speak it.

> The authoritative word demands that we acknowledge it, that we make it our own.... [It] is located in a distanced zone, organically connected with a past that is felt to be hierarchically higher. It is, so to speak, the word of the fathers.

Dominating Bakhtin's work is a reversal of those aspects of print literacy that lie at the center of an older, more encompassing Western tradition embedded in print literacy. Bakhtin's crowd is not like the one in Shirley Jackson's classic story, 'The Lottery', a force for the thorough, often brutal, and, at least for cultural conservatives, at times necessary suppression of the individual; nor does his authority have anything in common with the established philosophical and political Western traditions of intellectual criticism and social dissent, that system of values and institutions that, to choose just one example, underlie Thoreau's 'Essay on Civil Disobedience' (a work commonly taught within the 'authoritative discourse' of the school). Whatever individuality we manage to achieve, as Wayne Booth explains, it is 'never a private or autonomous individuality' but one that results from our remaining true to the 'chorus of languages' (1984, p. xxi) we all speak. Authoritative discourse in Bakhtin that denies such multiplicity seems to be associated, not with Western academic tradition that at least since the Brothers Grimm has been almost consumed by a fascination with the wisdom of the folk, but with the kind of clumsy, deadening, malevolent rhetoric of Stalinist bureaucracies, a fearful totalitarian discourse that, at least in the United States, has more often been associated with such flights of right-wing paranoia as *Red Dawn*, a film that in the best anti-intellectual tradition sees the greatest threat to America in its leaders and its ultimate salvation in the spirit of freedom (and the guns) of the silent majority.

Bakhtin, as it were, turns the world of print literacy on its head, and in so doing becomes a rallying point for all language educators — both those committed to and those largely ignorant of networked classrooms — who want to move beyond the pedagogic and, at a deeper level, the moral limits of print literacy. The specific appeal of the networked classroom is that it literally embodies the structure of post-print literacy. Such a classroom, for example, automatically seems to refute one of the principal tenets of print literacy, that of the writer as isolated individual, replacing it with a parallel tenet of online literacy, that of writing and knowledge generally as social construction — or as juxtaposed in the two-part title of Carolyn Handa's essay, noted in Chapter 1, 'Politics, Ideology, and the Strange, Slow Death of the Isolated Composer or Why We Need Community in the Writing Classroom' (1990b). The operative term in this essay advocating networked classrooms is *collaboration*, a concept Handa sees as involving 'a move outward from the writer to others who provide response and input', a move that is supported by the tendency of a network, as we have seen, to treat the written exchange or dialogue occasioned by a text as at least as important as the text itself. Collaboration, for Handa, represents a 'move away from solipsism' (1990b, p. 162), a loaded term that suggests a kind of self-absorption and moral blindness. 'Collaboration is a spirit that makes an author eager to talk over his work with others, makes him distrust his own work for the blindness he knows it contains.'

While it is difficult to openly support solipsism — or openly oppose cooperation — it is also difficult to know just what to make of this new emphasis on collaboration in Handa and in two other writers she relies on, Anne Ruggles Gere and Karen Burke LeFevre. What one must first recognize is how in these writings, the underlying terms of the debate themselves undergo a radical revision. A continuum that seems to offer writers only a choice of *solipsism*, with the suggestion of self-absorption and narcissistic selfishness, or *collaboration*, with the suggestion of cooperation and a generous, giving temperament, has already remapped the landscape of print literacy, largely in accordance with a new political sensibility — one that, as will be examined below, pits the self-interest of industrial capitalism against the community-mindedness of some generalized post-industrial economic order. Or as Handa writes, the collaborative classroom 'challenges the assumptions that characterize both capitalistic societies and academia, as well as theories of knowledge reinforced by textbooks built on certain traditions and reactions to those traditions' (1990b, p. 168).

Such impassioned rhetoric, not surprisingly, can disguise as well as reveal the ease and seeming efficiency with which key cultural concepts and terms can be transformed. Such quiet transformations, as noted in earlier chapters, have occurred before — the radical shifts in such central terms as *original* two hundred years ago and *reading* at the end of the last century. We should hardly be surprised that equally momentous historical changes now occurring should produce equally profound redefinitions. As we have seen, only a generation ago the computer itself, now depicted as a facilitator of new, more open forms of human inter-action, was more likely to be seen as a menacing new agent of social control. We should thus not be surprised to see the meaning of so central a term as *collaboration* shift. Only a half-century ago it was largely pejorative, suggesting among other things compliance with a hated enemy; today it is increasingly being trumpeted as a universal good, a sign of one's rejection of all the ills associated with an older world order (authority, patriarchy, subservience, conformity, …) and one's acceptance of all the promises of a new one (cooperation, tolerance, independence, resistance, …).

What is at stake here, as Karen LeFevre (1987) realizes, is the direct but frequently overlooked connection between classroom practice and economic pro-duction. What she calls the 'Platonic view of rhetorical invention' — the notion that 'ideas are created in the mind of an atomistic individual and then expressed to the rest of the world' (p. 1) — has prevailed, she contends, largely because of its underlying connection with an economy based on individual initiative.

> [I]nventional theory based on the assumption that individuals develop their own ideas from within and then claim ownership for what they invent … is certainly in line with the aims of Western capitalistic societies, in which ideas and discoveries, like nearly everything else, become property owned by individuals, able to be bought and sold (p. 20).

The stakes in this debate are high indeed, having as much to do with the reorganization of society as with any changes in instruction. In supporting increased collaboration, educators are countering what LeFevre sees as an unholy alliance between 'capitalism, individualism, and patriarchal assumptions' (p. 20). Or as Handa notes:

> choosing to keep a traditional, noncollaborative classroom could mean choosing to run the risk of preventing students from realizing their own power as writers and from challenging the competition, chauvinism, and class structure that have played such a major role in capitalistic societies and academia (1990b, p. 168).

The changes driving current reforms are equal in scope to the establishment of print literacy in the curriculum a century ago, and, as with that earlier shift, intricately connected to reformulations in how we define work and how we generate wealth. As noted in Chapter 2, we are at the end of an age that generated wealth, and overcame a host of social and natural problems, largely through the widespread application of creative, independent thought, usually in the form of scientific discovery, and at the beginning of a new, post-industrial age, one that sees progress in terms of both curbing industrial expansion and increasing our ability to interact productively in a new, intensely social, information-rich work environment. It should hardly be surprising that new pedagogic practices are evolving to meet these new needs, nor that the computer — one of the prime causative factors in this massive cultural transformation — is at the center of these practices. What is surprising, and what needs further explication, is the justification for such educational reforms, especially the ideological fervor which ignores all that may have been laudable about print literacy while glossing over all that is troubling about reading and writing online.

Advocacy of the networked classroom, therefore, often cannot be separated from a broader and more thorough-going rejection, not just of teacher-centered instruction, but of print literacy itself and, more often than not, the entire social apparatus it supports. And yet there is a potential contradiction here: there is much of value to salvage from that older tradition. The most determined critics of print literacy, for example, are often the figurative children of that tradition, their idealism and zest for reform, as Gouldner notes (1979, p. 70) like that of so many political revolutionaries this century, nourished in the very world they seem most intent on changing. And in both cases, there is a similar ploy — to sever the best of the older tradition from its historical roots, turning the tables, as it were, by assuming that the best of that tradition (in the case of print literacy, for example, the constant drive for reform itself) comes into being only in spite of specific practices of teachers or, as we shall consider later, parents. Author/reformers themselves become not the logical products of that older tradition, nor the students who have mastered the best lessons of their teachers, but (ironically, given the moral structure of the model of print literacy being rejected) the exception, liberated individuals who have managed to escape the throes of a deadening tradition. It is as if critics of teacher-centered instruction have themselves never been aided by strong, assertive teachers, but instead have arrived at their position only after having escaped the clutches of a lifetime of classroom tyrants. As a result, all that is worthy about print literacy — the sanctity it places on individual experience, its respect for privacy, its respect for innovation — become ungrounded universal ideals, readily transferable to the critic's new pedagogic scheme, in this case the new collaborative writing class.

What a strange and sudden bend in the road it is that so completely transforms the educational landscape! Where formerly the teacher had been the embodiment of critical thought, the one person able to create a safe space for nurturing the initially private thoughts and sensibilities of the more sensitive and insightful students, protecting them, as it were, from insatiable pressures to conform from society at large and from one's classmates in particular — now the teacher is seen as an extension of those same mindless, insensitive, authoritarian pressures. Meanwhile, the computer, no longer like HAL the embodiment of oppressive control, now becomes the instrument of liberation. Such a tactic has the desired effect of stripping print literacy of its legitimacy. Yet this legitimacy needs to be partially restored if we are ever to gain a balanced view of where literacy has been and where it may be going.

In print literacy collaboration was long considered inconsequential, but not in order to isolate students from one another, or to emphasize their subservience to the teacher, or to make them better skilled at following directions than thinking for themselves — nor even, as Handa states, drawing from the most polemical attacks of Richard Ohmann's *English in America* to make them better adapted to the needs of the military-industrial complex. Collaboration was not valued in the moral world of print literacy largely out of a keen sense of the power of any group to foster bland, mediocre thought, ideas that the high priests of print culture (its authors and critics as well as its teachers) suspected too often complied with the conformist, uncritical tendencies that were deeply embedded in modern consumer culture. As traced by Raymond Williams in his classic study, *Culture and Society* (1985), English studies throughout the nineteenth and the first half of the twentieth century was part of a larger critique of commercial culture and especially the values inherent in an open-market economy. From such a perspective only the most debased ideas ever received wide circulation.

Writing instruction, embedded as it was in English studies, saw its principal charge as helping the individual withstand the numbing onslaught of commercial culture, including new empirical academic disciplines, mesmerizing and dehumanizing popular culture, and, just as dangerous, peer pressure. Print literacy in its most rigorous form — the kind of critical reading, writing, and thinking that characterized the best college writing programs — was viewed as a safeguard against contamination by a world organized around the manufacturing, merchandising, and consumption of goods, organized, in a word, for profit. Public discourse was little more than a subtler form of mass advertising — the antithesis of the sincere expression of human experience one found (after a struggle necessary to ward off the insincere) in literature and anything else worth reading. Holden Caulfield, the 'hero' of J.D. Salinger's *The Catcher in the Rye* was the model of the sensitive, literate student, and Paul Goodman's *Growing Up Absurd* (1960), Edgar Freidenberg's *The Vanishing Adolescent* (1959), and David Reisman's *The Lonely Crowd* (1950) were his guides. As in Don Seigel's classic 1956 B-thriller, *The Invasion of the Body Snatchers*, students of print literacy faced dangers everywhere — fall asleep for a moment and you will become one of 'them', a faceless individual distinguishable only by a certain lethargy of spirit and a fierce, total, unquestioning commitment to the group.

In such a world, the first obligation of literacy was to be not a cooperative citizen, but an independent intellectual, someone who maintains sufficient critical distance from the commonplace (with the implicit understanding that the democratic — and capitalistic — body politic is healthiest when composed of a multitude of independent thinkers). The constant vigilance required by Seigel's doctor hero parallels the constant critical scrutiny of the intellectual. What is truly worth knowing — understanding when we read, creating when we write — is not the ordinary but the extra-ordinary. What is average — the collective wisdom of the group (what 'they' said) — is, in the final analysis, what education for print literacy is organized to overcome. In English studies especially, where such emphasis has been placed on resistance to popular misreadings, it was long felt (and in many quarters, still is) that reading and writing collaboratively is, in essence, reading and writing by committee — the surest path to mediocrity of thought and, ultimately, of social life.

With the proper ideological context, a value like the sanctity of individual experience that once helped to define print literacy and English studies this century can now be readily dismissed as 'solipsism'. As the analysis of Pirsig's narrator at the end of Chapter 2 demonstrates, such sanctity is hardly an absolute good, and as will be developed at length in Chapter 5, print literacy itself may finally be judged to have had as many failures as successes, giving us good reason to celebrate its transformation or possible demise; nevertheless, to dismiss print literacy summarily for its 'solipsism' is to reduce one of the great achievements of human culture to a caricature. Readers and writers of print did have to do much (though certainly not all) of their work alone, especially as writers of the age of industrial expansion, the high-water mark of print literacy, moved in the direction of more massive, and more psychologically intense, literary productions. There is a solitary path that one must venture down either to create or to read a lengthy, detailed, complex novel like Henry James's *The Ambassadors*. Yet one is not alone on that path; in words derived from the most traditional, most solidly print-based model of literacy, that of Matthew Arnold's, one is in contact with 'the best that has been thought and said'. Individuals were steered away from collaboration, not out of the belief that it was possible to read and write only to oneself, but in order that they could concentrate on communicating with kindred spirits, other individuals capable of appreciating what we had to say or, in turn, of informing us. Literacy, like Dewey's vision of schooling, was fundamentally social; its job, as Bowers explains, was to 'insure that only those elements of the past that strengthened the cooperative application of creative intelligence to social problem solving would be passed on to the young' (1987, p. 34). Even for the most reclusive writers — Dickinson, Kafka, Beckett — writing was clearly a form of what Handa calls 'a dialectic with others' (1990b, p. 162). The archetypal student of print literacy is the lonely adolescent who finds consolation reading Willa Cather's *My Antonia* and keeping a diary recording in meticulous detail all the comings and goings of her world as a means of preparing to write her own life story, a volume eventually to be shared with other readers.

We might want to counsel this adolescent to be more outgoing, to make more friends so that she could share her diary as she wrote it. Becoming more gregarious, more open in her feelings, less solipsistic (to use Handa's phrase) may be good advice as regards this person's overall emotional well-being — isn't that what we would want for our own child? But what is not clear is how any of this affects a basic assumption in Handa and others that doing so will somehow improve her 'literacy', at least as defined in terms of making her a more powerful reader or writer. As articulated by Rosenblatt, the charge before us as traditional English teachers of such a student (as teachers of print culture) moves us in an entirely different, but no less ethical direction: not how to be more engaged in the world, but how to experience it more deeply; that is:

> how can the study of literature enable students to understand themselves
> better and to see human beings and society in a broader context of
> emotions and ideas? In short, how can students be helped to achieve
> literary experiences of higher and higher quality (1976, p. 53)?

The individual is obliged in such a fundamentally liberal, Deweyean view of literacy, to escape social control, not for narcissistic or solipsistic purposes, in Bowers' words, not 'in order to exercise greater inner self-direction ... but [as a means] of acquiring a form of power that involves an increased capacity to reorganize experience' (1987, p. 35).

Handa basically finesses the complex relationship between being more social and more literate, noting that collaboration really does not have to be with other people, that it can be 'less interactive ... with people either living or dead through their ideas in books' (1990b, p. 162). Gere attempts to address the point more directly in her monograph *Writing Groups* (1987). For Gere, writing groups, what she defines as 'writers responding to one another's work' (p. 1), are less an innovation than an extension of the best aspect of traditional practices of literacy — a means of providing all writers, presumably an Emily Dickinson or a Franz Kafka as well as our introspective adolescent, with that vital component of the writing process, a sympathetic audience. Gere does not discuss computers and various forms of electronic conferencing, but the implications for her work are clear. If what she calls the 'social dimension of writing' (p. 3) really is the basis for literacy, then any technology that places people in closer contact with one another would, by definition, enhance literacy.

Why is it now in our interest to move away from the solitary experience of print literacy? Gere resolves this dilemma in much the same way that new classroom practices are being promoted in general, by a rhetorical appeal to a new, post-industrial moral framework in which older forms of social relations get stigmatized (largely as hierarchical and authoritarian) and new forms get validated (largely as collaborative and autonomous). On one level, the struggle over good and bad classroom practices becomes part of a larger epistemological struggle between good and bad conceptions of knowledge.

> Knowledge conceived as socially constructed or generated validates the 'learning' part of collaborative learning because it assumes that interactions of collaboration can lead to new knowledge or learning. A fixed and hierarchical view of knowledge, in contrast, assumes that learning can occur only when a designated 'knower' imparts wisdom to those less well informed (pp. 72–73).

Here is a struggle that extends beyond the conflict between good knowledge and bad. Gere's writing groups represent more than an effective instructional practice; they are centers of post-print literacy and post-industrial ideology. In rejecting fixed knowledge, they also reject the accompanying evils of hierarchical culture, including its limiting notions of language and authority. Clearly, the teacher referred to above, in choosing the wrong side, assumes the mantle of the self-absorbed pedagogue, one who mistakes the little that he or she knows and is attempting to drill into the heads of students with the dynamic, ever-expanding world of knowledge. There is a certain smugness in teachers whose methodology suggests that knowledge is hierarchical, that they are on top, and that they know more than students. Someone who thinks that way, Gere suggests, has a corrupted view of language itself, seeing it as 'a medium, the vehicle through which knowledge is transmitted', and thus 'on the margins of knowledge' (p. 73). 'The socially constructive view, by contrast [*sic*] places language at the center of knowledge because it constitutes the means by which ideas can be developed and explored.'

Hierarchical organization did place the teacher above the student, not as an act of authority (for example, to teach obedience), but out of the defining belief that what was most worth knowing was to be found — or created — furthest from (above or below) the commonplace. Nor was this knowledge to be communicated in some transparent way by language. On the contrary, print literacy elevated the well-wrought text to its highest standing, while resisting all attempts to reduce the meaning of such texts to a paraphrase. The purest form of communication, therefore, is in writing and reading such texts — in generating the new knowledge or understanding that is embedded in such well-wrought texts (and nowhere else) and in the complex act of interpreting them. While it may have been important for readers and writers to have all sorts of personal and professional relations — family, friends, and colleagues — to offer them support and encouragement, as well as helping to fulfill the many emotional needs we all have, none of these common social dealings can approach the importance of creating texts as writers or readers.

What is at stake in Gere's contrast between hierarchical and collaborative modes is, in the final analysis, a conflict between alternate ways of being in the world. What Gere and, by extension, more direct advocates of computer-mediated writing are promoting is a new form of social relations — the world of print is rejected mainly for its moral deficiencies. The issue is not whether a class-room based upon the trio of evils, 'hierarchy, competition, and isolation' (p. 51), might produce a higher level of literacy — more compelling literate texts, for example. The pedagogic tradition of the master class, with its intense competitive pressures to emulate and impress the teacher, is dismissed out of hand, not explicitly for failing to produce future masters of the craft, for example, but implicitly for creating the wrong kind of student — one too bound up in compe-tition, too eager to please, and presumably, too unwilling to think and act on one's own. The assumption in such thinking is that the quality of the product — just how good a writer (or artist) one produces — is not really the issue. All that matters is what sort of person is produced, and a methodology based on imitation, what Piaget argues is along with play one of the two great instruments of human learning, could only produce an imitative, noncritical person.

Such a conclusion, however, flies in the face of much of our own experience. Consider, for instance, the story David Bartholomae tells about his own educational struggles when contemplating the task of constructing an English curriculum to ensure full literacy for underprepared college students.

> The most dramatic educational experience I had was my contact with Richard Poirier in my first year of graduate school. The first three years of graduate training were driven by a desire to be able to do what he did — to be able to read and speak and write like him. I would, for example, copy out difficult or impressive sentences he had written in order to get the feel of them. I can feel them now in sentences I write. It is a mixed feeling. I state it simply, but it wasn't simple at all. I tried for a whole semester to write a paper using the word 'language' as he used it in talking about how the language 'worked' in 'Upon Appleton House'. It took me a whole semester to use the word in a sentence that actually made sense to me, in a sentence I felt I could control. I felt that I had gained access to a profession by exercises like these. At the time it didn't feel like surrender. It was inspiring to feel that I could use language and mimic, as I could, his way of reading and writing (1986, p. 115).

What Bartholomae is testifying to here is only what many others have experi-enced, the important role that modeling plays both in forming character and, as Piaget argues, in less obvious ways, in spurring cognitive development as well. 'You cannot write or teach or think or even read', Bartholomae quotes Harold Bloom, 'without imitation, and what you imitate is what another person has done, that person's writing, or teaching or thinking or reading.' Has any of us ever excelled at anything — or at least, worked at excelling, from playing double-stops on the violin to hitting top-spin backhands in tennis — without having had such models in mind to help sustain us through hours of arduous practice? What have we worked for during those times if not to emulate what to us seemed perfection (what educators now dismiss as the ideal text)? And at the moment of greatest success, at the instant that we have most completely lost ourselves in the demands of our new discipline, did we not also feel what Bartholomae felt — a sense of exhilaration, a feeling of personal accomplishment, and, what may seem strange to those who confuse logic and emotion, a momentary glimpse into that strange state we call human freedom?

Gere's dichotomy of individual and social, like that between collaboration and solipsism, obscures rather than clarifies the central issues. The writer in the midst of such a literate performance is truly self-absorbed, focused on maximizing personal expression through mastery of craft, and is thus cut off from the support structure of family, friends and colleagues that help us manage our daily affairs — much as a dancer or other performer may have to appear before the public on stage alone, having internalized such support. And as with the solo performer, there seems to be no easy place to raise questions about morals, much less manners, apart from the values embedded in the performance (or the text) itself. Print literacy, like art, is an arena of intense personal freedom, a place where one can escape many of the most superficial and wearing demands to act correctly that are an unavoidable part of ordinary life. Quite simply, in art as in literacy in its most intense form, we do not have to be the nice, accommodating person all our friends expect us to be — in escaping from our normal self we are free to express another, more vital part of ourselves.

Critics of print literacy would have us rein in such freedom in the guise of saving us from isolation, competition, authority and alienation. No longer is the writer to be allowed to be perverse and in stark opposition to the group, indifferent to the needs of readers, in a word, extra-ordinary. The condition of standing utterly apart, like Pirsig's persona, becomes for Gere a form of alienation leading to 'feelings of isolation, powerlessness, and meaninglessness' (p. 62), apart from the quality of the writing that may result. It is as if all writing is improved by becoming more immediately socialized, more palatable to the group, more able to help writers 'remember what their readers need to know and to find the right words to make their ideas most accessible to those readers' (p. 68). Clearly certain forms of writing can succeed only by meeting the demands of the group, but the implication throughout Gere's treatise — and throughout much of the ideology of collaborative learning — is that learning how to adjust to the needs of the group is a necessary condition of *all* writing and, more to the point, *all* writers. There is no ideal text, Gere joins many others in assuring us. 'Participants frame comments in terms of their own experience with the writing rather than some "ideal" text, and in so doing they avoid standardized comments that can be transposed from one piece of writing to another' (p. 74). Yet without some kind of general standards, we might ask, how are we to respond to any work that goes beyond the dim light of our own Platonic cave? The answer that Gere offers can be read as a sobering renunciation of the very core of print literacy — namely, that individuals have no business leaving the group to stare into the bright light. 'In the collaborative view individual genius becomes subordinate to social interactions and intellectual negotiations among peers' (p. 75). The goal of literacy becomes, not the creation or comprehension of an artifact, no matter how inspired, but social adjustment: 'to change oneself, to leave one community and join another' (p. 103). Here is another, perhaps more chilling view of the world of print turned upside down, with the best adjusted person, be it future sales-person or politician, deemed, by definition, the most 'literate', and the least adjusted, Pirsig himself and other 'geniuses' of print, deemed most in need of remediation. When the text is reduced from a realm of personal freedom to 'polished prose', what remains of literacy is 'the process of the group, the means by which individuals experience and eventually become part of a literate community' (p. 123).

Gere obviously does not see herself as radically altering literacy, reducing it as it were to a form of social adjustment, nor apparently does she recognize the role of adjustment in her collaborative model of literacy. After all, the key to the new collaborative practice is to arrange things so that everything is freely chosen by autonomous individuals. Yet the crux here is how one is to arrange such a world, and as Gere realizes, it often does not happen on its own; instead, the teacher must work carefully to create an atmosphere 'where no one individual constantly dominates, where all members are supported, and where individual contributions are developed upon by other members' (pp. 68–69). But what is such orderly, constructive behavior but a new ideal — what is at work here but the substitution of a model of ideal behavior for that of the ideal text? And what is the charge for teachers but to work as rigorously in enforcing this new ideal as they have formerly worked in enforcing the old? 'Teachers can prepare for writing groups,' Gere concludes, 'by transforming the class into a community where all members feel secure' (p. 103), by creating through the manipulation of the classroom environment, if not the direct exercise of authority, a new post-print community. 'This means establishing a climate where put-downs are disallowed, where people are encouraged to express their ideas without fear of recrimination, and where diversity is appreciated, not depreciated' (p. 103).

And while all of us might agree it is better to have sensitive, caring students than boorish, self-absorbed ones, what is at stake is the amount of indirect authority that is involved in moving students 'away from positions articulated as "What right does another student have to comment on my paper?" ... toward positions articulated as "I value the comments of my peers"' (Gere, 1987, p. 52)? Where, we must ask, does this solicitous, orderly concern come from? The implication in post-print pedagogy is that in Rousseau-like fashion all things fall into place once the oppressive authority of the teacher is removed. It is as if the spirit of cooperation really is the defining characteristic of human nature — and no doubt it is, albeit in the same sense that the spirit of competition is also the defining characteristic of human nature, or at least, was often thought so when such an aggressive attitude had a clear economic benefit to individuals and society at large.

For James Berlin, one of the most articulate theorists of new classroom inter-action, a new world of increased democratic involvement seems to flow out of the recognition that all truth is ideological. In liberating students from all forms of tradition and authority, Berlin problematizes all universal truths (except perhaps its own founding principle) by asserting that knowledge must be seen 'as an arena of ideological conflict'. What are the consequences of any belief? we are instructed to ask. Who benefits, gains material power, from our beliefs?

Because there are no 'natural laws' or 'universal truths' that indicate what exists, what is good, what is possible, and how power is to be distributed ... [such decisions] must be continually decided by all and for all in any way appropriate to our own historical moment (Berlin, 1988, pp. 489–90).

The implication throughout his discussion is that traditional, teacher-based pedagogy, such as lectures or teacher-led discussions (including those with a Marxist perspective) hides such questions and distorts the true interests of students to create their own truths. Berlin's position is thus a grand extension of Marx's famous dictum — only now organized education, not just organized religion, is an opiate for the masses.

The unanswered question in Berlin's classroom, and in Gere's (and in their larger worlds), is what in fact happens to truth, justice, and social relations when (or if) print literacy is entirely overthrown. What happens if the authority of the teacher and the author (and, by extension, the transcendent truths such authorities imperfectly embody) is removed? No one can deny that even the most enlightened teachers and social institutions as a whole are imperfect instruments for social justice. That despite their fiercest revolutionary intentions all teachers in fulfilling their professional roles also promote models of social stability, mainly by working against the free and unrestrained (some might claim, anarchical) exercise of the popular will. The institutions of print literacy, grounded as they are in vertical notions of truth, have always cast a wary eye on the expression of such popular will, especially in its most visible form of consensus. Upholders of the institutions of print literacy have felt that group action unenlightened by the ideal of social justice and the imaginative capacity for human compassion (two transcendent values language educators were traditionally charged with instilling) could result as readily in reaction as in progress — that the tyranny of the crowd is a short step away from mob rule. The value of authorities — teachers (and parents) as well as authors — was in legitimating higher (if not, universal) standards of conduct.

Yet what we find in Berlin is a forthright assertion, in the name of social progress, that 'there are no arguments from transcendent truth' (1988, p. 489). All claims, he suggests, are inevitably distorted by their association with all institutions of authority, including those with the highest revolutionary intentions. Behind Berlin's social-epistemic rhetoric is the belief that the free play of individuals acting without the efforts of authorities to impose ideals, 'inevitably support economic, social, political, and cultural democracy' (1988, p. 489). Democratic practice, it turns out, is the one certain path to overcoming false consciousness.

What, one might ask, happens if Berlin is wrong, if a group (as many have in history) turns mean, counter-revolutionary, becomes misdirected by false consciousness? What does the teacher do if the class consensus is in violation (vigorous proclamations notwithstanding) of what clearly stands as the transcendent truth, and the hidden ideological agenda, at the core of collaborative rhetoric — that people should act together to extend social justice? 'At the foundation of well-founded belief', writes Ludwig Wittgenstein, 'lies belief that is not founded' (1969, p. 33e), an assertion that presumably applies even (or especially) to the most radically suspicious, most self-questioning systems of belief like that of Berlin.

Social-epistemic rhetoric is an alternative that is self-consciously aware of its ideological stand, making the very question of ideology the center of classroom activities, and in so doing providing itself a defense against preemption and a strategy for self-criticism and self-correction (1988, p. 478).

But what happens if the self-criticism and the self-correction and, more importantly because here unstated, the social criticism and the social correction, all stop, or wander off course? What propels the group forward in its criticism; what keeps it on track — constantly forcing it to revise all received interpretations in what Berlin describes as 'the interests of the greater participation of all, for the greater good of all' (1988, p. 490)? What is it that guides social action in the classroom? And here only two answers come to mind. It is either an unfailing (tautological?) faith that the response of the group is always right, always socially progressive, or, all protestations notwithstanding, the authority (literally, the violence) of the teacher grounded in the mastery of a widely valued academic and moral tradition.

Before considering the theoretical response of social philosophers to such questions, it may pay to look at the more practical resolution of these issues in a closely related environment, the new, computer-mediated workplace. Shoshana Zuboff's *In the Age of the Smart Machine* (1988) reviews the implications for the productive application of the malleable, de-centered electronic text. When texts in a corporate environment are accessed through networks their essential character changes in ways indicated in Chapter 3. First, their individual character, their sense of having a boundary, disappears; they become 'not discrete but comprehensive and systemic'. Instead of 'individual events converted to text', we now have 'systems of events that are revealed comprehensively.... The organization's work is made visible in a new way' (Zuboff, p. 179). Second, the individual texts can be integrated in ways that reflect the integrated knowledge of the corporation as a whole, as compared to that of any one unit. 'The structure of the text, as well as its content, reflects material that had been private and implicit.' The electronic text, although seemingly centralized in a single network file server, is in fact available to any employee at any place at any time. 'The contents of the electronic text can infuse an entire organization, instead of being bundled in discrete objects, like books or pieces of paper' (p. 180). The result is that all employees can interact with textual information in new, potentially creative and playful ways. As a substitute for what Zuboff calls 'bodily presence' (p. 181), interaction with electronic text not only frees us *from* 'having to participate in the immediate demands of the action' but frees us *to* gain greater control over our work. 'The automating capacity of the technology can free the human being for a more comprehensive, explicit, systemic, and abstract knowledge of his or her work made possible by the technology's ability to informate.'

When Zuboff looks closely at the workings of DIALOG, a computer conferencing system within the research and development division of a company she identifies as DrugCorp, she finds the same kind of openness and collaborative spirit advocated by Handa, LeFevre, Selfe and other language educators. She recognizes that the most valuable knowledge (here, the creation of new products) is best facilitated by increased social interaction. '[I]nterpersonal communication provided researchers with their most important channels of access to information and stimulation for new ideas' (p. 363). The anecdotal evidence of the workers themselves certainly supports the benefits of informal collaboration.

> Many of DIALOG's participants thought that the medium worked most effectively in facilitating the examination of issues from a range of perspectives. They spoke of using the system for thinking rather than for taking positions, and they found that it encouraged divergence and inhibited convergence on a single line of reasoning (p. 368).

Or, in the words of one enthusiast:

> DIALOG lets me talk to other people as peers. No one knows if I am an hourly worker or a vice president. All messages have an equal chance because they all look alike. The only thing that sets them apart is their content. If you are a hunchback, a paraplegic, a woman, a black, fat, old, have two hundred warts on your face, or never take a bath, you still have the same chance. It strips away the halo effects from age, sex, or appearance (p. 371).

And, as we have seen before, it strips away other traditional components of texts as well. 'You don't have to be highly verbal to use DIALOG', a worker adds. 'Spelling and grammar really don't matter. They did at first, but nobody cares anymore. We learned to separate formal from informal' (p. 369).

More than an extension of traditional textual practices, DIALOG can be seen as an extension of traditional informal interaction — what one employee referred to as 'the closest thing I know to running into someone in the hallway' (p. 370), and what another described as 'meandering through the conferences to hallway conversations, experiencing the same degree of serendipity and stimulation' (p. 369). It is hardly a surprise that the single most popular conference on DIALOG was known as the Computer Coffee Break. 'Computer conferencing', Zuboff writes, 'transformed this transient talk into a concrete presence. It was as if the ether of sociality that once filled the hallways had suddenly congealed' (p. 376).

Yet it is this most informal, most collaborative world of employees electronically gathered around a virtual coffee pot that reveals many of the tensions inherent in Berlin and Gere. On the one hand, as Berlin would be the first to note, any collaborative arrangement is already located within a given historical setting, one that may not always be entirely receptive to such informality. Businesses, like classrooms, do not exist in isolation; whatever freedom they allow falls within the control of higher authorities, who, in the most sinister of scenarios, can use the 'openness' of collaboration as a means of spying upon employees. The privacy of electronic communication, especially within a corporation or a school, is not well protected in law; such a guarantee, were it afforded, would then entail the kind of establishment of authority (with the power to discipline) that goes against the grain of collaboration in the first place. Employees themselves also soon realized that there is a stream of non-normative behavior, at times expressing resentment of others, at times expressing erotic desires (as in dirty jokes) — all potentially fertile grounds of imaginative thought and liberation from authority — that cannot be easily sanctioned on an open network. To engage in private thoughts openly, participants essentially had to re-create Lucy

Snow's attic in Charlotte Brontë's *Villette*: they started a new, secret conference with severe limitations as to who could write or view a message.

Such events raise one of the profound questions of networked communication: how do we express the anti-social in a medium designed to promote social cooperation? What happens to *anomie* in a world where our comments are monitored by our colleagues, and where the clearly articulated unnecessary-goal of communication is cooperation? Or, as Zuboff herself asks, in a most telling section, 'Dissent from Wholeness', 'Is there a dark side to this vision of a wholistic [sic] organization with its emphasis on relationships that are intricate, dynamic, and constructed ad hoc? What new psychological costs might it imply?' And, most important of all, 'What new mechanisms might be required to ensure justice and equity?' (p. 402). In traditional labor relations, Zuboff notes, blue-collar workers, somewhat like students in a teacher-centered classroom, 'know exactly what is required of them and, in return, what rights they possess. The worker's first obligation is above all to the job [as that of the traditional student is to the assignment] — to perform it competently and completely' (p. 403). Unlike managers, or participants in collaborative jobs, workers (and students) in traditional settings have no overriding obligation to the enterprise as a whole, no need to 'buy into the purposes or values of the organization in order to ... enjoy the rewards he or she has earned. There is no pressing need to be liked by those around you, either superiors or peers, when one's primary obligation is to fulfill the demands of a narrow job description' (pp. 403–4), or, by extension, a narrow paper assignment. Where proponents of a new collaborative spirit see only openness and sharing, traditional workers see only a world of 'unlimited demand', where managers (and other workers and students invited into the circle):

> must conform to company ideology. Instead of the feistiness and pluralism that characterizes the labor-management relationship, many workers see in the manager's world overbearing demands for ideological unity, loyalty, and the submergence of the self (p. 404).

Here, ironically, we can most clearly see the clash between traditional workers, in the idiom used by Zuboff, proud of being 'one's "own man"' (p. 404), and the new collaborative classroom envisioned by Gere, a place where 'the process of the group' is more important than the text or any other isolated work. One cannot question the sincerity of Gere's commitment to 'transforming the class into a community where all members feel secure', but what do we do with those who feel secure only outside the group, either those who want only to read and write as little as possible so as not to be co-opted by the teacher, or those who see in reading and writing a means of coming to terms with our deepest fears and passions, emotions that, like the moment of our own conception, not even a liberated society may want to view collectively? What, in other words, do we do with those who see collaboration as a new, more insidious form of social control. Who see it, in John Trimbur's (1989) words, as 'new versions of an older industrial psychology adapted to late capitalism — human relations techniques to bolster morale, promote identification with the corporation, legitimize differential access to knowledge and status, and increase productivity' (p. 611)?

The answer suggested by Berlin, and apparently supported by Trimbur himself, lies in the belief that the individual's and the group's interests are finally one — that new forms of collaboration as endorsed by Gere and others will in fact lead to strengthening the critical, distancing powers of individuals, that in renunciation of authority and increased social interaction comes a stronger sense both of the community and of individual autonomy, that somehow there is an affinity of interests between all groups that meet in a writing class — between students, women, and ethnic minorities — that subsumes the question of individual and collective identity. The computer, even with the connectivity offered by its networking capacity, is not the principal issue. What does matter in the end is the human potential of education, and presumably, all human interaction, based on a new form of social organization. Gone is a hierarchical, authoritative discourse concerned with generating truth, based on the notion of truth as an ever more powerful transformation of nature, to be replaced by a collective dialogue among equals, one facilitated by computer networking and based on the notion of truth as the product of continuous negotiation between groups. The notion of ideology as a distortion of truth, as the hegemonic efforts of the powerful to universalize their own practice, and thus of the principal task of education as the relentless effort to overcome such distortion (in part through deep critical reading and analysis), has been replaced by the notion that all truth is ideological. One no longer replaces the prevailing ideology of the powerful with the truth as revealed by an authoritative critical analysis (usually generated by an intellectual elite). Instead, one restructures social practice so that there are no authorities in the belief that large numbers of disenfranchised minorities, previously without voice, will now have the chance to forge their own collective ideologies. And presumably such ideologies will have a better chance of prevailing in a more open, democratic marketplace of people and ideas, in a classroom, and, by extension, society at large, where (in the words of writing theorist Olivia Frey) standards of acceptability are not 'generated out of a cultural, political, or social context that was (and is) largely patriarchal, white, privileged' (1987, p. 98).

The educational application of computer networking in the language classroom has the broadest possible cultural implications, including (to be considered in the next chapter), ways in which post-print literacy is associated with the de-centered, non-authoritarian economy of post-industrial capitalism. Almost as broad, and more immediately connected to the questions in this chapter, are the implications of the new collaborative classroom for the one institution that, at least in the past, has had as great a responsibility for education as the school — the family. The effort to de-center the teacher can be read as part of the larger cultural effort to replace all hierarchical authority, including that within the family, with the dialogue of equals. It is an effort to replace a situation where the teacher or parent is perceived, in Frey's words, 'as the judge on the side of the system' — a system that does 'violence' to students, 'although we never raise a hand' — with what she calls 'the peaceable writing class' (p. 100). Although not devoid of conflict or failure, the peaceable writing class is a model of the new family, a place where if young people do fail they do not do so 'in the usual sense, feeling humiliated, confused, angry' (p. 101), a place where the instructor is 'more a guide than an authority figure' (p. 100), a place where people of different ages and levels of authority 'can come to know each other' (p. 99).

At the core of the new peaceable social unit, be it classroom or family, is a radical realignment of individual and collective action. Yet in the name of transferring power to the disenfranchised group, the right of individuals to act counter to the interests of the group is curtailed, even when such actions are grounded in claims of universal justice. The intent here is clearly to curtail the power of the teacher-parent while increasing that of the student-child, but the effect is hardly so simple or unambiguously benign. What is lost in this new social arrangement is the educational value of the model of a strong individual, albeit teacher or parent, able to act against the immediate needs of a group, at times, against pleasure itself, out of some larger sense of justice. It is now the child, argues cultural historian Christopher Lasch (1977), who 'masters the world more easily than his parents' (p. 75), or his or her traditional teachers, by learning the secret of the new peaceable kingdom, not how to resist, but how to get along with one's peers. Under such conditions, Lasch argues, there is a kind of peace. 'The traditional turmoil of adolescence subsides. Instead of withdrawing into himself or trying to overcome his loneliness through passionate friendships and love affairs, the adolescent now prefers the casual, easygoing sociability of his peers.' The adolescent, who in the height of print literacy had been converted into the archetypal rebel, under the pressure of new social relations now, as Lasch cites Edgar Z. Friedenberg, 'has abandoned the task of defining himself in dialectical combat with society and becomes its captive and its emissary' (p. 32).

Lasch quotes German social theorist Max Horkheimer who noted over forty years ago, when the attack on authoritative educational structures was already under way, that the traditional family (like the traditional class) is related to society 'in an antagonistic no less than a promotive way'; it 'not only educates for authority in bourgeois society; it also cultivates the dream of a better condition for mankind' (p. 91). Or as Lasch concludes, the authoritative family unit, while it did give 'rise to a crippling sense of guilt, ... also gave rise to ideals by which bourgeois society itself stood condemned'. Instead of being a 'haven' from capitalism economic pressure or ideology, or better still, a source of resistance, the family — and, by extension, the classroom — are now in danger of becoming their extension. When all truth is socially constructed, neither the school nor the family — nor, alas, the individual conscience — is free from ideological struggle, and public scrutiny.

> Today the state controls not merely the individual's body but as much of his spirit as it can preempt; not merely his outer but his inner life as well; not merely the public realm but the darkest corners of private life, formerly inaccessible to political domination. The citizen's entire existence has now been subjected to social direction, increasingly unmediated by the family or other institutions to which the work of socialization was once confined. Society itself has taken over socialization or subjected family socialization to increasingly effective control. Having weakened the capacity for self-direction and self-control, it has undermined one of the principal sources of social cohesion, only to create new ones more constricting than the old, and ultimately more devastating in their impact on personal and political freedom (Lasch, 1977, p. 189).

What most concerns Lasch — and as we shall see in Chapter 5, concerns Marxist theorist Fredric Jameson as well, but seems not to worry proponents of the networked classroom — is the totality with which capitalist economic forces and its ideological component of free choice can sweep through all social negotiations, even between parent and child, and teacher and student, between any well-meaning individuals trying their best to help each other. As Gouldner notes, the private sphere is precisely that 'arena from which public rationality is excluded' (1976, p. 104), and, one might add, its frequent handmaiden, free-market economics. The nurturing of the private sphere in the modern world is for Gouldner basically an act of resisting 'a public sphere which can become powerful enough to intrude on and control the private person' (1976, p. 104). The open negotiation of justice that so concerns Lasch becomes justice subject to the regulation of public rather than private values, and as such may wind up no fairer than the deal-making and collusion (often under the illusion of choice) that characterizes so many of the transactions of the 'free market'. And like the most ardent upholders of free market economy, we seem on the verge of seeing all exercise of authority based on principles other than open negotiation as an expression of what Lasch calls the 'divided father', that is, authority projected as either 'incompetent or malevolent' (p. 178).

Americans who weathered the Reagan-Bush years should hardly be surprised to discover that the disestablishment of overt authority — for example, the regulative role of government — does not necessarily lead to the increased empowerment of marginalized groups. By extension, it is at times difficult to account for the revolutionary expectations that language educators see as the inevitable consequence of substituting consensus for the informed judgments of authorities. 'What defines a relationship of power', notes Foucault, 'is that it is a mode of action which does not act directly and immediately on others. Instead it acts upon their actions; an action upon an action, on existing actions or on those which may arise in the present or the future' (1983, p. 220). We are always controlled by power relations; the social structures of print literacy, including the private reading space and the traditional classroom, represent attempts to create private spaces less immediately subject to the economic forces that increasingly seem to control all human experiences, forces that are just as likely to be represented in the consensus of a class as in the attitude of the teacher. 'Power relations', Foucault adds, including presumably those in the networked classroom, 'are rooted deep in the social nexus, not reconstituted "above" society' (1983, p. 222). A society without such relations he calls an abstraction. If consensus and, indirectly, the networked classroom are to have real transformative power, new teaching strategies must come to terms with, not simply reject, the best of the older tradition of print literacy. One model of such a synthesis is John Trimbur's rehabilitation of the notion of consensus.

While Berlin conspicuously abjures transcendent truth in promoting a social constructionist view of knowledge, Trimbur (1989) places such truth at the heart of his project. Consensus for Trimbur, what he refers to as 'the desire of humans to live and work together with differences' (p. 615), is a utopian aspiration, 'a dream of difference without domination'. It is not a state that can be achieved simply by removing authority; instead, Trimbur argues, drawing upon Habermas, it must be based on the 'ideal speech situation' of non-domination. Consensus is not 'an empirical account of how discourse communities operate but a critical and normative representation of the conditions necessary for fully realized communication to occur' (p. 612). It is finally based on the recognition of the overt claim of social justice, that 'we recognize the inexhaustibility of difference and that we organize the conditions in which we live and work [and teach] accordingly' (p. 615). Paraphrasing Marx, Trimbur charges collaborative learning with the highest possible task: 'not simply to demystify the authority of knowledge by revealing its social character but to transform the productive apparatus, to change the social character of production' (p. 612).

Such a high-minded charge to change as well as to understand the world carries with it direct, acknowledged ties to a utopian tradition of critical thought — a tradition co-extensive with that of print literacy, one that saw progress as the result of greater insight into our common historical condition. Trimbur even resorts to two of the mainstays of print literacy — the language of verticality and a suspicion of mass culture — admitting that:

> we cannot realistically expect that collaborative learning will lead students spontaneously to *transcend* the limits of American culture, its homogenizing force, its ingrained suspicion of social and cultural differences, its tendency to reify the other and blame the victim (p. 603, italics added).

Indeed, Trimbur goes so far as to articulate unambiguously the basic complaint print literacy has against consensus — the fear that 'once we give up extra-historical and universal criteria and reduce the authority of knowledge to a self-legitimizing account of its own practices, we won't have a way to separate persuasion from force, validity claims from plays of power' (p. 609). It is almost as if Trimbur is repackaging print literacy — and its single most important term, *critical* — under the new label of *consensus*. Consensus thus comes to be defined through 'conflict', through 'voices at the periphery of the conversation', through 'dissensus' (p. 608).

Collaborative learning in Trimbur is less a method than a goal, one guided by the 'utopian desire' (p. 612) of consensus. 'I do not believe', he concludes, drawing upon two terms from Habermas, 'removing relations of domination and systematic distortion, whether ideological or neurotic, from the conversation is likely to establish the conditions in which consensus will express a "rational will" and "permit what *all* can want"' (p. 615). Where there is a seeming vacuum of power in Gere and Berlin — only the unacknowledged belief that the group will meet the needs of the individual — there is in Trimbur still the teacher and the fully acknowledged charge to the teacher to undertake the radical transformation of first the student and then society at large. What Trimbur in the end calls for is the most active sort of teaching — the kind whose absence Isaac Asimov laments in his brief tale — teaching in the best tradition of print literacy that constantly organizes instruction so as to enable students to distinguish between reality and appearance, or, in Trimbur's words, 'between "spurious" and "genuine" consensus' (p. 612); it is a teaching based 'not so much on collective agreements as on collective explanations of how people differ' (p. 610). It is teaching, in other words, based on the one thing that the networked classroom with its socially constructed knowledge seems to lack — images of a better world charged with the force of an authorizing moral or artistic tradition. What remains unclear is how the ascendancy of online literacy across the culture, and not just in the networked classroom, will affect our ability to continue creating and responding to such images. Remaining to be addressed is what may well be the single most important question before us: what are the prospects for the critical imagination in the computer age?

Chapter 5

Imagining the Future

Where, after the metanarratives, can legitimacy reside?
Lyotard, *The Postmodern Condition*

In January 1990 Marcia Peoples Halio, until then a little known assistant director of the writing program at the University of Delaware, fired a shot across the bow of those in the profession who have been advocating greater use of computers in the writing curriculum. Computer-based composition, B.H. (before Halio), had been based on one comfortable premise — that computers, especially in the form of word processors, provided students with a powerful new tool for producing traditional texts. While it may not have been all that difficult, even from the early years of personal computers, to see the revolutionary, not just evolutionary, potential of such technologies as hypertext and networks, composition specialists as a whole seemed content to focus on the more immediate matter of using computers to help students in their task of producing the detailed, developed, insightful texts that have long been the norm in print literacy. The purpose of computers for them was to assist students in the arduous task of working through the writing process, finding what they want to say, and generating and organizing their ideas, using the electronic editing power of word processing to facilitate the recursive revising that underlies the writing process — the easier it is to revise, so the thinking went, the more thorough and complete will be the writing process.

What Halio reported was not that computers do not always help this process, or that they may hurt it — research suggesting as much had long been in circulation; instead, what she reported was something more troubling, and more controversial — namely, that the computer technology itself (specifically, the type of computer one was using) had a significant impact on the quality of what one wrote. The writing of students using Apple Macintosh computers, she reported, tended to diverge rather sharply from the model of detailed, well-developed writing students working on MS-DOS, IBM-compatible systems were still trying to achieve. Here is how she describes student writing on the Mac.

Paragraphs were brief, resulting in a lack of development of thought; and sentences, too, were short, obviating the need for complex punctuation. Word choice tended to be simple, spiced with slang and colloquialisms, accenting the simplistic and generalized nature of the thought.... Students were affecting a sort of pop-style of the kind found in advertising or in the mass media (1990, p. 17).

It was as if Mac students had stumbled upon a new model of writing.

It is not surprising that Halio's salvo aroused such controversy. Few aspects of computing stir passions as deeply as the relative merits of operating systems, word processing programs, and especially input devices (keyboard vs. mouse). Here apparently was some hard evidence of the superiority of function and cursor keys to mice, a command-line interface to a graphical one, the no-nonsense seriousness of the character-based past to the creativity and freedom of the image-based future. There was, not surprisingly, a sustained attack on Halio's admittedly limited research methodology and on the process by which her article was eventually accepted for publication — much was at stake, including the recommendations of university administrators regarding the purchase of new computer systems. That there was a much larger issue at work here, however, was not immediately apparent.

Behind the firestorm surrounding the Halio article lies the growing sense (the shock of recognition?) that we were not going to be able to have the best of both worlds, the intensity of the page and the play of the screen, not going to be able to have a revolution in the technology of writing, one that completely transforms our notion of text, without also altering, not all in positive ways, traditional literacy practices. What made Halio's article so controversial was the possibility that, with regard to the future of literacy, the computer revolution may well be much like a zero-sum game with gains in some areas offset by losses in other areas. That a new computer medium with the potential for treating words and pictures alike would alter patterns of print literacy in profound ways should hardly be a surprise. Yet it is natural to focus on the positive side of change, to see only the great potential in giving students the chance to work with their 'writing', with its internal form and texture as well as its graphical appearance. It is easier and more comforting to inveigh against the quality of Halio's research than to consider the profound implications of the realignment in the traditional relationship between words and pictures lurking behind her low-tech research: that her two groups of students working side by side at the University of Delaware dramatize the conflict between print and online literacy soon to be played out across the culture at large.

What is this conflict, reduced to its most elemental level, but the struggle between text and graphics? The troubling truth in Halio's essay that most of her critics do not want to see, in part due to their loyalty to Mac computers, has to do with the increasing marginality of print literacy they themselves have been trained to support. Yet work like Halio's makes it difficult to continue denying a basic contradiction of print literacy — that the unadorned text which has been practically the sole concern for language educators the last hundred years has also been increasingly on the periphery of all other forms of communications. How else are we to explain the fact that while we have come to rely more heavily on pictures — at first still but now moving, even pulsating — literacy education has remained fixated on the unadorned, printed text as the embodiment of new experiences?

Consider a vivid example of this conflict. While graphic artists strive to design ads that will capture our attention in the pages of a magazine like the *New Yorker*, and the magazine's own art staff strives to create a strikingly attractive magazine, the stories, poems, and, with the exception of a small opening sketch, nonfiction articles are all outwardly unadorned, although presumably subject to extensive internal revisions. The model of text here may be represented by the Modern Library editions of great literary works — entire books whose graphic component is represented by an illustrated cover and a torch-beating colophon on the title page. The coded message here is not difficult to decipher. Graphic artists and consumers alike can be concerned with the surface, pictures — the true reader and the true author alike are concerned with a truth beyond the surface, one embodied in the purely abstract world of verbal meaning.

Likewise, in the high print literacy of the English curriculum, with the exception of the occasional Blake scholar, there has been little concern with graphics (just as there has been little concern with political oration and other formal forms of speech). Print literacy has been based on, not a pretty or expressive picture, nor a passionate, moving speech, but a verbal construction of a new way of describing the world. While liberal pedagogies stress content over form — to the point of derogating all concern with mechanical correctness — conservative writing pedagogies, those most concerned with largely pre-industrial notions of decorum, as set forth in tomes like the *Harbrace Handbook*, also have little to say about the appearance of a document (other than that it should be neat, and correctly spaced). Composition handbooks are differentiated across the political spectrum, not by their interest in the graphical component of writing, but by their tolerance toward informal usage. As a rule they are still devoid of basic information about page layout and design — they have nothing yet to say about columns, multiple margins, and tabs; nothing about fonts, pitch, point, and leading; nothing about graphic formats, cropping, and dithering. Although students born after World War II grew up with television — those in the last twenty years with color television, and those in the last ten years with the ability to make their own videos — school 'composition', at least beyond the elementary grades where drawing is often encouraged, has continued to be thought of as entirely lacking any graphic dimension.

While communications instructors encourage their students to explore the graphical potential of Mac computers in considering how texts and graphics can be effectively integrated, composition and literature instructors (that is, English teachers generally) — even those using Mac computers — are likely to see concern with graphics as a distraction from the more serious task of using written language alone to express and develop complex ideas. Yet these teachers are the Mac users most enraged by Halio's unremarkable but nonetheless revolutionary finding that a machine designed for online literacy undermines some of the guiding principles of print literacy. For other English teachers — those more open to the possibility that the literacy of the future might be substantially different from the literacy of the past, more than an extension or a deepening of print — the proper response to Halio's findings is not shock but excitement, tempered by disagreement with her interpretation of them. So what if students writing with a graphics-based computer system wrote shorter sentences, someone like Richard Lanham might respond — isn't this what one would expect, especially if the text is to be laid out with multiple fonts and formats and integrated with other graphical features?

For two such screen-oriented teachers, Nancy Kaplan and Stuart Moulthrop, the main problem with Halio is that she trapped within an overly narrow and, they hope, soon to be outdated paradigm of composition, a print-based model geared to the needs of 'business and academia' (1990, p. 100). What we need instead, they contend, is a new paradigm for composition that 'would situate language — spoken, written, and iconographic — in a much richer context than the typed or word-processed essay can provide' (p. 99). Such a course would still focus on argument and persuasion, what they call 'the native province of rhetoric from classical times to the present', and teachers of such a course would still teach writing, 'with all the mechanical and grammatical conventions that are essential to it' (p. 100). Such instruction, however, would be part of a return to a more exciting, richer historical moment for rhetoric, one where 'writing and textual presentation historically have encompassed more than the printed word' (pp. 99–100). At the base of 'literacy in the next century', they suggest, may well be the 'ability to compose in multiple discursive dimensions and across media' (p. 100); that is, English composition as multimedia composition.

For Kaplan and Moulthrop such a transition is natural and desirable, since they see English composition less in terms of the model of print, where the goal of discourse is the embodiment of a new (and deeper) understanding of the world, and more in terms of classical rhetoric, where the goal is the persuasion of a particular audience. And as is abundantly clear from the history and practice of modern advertising techniques and public relations — long the academic center and spiritual home of multimedia composition — the persuasive force of an argument (or message) is immeasurably enhanced by the effective mixture of graphics, animation, and sound with text. One does occasionally come across all-text print ads, or radio and television spots with a single voice reading text — but such unadorned uses of text obviously gain their effect of heightened sincerity and seriousness in contrast to the norm of razzle-dazzle graphics and multi-channel sound tracks. Whereas for most of this century, producing such multimedia 'compositions' was the province of advertising and production specialists, working on expensive equipment, continuing computer development is making many of the editing tools necessary for creating such multimedia presentations available to ordinary computer users.

We are at the beginning of a new age of multimedia computing. New, relatively inexpensive computer systems (utilizing technologies that will allow us to write to as well as read digitized video information from compact discs and other storage media) will soon make it possible to place in the hands of students tools for editing, combining, and linking hypertextually not just pictures and words, but video and music as well. All of us will soon have access to computer tools for producing true multimedia presentations as glitzy as the latest Diet Pepsi commercial or as moving as Ken Burns' documentary on the American Civil War, products that we now consider from the perspective of viewers, not creators. Does not our role as teachers of rhetoric, Kaplan and Moulthrop ask, require us to teach our students to use such technologies productively? '[I]f we English teachers are unwilling to expand our notions of writing, we relegate ourselves to the study of the past and the instruments of the past' (p. 101). In light of technological changes, we are obliged, they rightly assert, to confront some 'profoundly serious questions', including how we should 'define writing, composition, and rhetoric as college subjects', and thus, as a matter of course, how we should define literacy.

Halio's article and Kaplan and Moulthrop's response at once raise the broadest and the most immediate questions about computers and 'the future of literacy'. Beneath the controversy over IBM and Mac computers lies the important issue of the replacement of character-based computing with a graphical-based system, what seems to be the first in a series of steps moving us inexorably toward an entirely new paradigm for literacy. Apple computers began this process some ten years ago by using a graphics-based operating system for the new Macintosh model that in effect drew the letters of a text on the screen instead of representing them by a predefined character set. Predefined character sets are exceedingly efficient — press a key and the computer displays a letter with a predefined shape on the screen — but greatly limited in the ability to display different styles and sizes of letters. Italic letters look the same as Roman; Courier font the same as Prestige; 24-point headlines the same as 7-point fine print — indeed, for a number of years character-based systems had difficulty just displaying underlining on the screen. Perhaps most importantly for the immediate future, character-based systems have no easy way of displaying the proportional spacing between letters of varying width — the system of spacing letters that in the past readily distinguished whether a text was professionally printed or just typed. When proportionally spaced, for example, the seven-letter word *Wyoming* is considerably wider than the eight-letter word *Illinois*, when printed or when displayed on the screen; with a fixed font, obviously, *Illinois*, or any eight-letter word, is one character wider (usually one-tenth or one-twelfth of an inch) than a seven-letter word like *Wyoming*.

Proportional font	Fixed font
Illinois	`Illinois`
Wyoming	`Wyoming`

In order to display proportionally spaced letters on the screen, a computer system (and, by extension, a print culture) has to be entirely reconfigured. At least in terms of computer storage space, it turns out that a single picture is literally equal to a thousand words. A printed double-spaced page of about 250 words stored strictly as text takes up on average about 15,000 bits (the individual yes/no, off/on binary decisions that form the essence of computer computation). That same single page stored as the kind of black-and-white graphic images used for FAX transmission takes up a half million bits; that same page stored as a single color television image takes up 15 billion bits. Without a means of compressing data, storing just the graphic information generated by a single typed page would require the equivalent of ten 40-megabyte hard disks.

Matters are just as complicated when it comes to displaying graphics on a computer terminal. The screen of a character-based operating system consists of a regular grid pattern of eighty columns and twenty-five rows, an arrangement of 2000 spaces each of which is capable of displaying a single predefined, preshaped character (usually from a set of some 200 plus characters representing upper and lower case letters, common punctuation marks, a scattering of accented vowels used in languages other than English, and basic graphic characters that when combined can produce lines and boxes). To control what's on a monochrome screen, a character-based computer system need only keep track of these 2000 spaces and 200-plus characters, as well as whether or not the single color is on, off, or at half brightness. With a graphics-based system, the complexity increases exponentially, within a general spiral of increasing capability. The graphics standard of IBM-compatible computers, available since 1988, and soon to be replaced by a higher one, displays a 800 by 600 grid, or nearly a half-million spaces (called *pixels*), each of which displays not predefined characters but colors or, in the case of monochrome monitors, shades of gray, selected from an ever increasing palette. We still have a way to go but seem headed in the direction of displaying a full page (8.5 × 11 inches) on a screen with the same clarity as a printed page, a grid of 3400 by 4400 pixels, each pixel capable of displaying any one of thousands of colors.

With the graphical interface of the Mac, as well as the new graphical interfaces like Windows now being marketed for formerly character-based IBM-compatible systems, writers are being offered a whole new set of tools for representing and editing proportionally spaced characters of different sizes and different styles on the screen (and, with the ever-widening availability of laser printing, for printing this output as well) that may prove difficult, if not impossible, to set aside. One can argue that providing access to new tools is not the same as forcing people to use them — the technology, we can argue, is neutral. With what-you-see-is-what-you-get editing, called *wysiwyg* (pronounced WHIZ-ee-wig), writers theoretically can go about their business of embodying new experiences, never bothering to learning anything about fonts and styles, point and pitch, leading and gutters.

No wonder that the eyes of anyone fully acculturated into the world of print literacy immediately glaze over with any discussion of proportional fonts — for such a person (and for the last few generations of English teachers) the goal of the writer is not to dazzle an audience with fancy print or graphics but to use writing to organize one's thoughts. Such are the people who write traditional composition handbooks, and for whom such handbooks are written. For them, the one great advantage of the printed text (over a handwritten one) was its clarity, its unobtrusiveness; the well-displayed text was one that acted as a clear pane of glass for its content, as Lanham cites a book designer, 'as a fine crystal goblet stands to the wine it contains' (1989a, p. 266). Certainly, individual writers will make such decisions, just as certain individuals have always resisted the lure of two other inventions that have transformed modern life, automobiles and television.

For the foreseeable future there will be writers, and writing teachers, who continue to concern themselves only with the internal meaning of the text itself. What is harder to imagine is how such concerns with page layout and design can be kept out of the writing curriculum entirely, assuming that one wanted to — many of the 'improvements' and increased power of personal computers for the foreseeable future will be concerned largely with extending our power to integrate text and pictures, in time, moving as well as still. The reverse is also true. For writers with no interest in graphical computing, that is, for anyone content to use computers solely to enhance print literacy, technologically speaking the computer revolution for all intents and purposes is already over!

Yet who but the most committed apostle of the abstraction of print could believe that with text-based word processing the computer revolution really is over? Who but such a person could fail to see the introduction of graphics-based computing as signalling anything but the beginning of a new form of literacy? In an age when students increasingly will edit text at the screen with the same tool they also use to construct multimedia presentations, college composition seems to be heading for a crossroads, one that lacks a clear, safe path. On the one hand, writing teachers can heed the warning implicit in Halio's article and continue to remain entirely focused on textual meaning, allowing students to gain document design and eventually multimedia presentational skills elsewhere in the curriculum, possibly in a new breed of communication courses. In remaining true to our recent past, we face the danger of moving from the center to the periphery of the university curriculum. On the other hand, we can heed Kaplan and Moulthrop's advice and become more concerned with design and presentational issues inside our composition classes. In reestablishing ties to our older rhetorical tradition, we face the danger of losing our philosophical and institutional connection with the imaginative texts that constitute print literacy, becoming as it were the very communications department that we have held in such low esteem for the last century precisely for not privileging the deep, inner psychological complexity of writing. The issue is whether or not we will eventually remake college composition, and by extension higher level literacy, as multimedia communications or surrender the central space within the curriculum that English as the embodiment of print literacy has long occupied. Our choice, simply stated, is to be transformed or marginalized.

The clash of industrial and information technology will likely play itself out in very concrete battles within the curriculum. While technical writing courses invariably become more concerned with both desktop publishing and various forms of online documentation, the key struggle will be over the nature of first-year composition, the one course that is required in most colleges precisely because of its longstanding historical connection with print literacy — this is the place where students are trained, or at least certified, in higher reading and writing skills. Soon the teachers and directors of such courses will be forced to consider the seemingly mundane question — how much time to spend on such matters as page design and desktop publishing — while authors and publishers decide how much space to devote to such matters in first-year textbooks. Today, as noted in Chapter 1, there is little time or space devoted to such matters, and defenders of print literacy will rightly see time devoted to teaching such manipulative skills as time taken away from other, presumably more serious (or at least more traditional) concerns.

As with hypertext discussed in Chapter 3 and networking in Chapter 4, the most inviting initial response is to resist the positing of an either-or alternative, to point to ways that the new computer technology, be it hypertext, networking, or multimedia, can in fact expand (deepen) traditional literacy instruction. An interactive videodisc like *A Right to Die*, for example, in placing students in life-like situations where the options before them change as they make their choices, becomes a powerful prewriting tool. Yet here too there is the awareness that although often designed and initially used to expand current practices — for example, allowing students to write more engaged, more focused, more detailed, more persuasive (what we have long considered 'better') responses to ethical dilemmas involving the right to die — the technologies seem to have the power to redirect instruction in other ways.

Langston and Batson discuss the *Right to Die* videodisc as a heuristic device for producing 'better' writing, but as we have seen in Chapter 4, our notion of writing begins to change immediately once our principal task becomes continuing an online conversation rather than composing a printed text. How much more radical will this change be when the response is no longer limited to written conversation but includes integrating the sound and graphics of the new medium itself? As Kaplan and Moulthrop note, new learning tools like *The Holy Land*, from ABC News Interactive, present a wealth of materials on videodisc that students in hypertext fashion can respond to, comment on, and rearrange. 'Using such features in conjunction with presentation management software, students in rhetoric courses could create multimedia essays that would combine their own written commentary with graphics, sound, and video' (p. 99). For better or worse, such students are now engaged in preparations of real-time multimedia presentations, an activity with obvious connections to an older rhetorical tradition but seemingly at odds with the different traditions of print literacy.

The choice before us may be no different from that recently faced by newspapers over whether they are in the business of publishing a newspaper or disseminating information. 'Most who chose the newspaper business', Lanham reminds us, 'are no longer in it' (1989a, p. 270). Lanham's point here is that we need to recognize that as composition teachers we are really in the business of teaching students, not to write five-paragraph essays, but to communicate effectively within their world, and, by extension, that as English teachers we are in the business of imparting a broad cultural heritage involving multiple forms of communication and not just a narrowly defined literary tradition. The situation of English studies today is not unlike that faced by classics in the nineteenth century. Then liberal educators like Thomas Arnold argued that the key to a classical education was not learning Latin declensions but the moral values of Thucydides. As education became more broad-based and fewer students had any sustained contact with their own national literature, educators working in the spirit of Arnold were prepared to undertake the seemingly radical shift of having students seek the same kind of moral training in Milton and Shakespeare, Dryden and Pope.

Within a generation, English as if out of nowhere became the focus of the college-level humanist education while those classicists who remained true to the form of their discipline retreated, at least in terms of numbers of students, to the periphery of the undergraduate curriculum (remaining visible today mostly in those institutions with strong, academic traditions antedating the rise of formal English studies). Similarly, teachers and society as a whole may soon be out of the business of 'classic' print literacy anyway; it may be inevitable that the mass of students learn to communicate effectively in the emerging multi-media environment, while the traditional study of print culture becomes a distinct and eventually specialized field of study, perhaps occupying a position not unlike that of American history today — a subject widely recognized as important but one expressly taught for only one year in most high schools (and only as an elective in most colleges). Yet aside from the uneasiness normally associated with such a radical change, should we really care?

Here then is the central question before us as educators and as citizens. What, if anything, are we in danger of losing — or conversely, what might we gain —

when students in large numbers and eventually people throughout society begin 'writing', not just by linking items in a database or conversing online, but by integrating words with pictures, moving as well as still, and sounds? Here, at one level, the initial answer is obvious, if seemingly circular. It depends mainly on one's attitude about the tradition of print literacy. For those committed to this tradition as it has been established this century, and fearful of the future, we are in danger of making a bad bargain, swapping the great tradition of high-print culture — the thick tomes of richly textured, psychologically probing literary, historical, and scientific masterpieces, works like George Eliot's *Middlemarch*, that for many contain the most detailed self-portraiture that we as humans have ever created — for the glib and glitzy superficiality of MTV. Conversely, for those disenchanted with the excesses — political, economic, and social — of the present, we stand to free ourselves from the limitations of a deadening, largely patri-archal, exploitative, relentlessly and unimaginatively pedantic literary and histori-cal tradition — to free ourselves, that is, from the spiritual shackles of George Eliot's arch-pedant, Edward Casaubon, so that we might communicate with each other via computers in a more open, more flexible fashion.

The seemingly straightforward question 'Should we care about the trans-formation of literacy?' quickly leads to a series of probing, troubling questions about our individual and collective attitudes toward where we have been, where we are now, and where we seem to be heading. Print literacy is an expression of the best and the worst of the intellectual dimension of modern, industrial culture, just as online literacy seems to promise (or threaten) us with the best and the worst possibilities of a postmodern, post-industrial world. The question of the future of literacy, therefore, is intricately interwoven with the prospects of culture generally, or, more to the point, our attitudes about imminent cultural changes. While some proponents of a new model of computer literacy see such technologies as hypertext, networking, and multimedia strictly as a means of expanding print literacy, somehow deepening the intensely personalized experi-ence at the center of traditional reading and writing, the most passionate and most convincing proponents, thinkers like Richard Lanham, see such new technologies as historic opportunities to effect a radical break with a moribund print tradition. For them, online literacy does not so much complete as refute print literacy, correcting as it were the gross deficiencies of two centuries of modern, industrial culture (and perhaps two millennia of Western, writing-based culture), while connecting a new computer-based practice of literacy with far older, pre-Socratic and possibly non-Western traditions of human communication and patterns of social organization. As has been suggested throughout this study, this critique of print literacy, although at times shallow and oversimplified, cannot be simply brushed aside. Guardians of the best traditions of print may see in computers only an approaching apocalypse — in the words of Sandberg-Diment, our

> heading toward a future filled with the emperor's new words, where word processing cranks out fast-food prose, becoming to writing what xerography has become to the office memo: a generator of millions of copies of countless phrases assembled for appearance's sake — rarely read, much less reflected upon (Heim, 1987, p. 250).

Yet traditional reading and writing practices are being transformed, some might argue collapsing, from their own weight, from limitations that seem to be inherent to print literacy itself.

The Historical Limit of Print Literacy

Perhaps the single greatest indictment of modern literacy is its historical connection with the limitations as well as the strengths of industrial culture, an historic epoch whose noblest, most liberal sentiments — what Habermas sees as its pursuit of scientific truth, its building of democratic institutions, and its support of private aesthetic, literary experience — are all grounded in a constant struggle with, and finally domination of, nature. For the last two centuries we have asked students to dig more deeply into texts, and themselves, as readers and writers, just as we have asked mineral explorers to dig more deeply into the earth. In both cases our goal has been models of production (literary or industrial) that are ever more powerful and ever more efficient.

There is a neurotic restlessness at work here. So what if Mozart's piano concertos expressed a timeless perfection and inner harmony — the modern temperament that was to emerge in the nineteenth century wanted a more unified concerto form, one better suited to capture the more tempestuous if less perfected strivings of musical genius. While we obviously knew that on one level art does not progress — that the piano concertos of Bartok are not necessarily better than those of Brahms, and that those of Brahms are not necessarily better than those of Beethoven — we have been driven by models of history grounded in the notion of the future as a time of better, ever more efficient production. Even the great writers and conservative social critics of print culture who opposed what they saw as simplistic notions of progress embedded in the progressive theories of Marx or positivist social theory, still saw developmental explanations, often based in history and autobiography, as the secret to understanding and possibly eventually changing the world. All change may not have been progress, but all hope of progress was at least grounded in understanding and controlling the process of change.

Online literacy is part of the larger cultural process of postmodernism that is freeing experience generally from the past, from history itself, in much the same manner that hypertext and networking free the authors and writers from texts. Time, as Jameson notes, becomes 'a perpetual present and thus spatial'. The metaphor of mineralogical exploration, what Jameson calls the 'notion of "deep time", Bergsonian time' found in modern writers like Proust or Mann, now 'seems radically irrelevant to our contemporary experience, which is one of a perpetual spatial present' (Stephanson, 1988, p. 6). Instead of struggling with nature, or with the past, instead of constantly digging to find or create something new, we have now a sense of play and manipulation of objects that are on the surface. The new creator in this postmodern age, Bolter's 'Turing's man', is best seen as the programmer, that person who manipulates not the physical world but computer codes and symbolic objects represented by such codes. Online literacy, in other words, escapes the fundamental contradiction, some would contend, the neurosis, of print culture, what E.F. Schumacker describes as 'the single-minded pursuit of wealth', an attitude that 'does not fit into this world, because it contains within itself no limiting principle, while the environment in which it is placed is strictly limited' (1937, pp. 29–30). As Bolter adds, it is an ironic situation, with print culture, based upon infinite exploration of a finite resource (ultimately, nature itself), leading to what many now see as pending ecological collapse, and with online culture, based upon the finite manipulation of the infinite resource of digitized information, a situation that seems to offer us two undisputable advantages.

The first advantage is the capacity to create and play against a virtual reality — an infinitely flexible, inexhaustible computer-generated simulacrum — instead of what is becoming ever more clearly a limited, exhaustible natural world. With modernism, the abstract, purely symbolic text and the concrete, physical world stand fundamentally apart, connected only in our ability to find, apply, and test one against the other. The dual danger we face in modernism is our texts becoming more self-referential and further removed from any practical concerns while our involvement with an often exploitative economy remains unmediated by critical understanding — the danger of having writers off in the woods composing elegant but largely unread tracts inveighing against the destruction of the wilderness while in the next valley timber companies, directed solely by material needs, are clear-cutting the forest. With online literacy, the text itself, at least in its hypermedia format, is capable of becoming an ever closer representation of the world itself, so that both 'writers' and producers are working with the same medium — in the example above, a computer-based ecological model of this particular wilderness area as it responds to different patterns of development. A simulation such as this is, according to French postmodern critic Jean Baudrillard, less a map of what is than a projection of what can be. 'The territory no longer precedes the map, nor survives it', writes Baudrillard, in the new process he refers to as the 'precession of simulacra' (1984, p. 253). In what he calls 'the fable today', it is not just that the territory is in serious decay (becoming '*the desert of the real itself*') but that the basic distinction between the two — between the 'poetry of the map' and the 'charm of the territory' — is itself disappearing, that what is being lost is the defining dichotomy (the 'representational imaginary') of print literacy and the entire modernist project itself.

Besides being at once less exploitative and less detached from nature, the other historical advantage of online literacy has to do with the increasing emphasis being placed on our ability to deal effectively with an entirely new kind of human interaction: complex, real-time, interpersonal negotiations between diverse parties. 'We have to save mankind from an almost certain and immediately approaching doom', warns Ted Nelson, 'through the application, expansion and dissemination of intelligence' (1987, p. 0/13). Nelson is apocalyptic on this matter, banking the future of the human species on its ability to get much better at negotiations, in large measure by this new ability to access vast amounts of information instantaneously and in turn to be able to build complex but readily understandable models with that information in the process of negotiating such complex but historically vital matters as nuclear disarmament agreements or treaties regulating the uses of the ocean. Terry Winograd, in *Understanding Computers and Cognition* (1986), is less dramatic but no less convincing in painting a new model of historical understanding, one geared less toward understanding the past than an historical present with all the irregularity of the shapes studied in the new fractal geometry. To understand the challenge to historical understanding, Winograd suggests, imagine that you are one of fifteen people engaged in a heated discussion. 'You cannot avoid acting'; 'you cannot step back and reflect on your actions'; 'the effect of actions cannot be predicted'; 'you do not have a stable representation of the situation'; 'every representation is an interpretation'; 'language is action' (pp. 34–35). While there may be a place for traditional historical understanding of this situation, what Lyotard would call a 'meta-narrative' of modernism, such insight, as Hegel suggests in his famous aphorism, is likely to come only after the fact, at twilight. Meanwhile, as we try to act in the midst of this heated discussion, it is not the reflective mode of print literacy that we will find ourselves relying on but the hypertextual selection and arrange-ment of information, the electronic mail and conferencing of computer networks, the model building of hypermedia. The primary goal of these activities will not be detached ('scientific') understanding, no matter how powerful, but historical efficacy, the very building of the effective network ties and interpersonal relations that in the age of industrial expansion has too often been dismissed, although now more likely proudly claimed, as a less masculine, more feminine way of knowing.

People have had such heated discussions for thousands of years — without the computer tools of postmodern literacy. Why, we might ask, are things all of a sudden different? A question that directs us to an old problem. Why is it that the tools for printing speech existed for hundreds of years (and the tools for transcribing speech for thousands more) before modern literacy itself became widespread? The answer to either question lies in the observation of Marx, that new modes of production — whether nineteenth-century industrialism or twenty-first century information management — control most aspects of social life.

> In acquiring new productive forces men change their mode of pro-duction; and in changing their mode of production, in changing the way of earning their living, they change all their social relations. The handmill gives you society with the feudal lord; the steam-mill, society with the industrial capitalist (1963, p. 109).

The computer, we might add, gives us the complex negotiations of competing specialists and interest groups that now characterize such routine administrative tasks as enforcing local zoning ordinances. As Marx states, 'The mode of production of material life determines the general character of the social, political and spiritual processes of life' (1964, p. 57). A new economic order, one based on the management of information, may offer the best hope for developing what sociologist Stanley Aronowitz (1988) calls an 'alternative science', one that has 'to imagine, as a condition of its emergence, an alternative rationality which would not be based on domination' (p. 352).

Online literacy offers us a new, positive means of intervening in a local zoning process, as well as large-scale global planning, by modeling pending zoning changes and by effectively managing the wealth of information (textual as well as graphic) that today even a relatively simple bureaucratic matter generates. Online literacy thus offers promise for solving what many, including educator C.A. Bowers, see as our most pressing human problem, that of 'bringing our incessant drive to press outward on the frontiers of basic research, technological innovation, and a consumer-based standard of living into line with the requirements for long-term habitation of the planet' (1988, p. 10). That we may have been able to manage such processes in the past with a text-based model of literacy is hardly convincing evidence, either that we did such management well (and, of course, for practically all matters relating to the wise management of limited human resources we did poorly) or that the print-based practices of the past will be much good in the future.

The Ethical Limit of Print Literacy

Online literacy also promises a major realignment of the ethical dimension of print culture, a response to what H.G. Wells, in *A Modern Utopia*, refers to as 'the plain message physical science has for the world at large'.

> [T]hat were our political and social and moral devices only as well contrived to their ends as a linotype machine, an antiseptic operating plant, or an electric tramcar, there need now at the present moment be no appreciable toil in the world, and only the smallest fraction of the pain, the fear, and the anxiety that now makes human life so doubtful in its value (Sussman, p. 165).

Here is the suspicion that any enthusiast of print literacy must feel regarding the connection between the control of the world noted above and our ability to act wisely and decently in it, on either a collective or an individual basis. We continue to draw upon a tradition of print that sees literate discourse as inherently liberal, in the words of C.A. Bowers, as always 'on the side of truth and progress, and only engaged in a power struggle for the purpose of liberation' (1987, p. 8). What is the source of this belief if not the sense of power that literate discourse, as discussed above, has always found in its common origin with the larger program of invention and discovery charged with freeing itself from common practice as a means of achieving an ever more powerful control of nature? It is a discourse that, in Gouldner's words, 'experiences itself as distant from (and superior to) ordinary languages and conventional cultures.... [It] claims the right to sit in judgment over the actions and claims of any social class and all power elite' (1979, p. 59). And it is this right to judge others, especially any work deemed 'journalism', based on the superiority of their own discourse that contemporary intellectuals, for all their protestations about the playfulness of language and the indeterminability of meaning, seem most reluctant to forswear.

But why, we need to ask, to refer back to Wells, does goodness and social justice not flow automatically from such epistemological power? How do we explain the contradiction between high standards of literacy and what Bowers calls the 'deepening of the ecological crisis, the loss of meaningful community life, and the nihilism that now permeates the moral and conceptual functions of society' (1987, p. 2)? Why is it that, as repeatedly probed by George Steiner, the connection between high levels of literacy and high standards of personal conduct seems to be anything but simple and direct? Who could claim, for example, that because of their craft writers are better spouses or better parents, more loyal friends or more committed citizens, happier or more decent human beings? There is no doubt that with the intellectual acumen that developed from the writer's sustained isolation with texts came a sense of ethical superiority, a sense grounded in the Enlightenment ideal that a clear understanding of the world (an 'enlightened' view) is the surest basis for sound social and moral judgment. Nor did things change radically with Romantic notions that such judgment was grounded, not in general educational principles, but in the insights of poets and other unacknowledged legislators of the world. In both cases, judgment was to be guided, not by common practice and tradition, but by the educated, eloquent experiences of others as embodied in texts. But what, we must ask, is the connection between an individual's new, heightened power to see and that person's ability to act wisely and justly, presumably — and here is the key — free from ideological bias? Authors of books have much to tell us about a host of possible ways of acting correctly in the world, ways that we can fully experience as readers, yet in the final analysis all that we know for sure that the literate writer or reader possesses is an enhanced ability, not to choose correctly for us, but only to describe those choices. The only thing we know for certain that writers can do well is write.

Much of the contemporary impetus to dethrone the author and to locate authority with the reader is in response to this ethical suspicion of literacy. As already noted in Chapters 3 and 4, online literacy in deflating the text and emphasizing collaboration and communication moves a new and higher ethical standard into the center of the literate experience. Hypertext, for all its technical flash, represents not just a new medium for handling information but also a new form of social collaboration. Likewise, Berlin's notion of the social construction of knowledge represents an attempt to redefine literacy as an ideologically charged rhetoric, one that in denying any privileged position to the literate author foregrounds the issue of motives and proper conduct, paying special attention to what it sees as the ideological bias of all human action. The study of literacy thus becomes the study of how, in the past, writing, and, today, all forms of communication are used by those in power to legitimate their authority while marginalizing everyone else — hence, the widely recognized radical political agenda of much postmodern criticism, of deconstructing all forms of authority, political as well as intellectual, while legitimating the myriad voices that had hitherto been silenced in the conversation of texts.

Online literacy represents a rejection of liberal ideology and its principal valorization of a political and, as we shall investigate in the next section, an educational system based on the normative status of the autonomous individual. In this it overcomes what C.A. Bowers sees as the great obstacle to educational reform — moving beyond the language of liberalism.

> [T]he assumption that change is inherently progressive, that the individual is the basic social unit within which we locate the source of freedom and rationality, that the nature of the individual is to be understood as either inherently good or amenable to being shaped by the environment, and that rationality is the real basis of authority for regulating the affairs of daily life (1987, p. 2).

It is a mistake, Bowers tells us, to assume that such an individual — a generalized version of the literate self — is the ideal social type, when the power to establish and maintain the semblance of independence from society is less the product of intelligence or character than of affluence and socialization into the ethos of a professional class (including that of college English teachers) whose prestige and economic value lie in its ability to maintain the pose of autonomy. Even Alvin Gouldner, the great theorist and, some might argue, apologist of intellectuals, eventually saw it as a 'flawed universal class', one with the 'vices of its virtues' — including a tendency towards 'stilted convoluted speech', the 'loss of warmth and spontaneity', and 'a structured inflexibility when facing changing situations' (1979, p. 84). What Gouldner at last condemns in intellectuals (and, indirectly, in print literacy) is a 'disruption of human solidarity' resulting from a susceptibility to 'dogmatism' and a '*task*-centeredness' that taken together 'imply a certain insensitivity to *persons*, to their feelings and reactions'. What is wrong with intellectuals, in other words, is their inherent connections to the same values — autonomy, authority, and a privileged language — that are targets for elimination in the new collaborative, networked communicative environment.

Such a world will no doubt have traditional intellectuals — those who use self-reflexive, critical discourse of essays and books to analyze their own experience — and there is no reason to suppose that these future intellectuals will be in any way ethically superior to the ones Gouldner condemns. Where the difference lies will be entirely in their normative position. 'Myths of the lonely rebel or nonconformists', writes Fredric Jameson, 'are patently antiquated' (1987a, p. 561). It is only the modern age that has so closely associated the intellectual with literacy, making the *writer* and the *intellectual* practically synonymous. In the pre-modern age, no one confused the lowly scribe with philosopher or the statesmen. The literate of the future will be neither the dutiful but unimaginative scribe, nor the powerful but at times heedless intellectual; the computer age will support a new literate, someone committed to working with others, indeed, inextricably linked with them, both literally through computer networks and metaphorically through common causes. It may well be based on what Bowers calls 'a metaphor of self that connects us with the larger cultural and biotic community, including a sensitivity toward nourishing worthwhile traditions and a sense of responsibility for insuring that the entire ecosystem has a future' (1988, p. 78). Whether such a new self guarantees a better, more just society, as it seems to do, is a matter yet to be considered; what it does guarantee is that all experiences, scientific or literary, not directly connected to our common concerns will be perceived as less important, having less to do with literacy. Online literacy, in other words, will be more practical, less theoretical, and new literates themselves valued to the extent that they are team players, not traditional intellectuals.

The Pedagogic Limit of Print Literacy

Anyone who struggles with the central democratizing task of modern composition education must at times be struck by what Lanham pointed out in Chapter 1 — the enormous, possibly undemocratic nature of the task of making all students, not just the most introspective and most sensitive, into creators as well as readers of texts. Not only must students be taught the demanding task of achieving mechanical, much less stylistic competence, but they must somehow be taught the more daunting task of commanding the attention of readers, offering, as it were, complete strangers competing and compelling visions of other ways of being in the world. 'Ours is the first society in history to expect so many of its people to be able to perform these very sophisticated literary activities', notes Mike Rose. 'And we fail to keep in mind how extraordinary it is to ask *all* our schools to conduct this kind of education' (1989, p. 188). A century of claims from progressive educators regarding the natural abilities of all students notwithstanding, anyone who teaches writing must confront the possibility that the sustained, detailed crafting of written language is too difficult a task, too removed from normal, informal, sporadic uses of oral language, to be the normative impulse driving a truly democratic language arts curriculum. Simply stated, the reading and writing of complex texts are not readily attainable skills, and to the extent that we make such activities the basis of literacy education, we doom many students to be labeled failures.

Consider the following affirmation of print literacy, written by the philosopher George Santayana during the height of industrial expansion, in 1924 (in *Reason in Art*), and cited by Louise Rosenblatt in her classic study of the psychology of complex reading, *Literature As Exploration.*

> The wonder of an artist's performance grows with the range of his penetration, with the instinctive sympathy that makes him, in his mortal isolation, considerate of other men's fate and a great diviner of their secret, so that his work speaks to them kindly, with a deeper assurance than they could have spoken with to themselves. And the joy of his great sanity, the power of his adequate vision, is not the less intense because he can lend it to others and has borrowed it from a faithful study of the world (pp. 228–29).

Here the implicit role of the reader — one is tempted to call it the *myth* of the literate reader for it is doubtful that it ever existed as more than an ideal — is as romantic novitiate, a priest in training, a person with the temperament and the physical space to isolate oneself from mundane cares. Now compare this temple of print with the world of today's high school students, described by Nancy McHugh and based on her thirty years of teaching in Los Angeles.

> Today's students seem paradoxically more sophisticated and younger. There is little that they have not experienced in what used to be called the adult world. They take drugs, they drink, and they talk about sex freely. Most of my students work, some because they have to, but many also because they want things: cars, clothes, skis; some contribute one half of the family income. They do not do homework; they do not 'have time'. They are 'into' many things and feel pressured by all of them. Many have little supervision; they belong to one-parent homes, or they live alone....
>
> Reading is in poor shape, except perhaps for honors and advanced placement programs. Students do not read outside of class; if they are required to, they use *Cliff's Notes* for novels and plays and refuse or bluff in relation to other materials. If they read in class, they read at such slow rates that lessons become impossible or three-ring circuses....
>
> Because students used to be read to and read, they came to school

with both some proficiency and some background. Reading could be assigned as homework and would be done for the next day's classwork. Today most teachers do discrete assignments, things that can be covered in one day. Absenteeism and shifting populations make such schemes, if not mandatory, at least conducive to survival (Elbow, 1990, pp. 67, 68, 69).

Certainly, almost all students, even the least prepared, can be taught to handle written language with some degree of success — to take notes, to express their thoughts, to write letters — but it is not obvious that students collectively, representing as they do the next generation of citizens in a democracy, have ever been uniformly able to meet the high standards of print literacy, or are in much of a position to do better in a future where writing will play less of a role as a source of either information or entertainment.

Standardized test scores of reading comprehension, vocabulary, and English usage remain depressingly low for large sections of the population and over the last thirty years have dropped precipitously for even the best prepared students. In interpreting *The Reading Report Card*, a synthesis of four different national assessments between 1971–1984, John Carroll concludes 'that somehow the nation will have to accommodate itself pretty much to the levels of reading skill now attained by various segments of the population' (1987, p. 430); that is, the conditions in the schools, in local and state governments, and, more importantly, in industrial culture generally, are not favorable for major changes in traditional reading skills, especially when the focus shifts from basic decoding skills to even the minimal sorts of comprehension tasks that constitute higher, critical levels of print literacy. That writing and language educators continue to discount the validity of the tests may be a more important indication of just how far we are moving away from the norms of print culture. Standardized tests are not so much dismissed for the imperfection with which they measure students' achievement of print literacy, for example, how well they can comprehend a reading passage, than they are for bothering to measure something as limited as print literacy in the first place. By concentrating on the mastery of print, such tests ignore the full range of what students can do with language in all its forms. In his response to two such critics, McLean and Goldstein, Carroll expresses the incredulity of a generation of language educators that regularly assumed that the standardized reading scores of students provided valuable information about their overall literacy. Being able to read a complex text (that is, to be able to answer questions about it), it was once assumed, was an integral part of being able to write one.

All aspects of standardized testing, as well as curriculum practices that are based on print literacy, have been in retreat for at least a generation, with sentence combining in the 1970s the last popular curriculum reform that placed principal focus directly on improving students' ability to manipulate texts directly. Until the recent concern with ideology and the social construction of knowledge discussed in Chapter 4, writing pedagogy of the last twenty years was dominated by a concern with 'process', a reform movement whose one common concern was to de-emphasize what for at least half a century has been the primary focus of college-level writing instruction — the product, or text, the one thing that in its internal complexity assures that literate exchange is fundamentally different from other forms of discourse. It is precisely this eagerness not to differentiate, or 'privilege', literacy that best defines most of the theoretical and pedagogic work that has had the greatest influence on the writing profession since William Labov's classic 1969 article, 'The Logic of Nonstandard English', a work that argued that the informal speech patterns of inner-city youngsters had all the formal complexity of, and often more expressive power than, the sanctioned, mainly middle class texts of print culture. Or as has been shown in the work of Shirley Brice Heath, it is the school, the primary institution of print literacy, that carries the main burden of the educational difficulties of the rural students she studied for its failure to recognize and build upon the rich patterns of indigenous language use. Heath's *Ways with Words* (1983), like Labov's work and that of so many others, casts print literacy as the villain in a vast cultural melodrama, a literal great divide in human history in which, in the words of Ron and Suzanne Scollon, 'the word comes to take precedence over the situation, analysis takes precedence over participation, isolated thought takes precedence over conversation and story telling, and the individual takes precedence over the community' (Bowers, 1988, p. 82).

What is prepared to replace the ideology and curriculum of print is a new, more democratic classroom practice, one that repudiates the central belief of print literacy that deeper, more profound readings are better. Such 'an agreement about a model for the typical English classroom' reports Peter Elbow, was the most crucial, specific outcome of the English Coalition conference.

> [N]ot a class that pushes for a single or best reading of a text [the traditional 'A' paper] but rather a class that pushes for multiple and various readings of the text and then devotes some time to reflecting on how one got to these readings. This is a call for teaching with less closure and less criticizing of bad or wrong readings and more affirmation of differences among readings (p. 39).

Here is a recipe for any class, even one without computers, to enact the principles of the networking outlined in Chapter 4. Here also is a class in which all students, including those described by McHugh above, have a better chance of succeeding, in no small measure because success itself, just like the governing model of literacy, has been redefined.

The Aesthetic Limit of Print Literacy

To these three flaws — historical, ethical, and pedagogic — we can add a fourth, one that goes to the heart of the issues of multimedia composition, namely, that print literacy may not be just too difficult but too narrowly focused, too removed not just from oral language but, in its sole appeal to the imagination, too abstract, too puritanical, too removed from the full range of sensual experience that life affords. No one can deny that for the engaged reader the traditional novel provides a range of imaginative pleasure that many find richer, more enjoyable than the most lavishly mounted film version — the rub is the adjective *engaged*. To the unengaged reader, the novel (except for the cover and what few illustrations it may contain) is without pleasure entirely, is a featureless series of identical pages, designed precisely not to catch our eye and hence draw our attention away from the meaning conveyed by the words. Nor is it an accident that the great monument of modern literacy, the novel, flourished at an historical moment (from the mid-eighteenth to the mid-twentieth centuries) that saw the triumph and now the eventual decline of middle-class life with its sustaining principles of sublimation and delayed gratification. Students of the future may still be willing to work their way through long, involved novels like *Middlemarch* and *The Magic Mountain*, but one must still face the possibility that far fewer people will be willing or able either to endure the isolation from all other sensory stimuli or to attend with single-mindedness of purpose for the uninterrupted hours at a time that such reading necessitates. It is at times difficult to believe that today's synesthetic world of compressed and disjointed artistic images — whether rock videos or normal television augmented by heavy use of a remote control channel selector — is only a little more than a century removed from the world in which the German composer Richard Wagner declared his long (four-plus hours), largely psychological music dramas as the art of the future.

The rejection of the aesthetics of print takes at least two forms, one directly and one indirectly connected to online literacy. The first form has already been forcefully stated by Lanham in Chapter 1, and suggested by Bolter above: that computer use is more immediately sensual and playful than traditional reading and writing. Print too has its games — puns, anagrams, riddles, and the like — but they have a minimal sensual component. There is no escaping the fact that there is just lots more to do — more fun to have — with a computer, starting with the simple task afforded by graphics-based operating systems of controlling on the screen the appearance as well as the content of the text. In responding to the implicit print bias in Halio, Kaplan and Moulthrop respond to the charge that decorating or 'gilding' a text detracts from its meaning, a charge they associate not with the print tradition but with 'a puritan or ascetic perspective'. It is time, they argue, for us to move beyond such thinking, in part by re-uniting with an older, pre-print tradition of writing, one that in referring to gilding's metaphoric sense of textual illumination, 'suggests that decorations infuse the text with a "light" that is as much discursive as aesthetic.' They reject the distinction basic to print literacy between *description* that is superficial and *depiction* that is integral to writing. 'The two have always been productively combined, and the evolution of electronic technology may enable even more valuable combinations' (p. 99). The pedagogic implication for such an approach is that students who are particularly good at design will collaborate with those good at more traditional writing tasks in completing a single project.

New computer-based techniques for manipulating writing provide one means of establishing a new aesthetics of online literacy, yet there is another area that may play a greater role in the long run (although for the last century it has been relatively inconsequential) and that is arts education. Stated differently, the reading and writing experiences of students using computers may well take on a more traditional aesthetic character, with a parallel narrowing of what has been a chasm between literacy and fine arts education. Curriculum specialists hoping to design a new pedagogy for online reading and writing would do well to turn to leading arts educators from Plato to Herbert Read for guidance as to the difficulties and possibilities before us. In this regard, the work of cognitive psychologist Howard Gardner provides a number of helpful suggestions concerning where we have been and where we may be heading in training students in art and, by extension, in literacy.

Gardner's work on human creativity was firmly based in the cardinal tenet of print culture — that what drives art and creativity in general is the nurturing of a restless, inquisitive spirit, what he labels 'the prevalent Western concept of the arts as cognitive, problem-finding, world-remaking activities' (1989, p. 14). The most valuable art, accordingly, is that which is closest to the tradition of print literacy, that which follows the pattern of cognitive growth elaborated by Jerome Bruner, for example, where symbolic thought builds upon prior sensory experiences. Gardner reduces his 'progressive' approach to arts education to a simple formula, one that works as well for literacy education: 'Exploration first, skill development later.' Yet it is precisely the premium placed on exploration that, as we see in the passage from Santayana, makes literacy (and presumably art) so difficult, and, as we have seen in Pirsig, so psychologically exhaustive; conversely it is precisely skill development in laying out, designing, and otherwise manipulating texts that the computer so boldly supports. A post-print aesthetics for Gardner would therefore require him to reverse completely his life-long commitment to what he calls the supremacy of 'transformative' to 'mimetic' activities, a hierarchy that is reflective in the Western practice of encouraging artistic expression in young children largely as a prelude to their mastery of written language.

Such a reversal turns out to be exactly what he experiences, through an analysis of various educational practices and his own personal experiences. In his earlier *Frames of Mind* (1985), Gardner already had exhibited a keen awareness of the connection between the underlying principles of a group's educational practice and how it generates its wealth. The high industrialism of print culture, he contends, privileges 'linguistic, logical-mathematical, and interpersonal forms of intelligence' (p. 384), while earlier stages of industrial development (the mercantile world of E.D. Hirsch, for example) place more emphasis on 'rote linguistic learning'. It is only in what he calls 'traditional agrarian society' that we see the kind of 'interpersonal, bodily-kinesthetic, and linguistic forms of intelligence ... highlighted in informal educational settings ... and featur[ing] considerable observation and imitation' that critics of print like the Scollons and Heath advocate as the basis of a new, more cooperative educational endeavor. Thus to the extent that Gardner could conclude that the computer is introducing a comparable economic transformation, he might well argue for new, more integrative educational practices.

That he does argue for such changes results less from the logical consequences of his own model-building, or from anything having to do with computers, than from an intense re-examination of his (and our) beliefs resulting from an extraordinary series of encounters with the more mimetic, more rigid practices of art education in China. What he discovered, in brief, is the saving value of a tradition that manages to balance an emphasis on competence and rote learning with respect for innovation and the individual, what we might interpret as the same balance that educators like Gere, Handa, and Trimbur are searching for in the new collaborative classroom. Establishing such a balance is hardly a simple or trivial matter, and can be seen in terms of the problem of meshing a new, post-print concern with the group with the high-print commitment to the individual. What is before us is a dilemma of the highest order, one that perhaps can be addressed best in a paraphrase of the classical paradox. If we are not for the group, what are we (other than the diverse individuals of print); if we are only for the group, who will speak for the individual, who will give voice to what is unsanctioned? Consider this general problem in terms of a specific case offered by Peter Elbow. A sub-committee during the English Coalition submitted a report that spoke of our need of nurturing 'a sense of common humanity', what some would argue needs to be the ethical foundation of any new model of literacy; yet others attacked the position.

> The phrase smacks of 'essentialism', they argued; that is, it suggests the dangerous notion that we are all the same; it's the kind of language that promotes intolerance of difference.... [I]f we agree about what is essential or about common humanity, then that agreement can serve as a fence to exclude certain people as outside what is essential or common humanity (pp. 62–3).

This ethical conundrum may possibly be solved by a grounding in the kind of arts education that Gardner found in China, one with the 'capacity to remain connected to the past ... while somehow opening oneself to and accepting the forces at work in the modern era'.

> It entails a respect for the old, for what has come before, for religious and even superstitious ideas, combined with a tolerance for those who are tied to, or cannot appreciate, these facets of an ancient tradition. It features a commitment to study, to scholarship, to artistic pursuits, accompanied by a belief that these activities are worthwhile for their own sake but also contribute to social connectivity and merit trans-mission to future generations. It makes allowance for individual dif-ferences, even eccentricities, but does not in any sense revel in them or project them at the expense of the sensibilities of others. One who exhibits this sensibility is willing to bend to the will of the wider community but not to sacrifice one's own sense of proportion and respect for individuality (1989, pp. 312–13).

Gardner's goal here is not merely to incorporate graphics into the curriculum, as suggested by Fortune in Chapter 3, to give students a new means of extending their critical thinking and writing skills beyond what 'is possible if we restrict writing instruction to verbal expression alone' (p. 160). Instead, it is to seek a new balance in education by re-establishing connections with the discipline and physicality of the fine arts. In important ways reading and writing need to be-come more like fine arts themselves, activities that are inherently self-gratifying and immediately pleasurable, in part for their rich sensory component and in part for their connection to a continuing crafts tradition.

In this regard, the new aesthetic dimension of literacy may well re-enshrine the teacher, not as an intellectual, but as a crafts master, possibly in a role not unlike the one in which Bartholomae cast his college professor, a role intimately connected to a larger pattern of the cultural transmission of knowledge and skills that Gardner sees as central to human culture.

> [W]e all feel in our own past the power of crucial traditional elements that have been important to our own development and prospering; that we see as lacking in the lives of the next generation, and sometimes in our own children; and that we believe must somehow be fused with the contemporary options if we are to feel at one with ourselves and linked with the larger world (1989, p. 316).

Here is a unifying vision of education as both a moral and a technical force, a process that requires us to master a concrete skill like drawing with our hand (or computing with our fingers) and a different set of communicative and imaginative skills with our hearts and minds. The craft is important in itself — as a craft it is aesthetically self-fulfilling — but it is also only a beginning of a life's journey and beyond. We must nourish the desire and the skill to pass this craft on to the next generation.

Transformed into such a context, literacy might gain much of the benefit of reading and writing online while retaining from the world of print what the horizontal webs and networks of computers seem to lack, the sense of linear time that informs the personal narrative that is our own lives. This is a vision of a literacy of the future that follows the spirit of Jameson's injunction 'to undo post-modernism homeopathically by the methods of postmodernism' (Stephanson, 1988, p. 17), that is, to use the power of the computer to critique computer-based models of literacy. Forging such a new model of literacy, one that exists online yet retains the critical edge of print, will not be easy. The four limitations of print literacy enumerated above are problems precisely because of the way each in turn privileges the critical component in effecting (1) more powerful transformations of nature, (2) more powerful explanations of human conduct, (3) more powerful readings of texts, and (4) more powerful, because more symbolic, renderings of experience. The answer must lie, not in abandoning critique, but in balancing it with the aesthetic playfulness and immediacy of interpersonal contact inherent in computer-based manipulations of information, text, and graphics. Word perfect, or the utopian promise of literacy, in other words, lies not in technological innovations themselves, no matter how spectacular and how liberating they may seem, but in the same practical task that in its undistorted form has motivated reading and writing in the age of print, that of remaking both our world and ourselves in accord with an imagined rendering, a verbal projection, of what we as human beings are capable of becoming. This is a vision of literacy online as an extension, not a rejection, of the literacy of print.

In January 1991, a wire-service story ran in newspapers about Kenneth Good, an anthropologist who spent ten years living with primitive Yanomama Indians in the jungles of Venezuela. 'It's a nice, balanced lifestyle', Good said. 'Their culture is probably closer to the way human beings were meant to live.' Nevertheless he was returning to America with his native wife, so that his kids would have the same choice between cultures that he had.

Those of us writing about computers and the future of literacy today, and at least for a few more years, are like Good in the unique historical position of straddling two worlds — we can explore the off-the-beaten-track allures of a new world (for us, that of online literacy) while being fully acculturated into an old world (here, that of print). Like K Good, our praise for whatever is new and different can be read as an implicit criticism of the familiar; and like Kenneth Good, we can venture into the unknown for a goodly number of years, even taking our family with us, and still come back to the world in which we grew up. In both cases the entire exercise can be seen on a practical level as part of one's academic career (namely, a means of getting published — and Good's own book, *Into the Heart*, appeared shortly after the news release) and on a more cosmic level as an instance, not of repudiation, but of enactment of that criticism of the familiar that is a defining characteristic of modernism itself.

The danger here is that we are too easily seduced into thinking that our attitude about some other condition — be it the Yanomama Indians or online literacy — is shaped by our direct experience of the world, that we are actually reporting on this other world, and not, as is the case, on a world as mediated by the critical spirit of print. All of us who read and write books about a new computer age are like Kenneth Good, tourists in exotic lands. It is unlikely that people without substantial experience of print literacy will discuss the future of literacy in the kind of terms raised here, just as it is unlikely that people fully acculturated into the life of the Yanomama will speak of giving their children a choice of cultures. The contemporary debate over computer-based literacy is as much a product of print as Good's experiment in lifestyles, and in each case we are faced with the same dilemma — of trying to filter out of that critique the restless, critical spirit that is so much a part of print culture, not the least because, as Fredric Jameson contends, it is so much a part of capitalist production itself.

> The dynamic of perpetual change is, as Marx showed in the *Manifesto*, not some alien rhythm within capital — a rhythm specific to those non-instrumental activities that are art and science — but rather is the very 'permanent revolution' of capitalist production itself (1984, p. xx).

Or as Robert Bellah adds in his collaborative study of the psychic strains of late-industrial society, 'Breaking with the past is part of our past' (1985, p. 75).

What we cannot so readily arrive at is what our future would be like if we really were successful in breaking with the past completely (and not just as a temporary means of achieving critical distance on that past), that is, what it would be like if suddenly our experiences of some exotic present — be it the world of online literacy or of the Yanomama Indians — were all of a sudden unmediated by our former paradigmatic experiences of print, that is, of experiences of complex, psychological journeys within the private space of texts. What if all of a sudden the character-based, private world of print were to vanish, and all 'writing' was collaborative and graphic-based — if all we knew was the world of the Yanomama Indians? We live with too little sense of the evanescent nature of the tenets and institutions of literacy, much like those educators a century ago who could only see classics as the basis of a college education, or who saw reading essentially in terms of recitation and writing in terms of penmanship. Alfred Kernan in *The Death of Literature* (1990), for example, contemplates comparable changes occurring now, independent of computers, regarding our attitude about 'the integrity of the literary work and its eradicable meaning'. Ideas that Rosenblatt found expressed in Santayana and Kernan finds fully articulated in a 1924 essay by Virginia Woolf — such beliefs that the literary work is 'complete in itself', that it is 'self-contained', and that it 'leaves one with no desire to do anything, except to read the book again, and to understand it better' — ideas that have today, he writes, 'disappeared as completely as if they had been vaporized' (p. 80).

Once traditions disappear, notes sociologist Edward Shils, they are gone. They are not, he writes, 'independently self-productive or self-elaborating. Only living, knowing, desiring human beings can enact them and reenact them and modify them' (1981, pp. 14–15). Even without reference to computers, Kernan wistfully sees signs of radical change everywhere. 'The great social issues the printed book provoked, literacy, censorship, originality, pornography, plagiarism, copyright, freedom of expression, are, after a final flare-up, beginning to look illusory' (p. 135). We are not far away from entering a radically transformed world, yet many critics of print culture envision the traditional literate world as a huge monolith, an impenetrable, undisturbable cultural tradition. As Kernan asks,

> Take away the works that are still for the moment agreed to be literature and what is left? Only a hodgepodge of institutional odds and ends without a center, a decaying instructional system, a set of professional arrangements, a library category, a high-culture avant-garde circle, a few publishers and reviewers, a few passing political and social causes (p. 212).

— that is, the institutions and issues of academic English, at one time the central concern of humanistic studies, now splintered and marginalized. What we need to come to terms with is the possibility that freeing ourselves completely from the remnants of print may well be like Kenneth Good, stuck in the middle of the Venezuelan rain forest, tossing out his compass.

For most advocates of online literacy there is no question: the hypertextual, networking, and multimedia capabilities of computers are important precisely in extending these same utopian aspirations; computers will make us better able to objectify new possibilities and to cooperate with each other in attaining them. Yet taking the lesson of television seriously, we should not be too hasty in confusing the power to project an image — clearly a strength of multimedia computing — with the power to imagine, or create, that image in the first place, and, more importantly, the power to connect that image to the realization of actual human goals. We need to connect promises about computers and online literacy, in other words, with the utopian promise of television only two generations ago, the possibility that, in the words of F. Christopher Arterton, 'Representative institutions will disappear; citizens will truly govern themselves' (1987, p. 14). Here was the chance to use modern technology to inform and involve citizens more directly than Jefferson or other ardent democrats could have envisioned. Yet what we have experienced over the last two generations is declining voter participation and an increasing apathy about most things political, symptoms of Nelson's 'video narcosis'. More recently there is the hope that global broadcasting would lead to the internationalizing of our sensibilities, our overcoming distrust and suspicion based on regional differences. It is easy and comforting to believe that with the spread of CNN and our ability to see war 'live' that we will be less willing to support aggressive, militaristic national policies. But wars in the past have often been waged by soldiers well accustomed to its sufferings, and supported by populations that, despite their extensive experience of the brutality of life, seem as bent as many were during the Persian Gulf war on claiming national heroes and forging a new collective identity.

The problems do not seem to have much to do with technology or with soliciting people's opinions — dictators, Arterton reminds us, regularly use plebiscites to legitimize their rule, and modern broadcast television is awash with scientific and informal polls. But all the technology seems to do is to manipulate hastily formed opinions while helping to break down such traditional democratic institutions as political parties. Just as the technologies involved in online literacy clearly have the power to allow us to formulate radical alternatives to the status quo, so too does television have the power to help us govern ourselves more rationally and to live together with other countries more peacefully. Part of the problem seems to lie in our faith that somehow technology itself, like miraculous new medical equipment for seeing inside the human body, will solve our problems — make us a healthier society — without having to be embodied in institutions of social reform. What we discover again and again, however, is that in the absence of such institutions just the opposite happens — that those in the best position to use the new technology do so for their own narrow interests while society as a whole suffers. 'The "distance shrinking" characteristics of the new communications technologies', write Gillespie and Robins (1989), 'far from overcoming and rendering insignificant the geographical expressions of centralized economic and political power, in fact constitute new and enhanced forms of inequality and uneven development' (p. 7). For anything socially productive to happen with computer-based literacy or other technologies, people must feel motivated both to envision a better world and to work through institutions still subject to human control to bring that world into being — and the crucial question becomes, not what a technology can do, but how people will be able to interact with it in shaping and fulfilling their own motives.

According to Piaget, people grow by alternately changing themselves and the world, through both play and constructive activity. Where computers, like television, seem to excel is in extending geometrically our ability to transform the world, especially through the playful transformations of simulation. The same computer power that readily allows us to preview how our writing will appear if printed in Times Roman or Helvetica allows us to reshape and recombine the world at large, cutting-and-pasting, as it were, through all human experience, creating realistic graphic representations of any imaginable combination of human experience. But if this power is to be any more constructive than the power to fashion our own television shows by channel-switching via remote control, it must have a direct connection with our acting in the world, our choosing one thing over another, as individuals and, more importantly, in conjunction with others. If online literacy is to rise above the level of the bells and whistles of high-powered Nintendo games, it must be in support of the same collective task of human transformation that has characterized our experience of print literacy.

Why shouldn't we be able to use computers, it seems logical to ask, to further the project of print — to think critically and imaginatively about who we can become, who we really are, as prelude to acting in the world? The obstacles here reside in part, as we have seen, in the technology itself, especially in the thoroughness and the ease with which computer-mediated transformations occur, and in part, as needs to be examined, in the larger historical forces that, as with industrialism in the age of print, may determine the possibilities and limits of any new form of literacy. As with print literacy, online literacy represents reading and writing practices that are grounded, not in the technologies of discourse — the printing presses and typewriters of the past, the computer networks and hypermedia databases of the future — but in the underlying modes of production. The industrial basis of print supported the formation of the model literate as intellectual-artist-innovator, as someone capable of re-imagining the world. Just what role, we want to know, will imagination play in a new, online literacy that is largely shaped by the needs and demands of a post-industrial economy?

Where television seems to have failed, and is thus a potential pitfall for online literacy, is in connecting thought and action, the hypothetical and the practical, the source of much of the transformative power print literacy has had for individuals and culture. What we need from online literacy is a comparable means of motivating the critical imagination, of strengthening within us the dual ability to objectify alternate worlds in language and to help organize ourselves to work toward constructing that world. What online literacy in its multimedia form must become is not fantasy but science fiction, that is, images attached to implicit programs of social reform. It must aid us in the projection of other, better ways of being by writers and readers as a means of initiating such constructive action; it must match the practical-utopian spirit that has always driven print literacy. Gregory Ulmer (1992) suggests that such a future may lie in our moving beyond narrative and exposition (the main modes of thinking in print) to what he calls 'patterns', a way of thinking best expressed through collages, and one that utilizes techniques now relegated to the 'lower' fine arts in reconstructing literacy.

Yet if patterning or anything else is to be the answer, then it must be social and practical as well as sensual and expressive; it must give us the sense of urgency that derives from the possibility that our projection of a world might be widely promoted as a proper model for change because it is perceived as 'deeper', more complex, more fully realized than ordinary understanding. Such a new literacy must overcome what even its proponents would be unlikely to disagree is lacking — the sense of author, and more importantly, author's vision, as authority. A new literacy, if it is to have the power of the old, will have to overcome the limits of postmodern attitudes and, what is too easy to overlook, the postindustrial model of economic production on which such attitudes are based.

What is necessary is to rehabilitate in some way the notion of progress that has underlain modernism and print literacy. Readers and writers of print interacted with each other through ever more complex, perfected texts, vying as it were for wider recognition as an authority — someone whose projection of the world was to be recognized as qualitatively 'better'. Today, things seems to have become completely reversed; in Kernan's words:

> with equal plausibility and equally well marshaled facts, everyone seems to agree that there are no works of art, only texts open to endless interpretation, that the authors have disappeared into a sea of intertextuality, that all writing is a part of the struggle for power to control interpretation (p. 80).

While a postmodern critic might intend such attitudes to be taken hyperbolically as critiques of the imperfections and hypocrisies of print culture (hoping all along that his or her own reading will escape this relativism, becoming in time a new authority), the technology of online literacy has the power to render such assertions literally true.

We are confronting an epochal transformation in human experience, not just, as Kernan suggests, the end of a literary tradition with which we have grown too comfortable, or, as has been discussed throughout this book, the end of print literacy, but as Fredric Jameson suggests 'the dissolution of an autonomous sphere of culture' itself, an event that he imagines not as a sudden disappearance but as an explosion:

> a prodigious expansion of culture throughout the social realm, to the point at which everything in our social life — from economic value and state power to practices and to the very stricture of the psyche itself — can be said to have become 'cultural' in some original and as yet untheorized sense (1984b, p. 87).

The abandonment of what Jameson calls 'the visual metaphoric depth' for 'a description of temporal disconnection and fragmentation' carries with it the loss 'of certain relationships to history and the past'; what we wind up with is a new kind of writing, 'a rhetoric of texts', characterized by 'the production of discontinuous sentences without any larger unifying forms' (Stephanson, 1988, p. 6). Here is the new world of online literacy that Jameson describes as post-modernism itself:

> that pure and random play of signifiers which ... no longer produces monumental works of the modernist type, but ceaselessly reshuffles the fragments of preexistent texts, the building blocks of older cultural and social production, in some new and heightened bricolage: metabooks which cannibalise other books, metatexts which collate bits of other texts' (1987b, p. 223).

Here is a world Jameson sees as characterized by the 'dead language' of pastiche, a type of writing that borrows the form of parody but not that form's 'ulterior motives', its larger satiric concern with social reform, without, that is, 'any conviction that alongside the abnormal tongue you have momentarily borrowed, some healthy linguistic normality still exists' (1984b, p. 65).

What is most disturbing here, most detrimental to the utopian possibilities of an online literacy that supports such an exploded cultural world, is the sug-gestion, echoed by Jameson and others, that this 'new' world of multiple, de-centered and un-authorized voices is precisely the world most supportive of a post-industrial economic order managed by a new breed of robber barons, the multinational, de-centered, largely invisible corporations of late capitalism. It is a world that Jameson sees as decontextualizing, hence subverting the critical or practical role of the imagination.

> [P]ast visual mirages, stereotypes or texts, effectively abolish[ing] any practical sense of the future and of the collective project, thereby

abandoning the thinking of future change to fantasies of sheer catas-
trophe and inexplicable cataclysm — from visions of 'terrorism' on the
social level to those of cancer on the personal (Jameson, 1984b, p. 85).

Images and texts — collaborative hypermedia — have the power to terrify us;
what they lack is the power to convince us to act collectively. Our principal
suspicion of postmodernism, as painted by Jameson, and of the online literacy it
supports, is that it may turn out to be little more than modernism minus critique,
little more, in other words, than a grand accommodation with the latest manifestation of global capitalism.

Here then is the basis of Lyotard's contrast of the defining characteristic of
print literacy — what he calls the 'old principle that the acquisition of knowledge
is indissociable from the training (*Bildung*) of minds, or even of individuals', a
principle that he sees 'becoming obsolete and will become ever more so' — and
an entirely new principle of knowledge, perhaps more accurately, information,
and a subsequent model for education based on the prevailing notion of totally
unfettered free market exchange.

> The relationship of the suppliers and users of knowledge to the knowl-
> edge they supply and use is now tending, and will increasingly tend,
> to assume the form already taken by the relationship of commodity
> producers and consumers to the commodities they produce and consume
> — that is, the form of value. Knowledge [information?] is and will be
> produced in order to be sold, it is and will be consumed in order to be
> valorized in a new production: in both cases, the goal is exchange.
> Knowledge ceases to be an end in itself, it loses its 'use-value'. (Lyotard,
> 1984, pp. 4–5)

Vast hypertexts and computer networks are after all the very modalities of late
capitalism, and we as consumers are ideally situated in this matrix when we have
total access to (the right to purchase) any individual item we want and no sense
whatsoever of how this vast system consumer network operates; for example,
who or what controls it. To understand the de-centered, open-ended postmodern
world, Richard Kearney asks us to imagine 'the man in the street, puzzled by the
enigma of inflation', who first goes to his local bank, then to a national bank,
then to an international one, with each 'in turn defer[ring] to each other or back
to themselves in a seemingly endless recursive circle'. 'It is as though the entire
monetary system of late international capitalism is without any single centre, a
criss-crossing network of connections, a hall of mirrors reflecting and multiplying
the diverse market forces from around the globe' (p. 298). It is as if we are all
living inside Jameson's version of a 'postmodern hyperspace', John Portman's
Bonaventura Hotel, a place that 'has finally succeeded in transcending the
capacities of the individual human body to locate itself, to organize its immediate
surroundings perceptually, and cognitively to map its position in a mappable
external world' (1984b, p. 83).

There is an analogy here between the postmodern geography and the landscape of online literacy. Both are rich with sensory details and de-centered,
undermining as it were the sense of some underlying or higher order. There are
images everywhere but little sense of their forming a coherent, larger pattern,
little faith in what Richard Kearney refers to as 'the modernist belief in the image

as an *authentic* expression' (p. 3). What is lost, in other words, is the sense of distinction between the *spurious* — that which is specifically produced, and hence valued, by a market economy for the sole purpose of being consumed — and the *authentic* — that which reflects an individual's ability to produce something of worth that goes beyond (deeper or higher than) free market value. Just as television, the communication miracle of the last half century, seems to have led, despite all expectations, to the decline of political participation, so too do graphics-based computers — what Kearney calls 'technological innovations in image reproduction [which] have made the imaginary more persuasive than the real world' (p. 252) — threaten the health of the critical imagination, blurring what Kearney calls 'the very distinction between artistic-image and commodity-image' (p. 4). It is a vision of the modern imagination awash in a consumer world of pseudo-choice, the habituate of the shopping mall who is seduced into thinking that the food court, instead of being the unified arm of a single conglomerate, offers the full range of human eating experiences, and, by extension, that real choice in dining (as in writing) exists in assembling a whole (a meal or a text) by selecting items from different concessionairess.

Although Kearney sees this threat to the imagination as 'one of the greatest paradoxes of contemporary culture', it can hardly be an unexpected paradox for anyone cognizant of the special historical connection between a well-nurtured imagination and the puritanical constraints of print literacy: The interiorization of industrial culture was accompanied by both the imaginary richness of print literature and the world-building (constructive) spirit of an entire professional class — intellectuals and critics as well as scientists and entrepreneurs. Online literacy seems on the verge of reversing this relationship, with the exteriorization of post-industrial (consumer-based) culture accompanied by the sensual richness of a virtual literature (or an actual mall) and the playful (deconstructive) spirit of a limited class of professionals who act only in language. Where before there were unadorned texts and introspective readers convinced that their individual acts of reading and writing were part of a larger project of transforming the world, there are now stacks of interconnected words and images and cooperating, supportive groups too often convinced that their collective act of reading and writing is part of a larger project by which the world is renamed but, as a solely linguistic entity, fundamentally unchanged.

There may well be a place for the imagination in online literacy, but for the imagination to have a critical dimension it must go beyond the ludic; it must not only be capable of projecting and comprehending new worlds, it must be capable of placing such worlds within the larger context of collective human action. Yet where does such a context come from in the emerging world of online literacy, lacking as it seems what Lyotard and others refer to as the master narrative, the larger historical explanation which helped individuals distinguish the authentic, often aesthetic experiences from spurious, commercial ones that seem to have been generated solely for the purpose of facilitating our adjustment in the world by overwhelming, thereby deadening, our senses? These are the master narratives that, despite their current unpopularity with the literates of late print culture, are nevertheless important in indicating to us what is possible beyond capitalism. As Jameson adds, it is such narratives that 'also "legitimate" the praxis whereby political militants seek to bring that radically different future social order into being' (1984a, p. xix).

Beyond a specific left-wing political agenda, narrative has a broader cultural function of encoding all human experience, of creating what Hayden White (1987) calls an awareness of 'a shared reality [that] can be transmitted' (p. 1). Narrative in this sense is the historical dimension of imagination, providing us as individuals and as a collective social unit with the stories of our lives. 'Is it not possible', asks White, 'that the question of narrative in any discussion of historical theory is always finally about the function of imagination in the production of a specifically human truth?' (1987, p. 57). What online literacy must provide us, if it is to replace and not merely subvert print, is a new way of fashioning that universal narrative of human history, a new way of re-telling the ongoing tale of our collective struggle to become what we are capable of imagining, a new way of shaping that most compelling image of who we want to be. What we must learn to do with the computer-based tools of literacy — hypertext, networking, and multimedia among others — is to connect ourselves to history, in the words of Richard Kearney, 'to remember the past and to project a future' (p. 392).

It is a task that we must begin by making certain that our electronic dreams, in words and images, grow out of and are constantly related back to the practical decisions of our daily lives. And it is a task that we must begin immediately, while the most highly literate among us still have solid contact with both worlds. Looking back from the world of computers, we are now able to see the serious limitations in the well-entrenched patterns and institutions of print; the literacy of print has exhausted itself as surely as the industrial culture that supported it has exhausted the natural world. Even those among us who, like Orwell's Winston Smith, are enamored of the very smell and texture of the printed page must recognize ways that our collective physical survival calls for new models of cooperation and interaction. Meanwhile, looking forward from the world of print, we are still able to see the importance of a critical edge in avoiding too ready and too easy an accommodation with what seems to be an increasingly market-driven world. Even the most ardent fans of computer technology must have some misgivings in face of the onslaught of sensory images, many commercially motivated, about to invade the hitherto abstract, private space of reading and writing.

For now many of us are straddling these two worlds, drawing strength from each — but for how much longer? At what point will students of print quietly begin retreating into Steiner's 'houses of reading' (if they have not already started), leaving the rest of us free to communicate — to interact, to negotiate, and to cooperate — entirely online? Perhaps, no one can say for certain. What we do know is that, if such a time should come, then we will have passed completely into a strange new world of online literacy, one from which we, unlike Kenneth Good and his children, are not likely to return.

Bibliography

ADAMS, H. (n.d.) *The Education of Henry Adams*, New York, Modern Library.

ADAMSON, W. (1964) *English Education, 1789–1902*, Cambridge, Cambridge University Press.

ADORNO, T. (1973) *Philosophy of Modern Music*, New York, Continum.

ALSCHULER, L. (1989) 'Hand-Crafted Hypertext — Lessons from the ACM Experiment', in BARRETT, E. (Ed.) *Society of Text: Hypertext, Hypermedia, and the Social Construction of Information*, Cambridge, MA, MIT Press, pp. 343–61.

APPLE, M.W. (1986) *Teachers and Texts: A Political Economy of Class and Gender Relations in Education*, New York, Routledge and Kegan Paul.

ARONOWITZ, S. (1988) *Science as Power: Discourse and Ideology in Modern Society*, Minneapolis, University of Minneapolis Press.

ARTERTON, F.C. (1987) *Teledemocracy: Can Technology Protect Democracy?* Newbury Park, Sage.

ASIMOV, I. (n.d.) 'The Fun They Had', in *The Far Ends of Time and Earth*, New York, Doubleday, pp. 308–10.

BAKHTIN, M. (1981) *The Dialogic Imagination*, edited by M. HOLQUIST, Austin, University of Texas Press.

BALESTRI, D.P. (1988) 'Softcopy and Hard: Wordprocessing and Writing Process', *Academic Computing*, February, pp. 14–17, 41–45.

BARKER, T. and KEMP, F. (1990) 'Network Theory: A Postmodern Pedagogy for the Writing Classroom', in HANDA, C. (Ed.) *Computers and Community: Teaching Composition in the Twenty-first Century*, Portsmouth, NH: Boynton/Cook, pp. 1–27.

BARRETT, E. (1988a) 'Introduction: A New Paradigm for Writing *with* and *for* the Computer', in BARRETT, E. (Ed.) *Text, Context, and Hypertext: Writing with and for the Computer*, Cambridge, MA, MIT Press.

BARRETT, E. (Ed.) (1988b) *Text, Context and Hypertext: Writing with and for the Computer*, Cambridge, MA, MIT Press.

BARRETT, E. (Ed.) (1989) *Society of Text: Hypertext, Hypermedia, and the Social Construction of Information*, Cambridge, MA, MIT Press.

BARRETT, E. and PARADIS, J. (1988) 'Teaching Writing in an On-line Classroom', *Harvard Education Review*, **58**, pp. 154–71.

BARTHES, R. (1974) *S/Z*, New York, Hill and Wang.

Bibliography

BARTHES, R. (1986) *The Rustle of Language*, translated by R. Howard, NY, Hill and Wang.

BARTHOLOMAE, D. (1986) 'Wanderings: Misreadings, Miswritings, Misunderstandings', in NEWKIRK, T. (Ed.) *Only Connect: Uniting Reading and Writing*, Upper Montclair NJ, Boynton/Cook, pp. 89–118.

BAUDRILLARD, J. (1984) 'The Precession of Simulacra', in WALLIS, B. and TUCKER, M. (Eds) *Art after Modernism: Rethinking Representation*, New York, New Museum, pp. 253–81.

BEGEMAN, M.L. and CONKLIN, J. (1988) 'The Right Tool for the Job', *Byte*, October, pp. 255–66.

BELL, D. (1975) 'The Social Framework of the Information Society', in DERTOUZOS, M. and MOSES, J. (Eds) *The Computer Age: A Twenty-Year View*, Cambridge, MA, MIT Press, pp. 163–211.

BELLAH, R., MADSEN, R., SULLIVAN, W., SWIDLER, A. and TIPTON, S. (1985) *Habits of the Heart: Individualism and Commitment in American Life*, New York, Perennial.

BENTHAM, J. (1983) *Chrestomathia*, edited by M.J. SMITH and W.H. BURSTON, Oxford, Clarendon Press.

BERLIN, J. (1982) 'Contemporary Composition: The Major Pedagogical Theories', *College English*, **44**, pp. 765–77.

BERLIN, J. (1988) 'Rhetoric and Ideology in the Writing Class', *College English*, **50**, pp. 477–94.

BLIVENS, B. JR. (1954) *The Wonderful Writing Machine*, New York, Random House.

BOLTER, J.D. (1984) *Turing's Man: Western Culture in the Computer Age*, Chapel Hill, University of North Carolina Press.

BOLTER, J.D. (1991) *Writing Space: The Computer, Hypertext, and the History of Writing*, Hillsdale, NJ, Lawrence Erlbaum.

BOLTER, J.D. (1992) 'Literature in the Electronic Writing Space', in TUMAN, M. (Ed.) *Literacy Online: The Promise (and Peril) of Reading (and Writing) with Computers*, Pittsburgh, University of Pittsburgh Press.

BOOTH, W.C. (1984) 'Introduction', in BAKHTIN, M., *Problems of Dostoevsky's Poetics*, Minneapolis: University Minnesota Press, pp. xiii–xxvii.

BOOTH, W.C. (1989) 'Foreword', *The English Coalition Conference*, Urbana, NCTE, pp. vii–xii.

BOWERS, C.A. (1987) *Elements of a Post-Liberal Theory of Education*, New York, Teachers College Press.

BOWERS, C.A. (1988) *The Cultural Dimensions of Educational Computing: Understanding the Non-Neutrality of Technology*, New York, Teachers College.

BRANDT, D. (1990) *Literacy as Involvement: The Acts of Writers, Readers, and Texts*, Carbondale IL, Southern Illinois State University Press.

BRONTË, C. (1979) *Villette*, New York, Penguin Books.

BURNHAM, D. (1983) *The Rise of the Computer State*, New York, Random House.

BUSH, V. (1945) 'As We May Think', *Atlantic Monthly*, July, pp. 101–8.

CALHOUN, D. (1973) *The Education of a People*, Princeton, Princeton University Press.

CALVINO, I. (1986) 'Cybernetics and Ghosts', *The Uses of Literature: Essays*, translated by CREAGH, P., New York, Harcourt, pp. 3–38.

CARLYLE, T. (1970) 'Signs of the Times', *Carlyle: Selected Works*, Cambridge, MA, Harvard University Press, pp. 19–44.

CARROLL, J. (1987) 'The National Assessment in Reading: Are We Misreading the Findings', *Phi Delta Kappan*, **68**, pp. 424–30.

CARROLL, J. (1988) 'The NAEP Reading Proficiency Scale Is Not a Fiction: A Reply to McLean and Goldstein', *Phi Delta Kappan*, **69**, pp. 761–4.

CHERRY, C. (1985) *The Age of Access: Information Technology and Social Revolution*, edited by W. EDMONDSON, Dover, NH, Croom Helm.

CLEVELAND, H. (1985) 'The Twilight of Hierarchy: Speculations on the Global Information Society', in GUILE, B. (Ed.) *Information Technologies and Social Transformation*, Washington DC, National Academy.

COLERIDGE, S.T. (1966) 'General Introduction or Preliminary Treatise on Method', in COLLISON, R., *Encyclopaedia: Their History Throughout the Ages*, New York, Hafner, pp. 238–95.

COLLISON, R. (1966) *Encyclopaedia: Their History Throughout the Ages*, New York, Hafner.

COOPER, M. and SELFE, C. (1990) 'Computer Conferences and Learning: Authority, Resistance, and Internally Persuasive Discourse', *College English*, **52**, pp. 847–69.

DAVIS, S. (1988) 'The Ragged Interface: Computers and the Teaching of Writing', in *Teaching Prose: A Guide for Writing Instructors*, New York, Norton, pp. 337–92

DE CASTELL, S. LUKE, A. and EGAN, K. (Eds) (1986) *Literacy, Society, and Schooling: A Reader*, New York, Cambridge University Press.

DITLEA, S. (1990) 'Hyper Ted', *PC Computing*, October, pp. 201–10.

DURKHEIM, É. (1956) *Education and Sociology*, Glencoe, IL, Free Press.

EISENSTEIN, E.L. (1983) *The Printing Revolution in Early Modern Europe*, Cambridge, Cambridge University Press.

ELBOW, P. (1990) *What Is English?* New York and Urbana, IL, MLA and NCTE.

ELDRED, J.M. (1989) 'Computers, Composition Pedagogy, and the Social View', in HAWISHER, G. and SELFE, C. (Eds) *Critical Perspectives on Computers and Composition Instruction*, New York, Teachers College, pp. 201–18.

ELLUL, J. (1964) *The Technological Society*, translated by J. WILKINSON, New York, Vintage.

EMERSON, R.W. (1883) 'Intellect', *Essays, First Series*, Boston, Houghton Mifflin, pp. 323–47.

English Coalition Conference: Democracy Through Language (1989) R. LLOYD-JONES, and LUNSFORD, A. (Eds) New York and Urbana IL, MLA and NCTE.

FARRELL, T.J. (1977) 'Literacy, the Basics, and All That Jazz', *College English*, **38**, pp. 443–59.

FORSTER, E.M. (1927, 1954) *Aspects of The Novel*, New York, Harcourt.

FORTUNE, R. (1989) 'Visual and Verbal Thinking: Drawing and Word-Processing Software in Writing Instruction', in HAWISHER, G. and SELFE, C. (Eds) *Critical Perspectives on Computers and Composition Instruction*, New York, Teachers College, pp. 145–61.

FOUCAULT, M. (1983) 'The Subject and Power', in *Michel Foucault: Beyond Structuralism and Hermeneutics*, 2nd ed. DREYFUS, H. and RABINOW, P. (Eds) Chicago, University of Chicago Press, pp. 208–26.

Bibliography

FOUCAULT, M. (1984) 'What Is an Author?' *The Foucault Reader*, edited by RABINOW, P., New York, Pantheon, pp. 101–20.

FREY, O. (1987) 'Equity and Peace in the New Writing Class', in CAYWOOD, C. and OVERING, G. (Eds) *Teaching Writing: Pedagogy, Gender, and Equity*, Albany, State University of New York Press, pp. 93–105.

GADAMER, H.-G. (1982) *Truth and Method*, New York, Crossroad.

GARDNER, H. (1985) *Frames of Mind: The Theory of Multiple Intelligence*, New York, Basic Books.

GARDNER, H. (1989) *To Open Minds: Chinese Clues to the Dilemma of Contemporary Education*, New York, Basic Books.

GERE, A.R. (1987) *Writing Groups: History, Theory, and Implications*, Carbondale, Southern Illinois University Press.

GILLESPIE, A. and ROBINS, K. (1989) 'Geographical Inequalities: The Spatial Bias of the New Communications Technologies', in SIEFERT, M., GERBER, G. and FISHER, J. (Eds) *The Information Gap: How Computers and Other New Technologies Affect the Social Distribution of Power*, New York, Oxford University Press, pp. 7–18.

GILLIGAN, C. (1982) *In a Different Voice: Psychological Theory and Women's Development*, Cambridge, MA, Harvard University Press.

GOODY, J. and WATT, I. (1963) 'The Consequences of Literacy', *Comparative Studies in Society and History*, **3**, pp. 304–45.

GOULDNER, A. (1976) *The Dialectic of Ideology and Technology: The Origins, Grammar, and Future of Ideology*, New York, Oxford University Press.

GOULDNER, A. (1979) *The Future of Intellectuals and the Rise of the New Class: A Frame of Reference, Theses, Conjectures, Arguments, and an Historical Perspective on the Role of Intellectuals and Intelligentsia in the International Class Contest of the Modern Era*, New York, Oxford University Press.

GRAFF, H. (1979) *The Literacy Myth: Literacy and Social Structure in the Nineteenth Century City*, New York, Academic Press.

GREENFIELD, P.M. (1984) *Mind and Media: The Effects of Television, Video Games, and Computers*, Cambridge, MA, Harvard University Press.

HAAS, C. (1989) ' "Seeing It on the Screen Isn't Really Seeing It": Computer Writers' Reading Problems', in HAWISHER, G. and SELFE, C. (Eds) *Critical Perspectives on Computers and Composition Instruction*, New York, Teachers College, pp. 16–29.

HABERMAS, J. (1987) *The Philosophical Discourse of Modernity. Twelve Lectures*, translated by F. Lawrence, Cambridge, MA, MIT Press.

HALIO, M. (1990) 'Student writing: Can the Machine Maim the message?' *Academic Computing*, **4**, pp. 16–19.

HANDA, C. (Ed.) (1990a) *Computers and Community: Teaching Composition in the Twenty-first Century*, Portsmouth, NH, Boynton/Cook.

HANDA, C. (1990b) 'Politics, Ideology, and the Strange, Slow Death of the Isolated Composer', in HANDA, C. (Ed.) *Computers and Community: Teaching Composition in the Twenty-first Century*, Portsmouth, NH, Boynton/Cook, pp. 160–84.

HAVELOCK, E. (1986) *The Muse Learns to Write. Reflections on Orality and Literacy from Antiquity to the Present*, New Haven, Yale University Press.

HAWISHER, G. and SELFE, C. (Eds) (1989) *Critical Perspectives on Computers and Composition Instruction*, New York, Teachers College.

HEATH, S.B. (1983) *Ways with Words: Language, Life, and Work in Communities and Classrooms*, New York, Cambridge University Press.

HEATH, S.B. (1986a) 'Critical Factors in Literacy Development', in DE CASTELL, S., LUKE, A. and EGAN, K. (Eds) *Literacy, Society and Schooling: A Reader*, New York, Cambridge University Press, pp. 209–29.

HEATH, S.B. (1986b) 'The Functions and Uses of Literacy', in DE CASTELL, S., LUKE, A. and EGAN, K. (Eds) *Literacy, Society and Schooling: A Reader*, New York, Cambridge University Press, pp. 15–26.

HEIM, M. (1987) *Electric Language: A Philosophical Study of Word Processing*, New Haven, Yale University Press.

HIRSCH, E.D., JR. (1987) *Cultural Literacy: What Every American Needs to Know*, Boston, Houghton Mifflin.

HORNE, H. (1989) 'Jameson's Strategies of Containment', in KELLNER, D. (Ed.) *Postmodernism/Jameson/Critique*, Washington DC, Maisonneuve Press.

HOWELL, R.P. (Ed.) (1989) *Beyond Literacy: The Second Gutenberg Revolution*, San Francisco, Saybrook.

JAMESON, F. (1984a) 'Foreword', in LYOTARD, J.-F. *The Postmodern Condition: A Report on Knowledge*, Minneapolis, University of Minneapolis Press, pp. vii–xxi.

JAMESON, F. (1984b) 'Postmodernism, or the Cultural Logic of Late Capitalism', *New Left Review*, **146**, pp. 53–92.

JAMESON, F. (1987a) '*On Habits of the Heart*', *South Atlantic Quarterly*, **86**, pp. 545–65.

JAMESON, F. (1987b) 'Reading Without Interpretation: Postmodernism and the Video-Text', in FABB, N. *et al.* (Eds) *Arguments Between Language and Literature*, New York, Methuen, pp. 199–223.

JANSEN, S.C. (1989) 'Gender and the Information Society: A Socially Structured Silence', in SIEFERT, M., GERBER, G. and FISHER, J. (Eds) *The Information Gap: How Computers and Other New Communication Technologies Affect the Social Distribution of Power*, New York, Oxford University Press, pp. 196–210.

JOYCE, M. (1988) 'Siren Shapes: Exploratory and Constructive Hypertexts', *Academic Computing*, November, pp. 10–14, 37–42.

KAPLAN, N. and MOULTHROP, S. (1990) 'Other Ways of Seeing', *Computers and Composition*, 7, pp. 89–102.

KEARNEY, R. (1988) *The Wake of Imagination: Toward a Postmodern Culture*, Minneapolis, University of Minnesota Press.

KELLNER, D. (Ed.) (1989) *Postmodernism/Jameson/Critique*, Washington DC, Maisonneuve Press.

KERNAN, A. (1990) *The Death of Literature*, New Haven, Yale University Press.

KNOBLAUCH, C.H. and BRANNON, L. (1984) *Rhetorical Traditions and the Teaching of Writing*, Upper Montclair, NJ, Boynton/Cook.

LABOV, W. (1973) 'The Logic of Nonstandard English', in KAMPF, L. and LAUTER, P. (Eds) *The Politics of Literature: Dissenting Essays on the Teaching of English*. New York, Vintage, pp. 194–244.

LANDOW, G. (1988) 'Hypertext in Literary Education, Criticism, and Scholarship', Providence, RI, Institute for Research in Information and Scholarship, Brown University.

Bibliography

LANDOW, G. (1990) 'Hypertext and Collaborative Work: The Example of Intermedia', in KRAUT, R. and GALEGHER, J. (Eds) *Intellectual Teamwork*, Hillsdale, NJ, Lawrence Erlbaum, pp. 407–28.

LANDOW, G. (1992) 'Hypertext, Metatext, and the Electronic Canon', in TUMAN, M. (Ed.) *Literacy Online: The Promise (and Peril) of Reading and Writing with Computers*, Pittsburgh, University of Pittsburgh Press.

LANGSTON, M.D. and BATSON, T.W. (1990) 'The Social Shifts Invited by Working Collaboratively on Computer Networks: The ENFI Project', in HANDA C. (Ed.) *Computers and Community: Teaching Composition in the Twenty-first century*, Portsmouth, NH, Boynton/Cook, pp. 140–59.

LANHAM, R. (1984) 'One, Two, Three', in HORNER, W.B. (Ed.) *Composition and Literature: Bridging the Gap*, Chicago, University of Chicago Press, pp. 14–29.

LANHAM, R. (1989a) 'The Electric Word: Literary Study and the Digital Revolution', *New Literary History*, **20**, pp. 265–90.

LANHAM, R. (1989b) 'The Extraordinary Convergence: Democracy, Technology, Theory, and the University Curriculum', *South Atlantic Quarterly*, **89**, pp. 27–50.

LANHAM, R. (1990) 'Foreword', in HANDA, C. (Ed.) *Computers and Community: Teaching Composition in the Twenty-first Century*, Portsmouth, NH, Boynton/Cook, pp. xiii–xv.

LANHAM, R. (1992) 'Digital Rhetoric: Theory, Practice, and Property', in TUMAN, M, (Ed.) *Literacy Online: The Promise (and Peril) of Reading and Writing with Computers*, Pittsburgh, University of Pittsburgh Press.

LASCH, C. (1977) *Haven in a Heartless World: The Family Besieged*, NY, Basic Books.

LEED, E. (1980) '"Voice" and "Print": Master Symbols in the History of Communication', in WOODWARD, K. (Ed.) *The Myths of Information: Technology and Post-industrial Culture*, Madison: Coda Press.

LEFEVRE, K.B. (1987) *Invention as a Social Act*, Carbondale, Southern Illinois University Press.

LEVINE, K. (1986) *The Social Context of Literacy*, Boston, Routledge and Kegan Paul.

LOCKRIDGE, K. (1974) *Literacy in Colonial New England: An Inquiry into the Social Context of Literacy in the Early Modern West*, New York, Norton.

LOUIE, S. and RUBECK, R.F. (1989) 'Hypertext Publishing and the Revitalization of Knowledge', *Academic Computing*, May, pp. 20–23, 30–31.

LUCKY, R.W. (1989) *Silicon Dreams: Information, Man, and Machines*, New York, St Martin's.

LYOTARD, J.-F. (1984) *The Postmodern Condition: A Report on Knowledge*, Minneapolis, University of Minneapolis Press.

MARX, K. (1963) *Poverty of Philosophy*, International Publishers.

MARX, K. (1964) *Selected Writings in Sociology and Social Philosophy*, New York: McGraw-Hill.

McCORDUCK, P. (1985) *The Universal Machine: Confessions of a Technological Optimist*, San Diego, Harcourt.

McLEAN, L.D. and GOLDSTEIN, H. (1988) 'The US National Assessments in Reading: Reading Too Much into the Findings', *Phi Delta Kappan*, **69**, pp. 369–72.

McLUHAN, H.M. (1962) *Gutenberg Galaxy: The Making of Typographic Man*, Toronto, University of Toronto Press.

McLUHAN, H.M. and POWERS, B. (1989) *The Global Village: Transformations in World Life and Media in The 21st Century*, New York: Oxford University Press.

MILL, J.S. (1969) *Autobiography*, edited by J. STILLINGER, Boston, Houghton Mifflin.

MILLER, H. (1941) 'Reflections on Writing', *The Wisdom of the Heart*, Norfolk, CT, New Direction, pp. 19–30.

MOSCO, V. (1989) *The Pay-Per Society: Computers and Communication in the Information Age: Essays in Critical Theory and Public Policy*, Norwood, NJ, Ablex.

NELSON, T. (1987) *Literary Machines*, Edition 87.1.

NELSON, T. (1992) 'Opening Hypertext: A Memoir', in TUMAN, M. (Ed.) *Literacy Online: The Promise (and Peril) of Reading and Writing with Computers*, Pittsburgh, University of Pittsburgh Press.

OLSON, C.P. (1987) 'Who Computes?' in LIVINGSTONE, D. (Ed.) *Critical Pedagogy and Cultural Power*, South Hadley MA, Bergin and Garvey, pp. 179–204.

OLSON, D.R. (1977) 'From Utterance to Text: The Bias of Language in Speech and Writing', *Harvard Educational Review*, **47**, pp. 257–81.

ONG, W. (1982) *Orality and Literacy: The Technologizing of the Word*, New York, Methuen.

ORWELL, G. (1961) *1984*, New York, Signet Classic.

PIAGET, J. (1954) *The Construction of Reality in the Child*, New York, Basic.

PIRSIG, R. (1974) *Zen and the Art of Motorcycle Maintenance: An Inquiry into Values*, New York, Bantam.

PROVENZO, E. (1991) *Video Kids: Making Sense of Nintendo*, Cambridge, MA, Harvard University Press.

PROVENZO, E. (1992) 'The Electronic Panopticon: Censorship, Control, and Indoctrination in a Post-Typographic Culture', in TUMAN, M. (Ed.) *Literacy Online: The Promise (and Peril) of Reading and Writing with Computers*, Pittsburgh, University of Pittsburgh Press.

RASKIN, V. (1992) 'Naturalizing the Computer: English Online', in TUMAN, M. (Ed.) *Literacy Online: The Promise (and Peril) of Reading and Writing with Computers*, Pittsburgh, University of Pittsburgh Press.

The Reading Report Card: Progress Toward Excellence in Our Schools (1988) Princeton, NAEP and ETS.

RHEINGOLD, H. (1988) *Excursions to the Far Side of the Mind: A Book of Memes*, New York, Morrow.

RICOEUR, P. (1981) 'Appropriation', in THOMPSON, J.B. (Ed.) *Hermeneutics and the Human Sciences*, New York, Cambridge University Press, pp. 182–93.

ROSE, M. (1989) *Lives on the Boundary*, New York, Penguin.

ROSENBLATT, L.M. (1976) *Literature as Exploration*, 3rd ed., New York, Noble and Noble.

ROSZAK, T. (1986) *The Cult of Information: The Folklore of Computers and the True Art of Thinking*, New York, Pantheon.

SCHOLES, R. (1988) 'Three Views of Education: Nostalgia, History, and Voodoo', *College English*, **50**, 323–32.

SCHUMACHER, E.F. (1973) *Small Is Beautiful: Economics as if People Mattered*, New York, Perennial Library.

SCHWARTZ, H. (1992) '"Dominion Everywhere": Computers as Cultural Artifacts', in TUMAN, M. (Ed.) *Literacy Online: The Promise (and Peril) of Reading and Writing with Computers*, Pittsburgh, University of Pittsburgh Press.

SCOTT, P. (1988) 'A Few More Words about E.D. Hirsch and *Cultural Literacy*', *College English*, **50**, pp. 333–38.

SELFE, C. (1989) 'Redefining Literacy', in HAWISHER, G. and SELFE, C. (Eds) *Critical Perspectives on Computers and Composition Instruction*, New York, Teachers College, pp. 3–15.

SHALLIS, M. (1984) *The Silicon Idol: The Micro Revolution and Its Social Implications*, New York, Oxford University Press.

SHILS, E. (1972) 'The Intellectuals and the Powers: Some Perspectives for Comparative Analysis', *Intellectuals and the Powers and Other Essays*, Chicago, University of Chicago Press, pp. 3–22.

SHILS, E. (1981) *Tradition*, Chicago, University of Chicago Press.

SHNEIDERMAN, B. (1988) 'Reflections on Authoring, Editing, and Managing Hypertext', in BARRETT, E. (Ed.) *Society of Text: Hypertext, Hypermedia, and the Social Construction of Information*, Cambridge, MA, MIT Press, pp. 115–31.

SIEFERT, M., GERBER, G. and FISHER, J. (Eds) (1989) *The Information Gap: How Computers and Other New Communication Technologies Affect the Social Distribution of Power*, New York, Oxford University Press.

SLATIN, J. (1988) 'Hypertext and the Teaching of Writing', in BARRETT E. (Ed.) *Text, Context and Hypertext: Writing with and for the Computer*, Cambridge, MA, MIT Press, pp. 111–129.

SOLTOW, L. and STEVENS, E. (1981) *The Rise of Literacy and the Common School: A Socioeconomic Analysis to 1870*, Chicago, University of Chicago Press.

STEINER, G. (1988) 'The End of Bookishness', *Times Literary Supplement*, July 8–14, p. 754.

STEPHANSON, A. (1988) 'Regarding Postmodernism — A Conversation with Fredric Jameson', in ROSS, A. (Ed.) *Universal Abandon?: The Politics of Postmodernism*, Minneapolis, University of Minnesota Press, pp. 3–30.

STREET, B. (1984) *Literacy in Theory and Practice*, New York, Cambridge University Press.

STUBBS, M. (1980) *Language and Literacy*, Routledge and Kegan Paul.

SUSSMAN, H. (1968), *Victorians and The Machine: The Literacy Response to Technology*, Cambridge: Harvard University Press.

TAYLOR, F.W. (1947) *The Principles of Scientific Management*, in *Scientific Management*, New York, Harper.

TRIMBUR, J. (1989) 'Consensus and Difference in Collaborative Learning', *College English*, **51**, pp. 602–16.

TUMAN, M. (1987) '*A Preface to Literacy: An Inquiry into Pedagogy, Practice, and Progress*', Tuscaloosa, University of Alabama Press.

TUMAN, M. (Ed.) (1992) *Literacy Online: The Promise (and Peril) of Reading and Writing with Computers*, Pittsburgh, University of Pittsburgh Press.

TURKLE, S. (1988) 'Computational Reticence: Why Women Fear the Intimate Machine', in KRAMARAE, C. (Ed.) *Technology and Woman's Voices Keeping in Touch*, New York, Routledge and Kegan Paul, pp. 41–61.

ULMER, G. (1989) *Teletheory: Grammatology in the Age of Video*, New York: Routledge.

ULMER, G. (1992) 'Grammatology (in the Stacks) of Hypermedia: A Simulation', in TUMAN, M. (Ed.) *Literacy Online: The Promise (and Peril) of Reading and Writing with Computers*, Pittsburgh, University of Pittsburgh Press.

VIDAL, G. (1984) *New York Review of Books*, March, p. 20.

WATT, I. (1957) *The Rise of the Novel: Studies in Defoe, Richardson and Fielding*, Berkeley, University of California Press.

WEBER, M. (1958) *The Protestant Ethic and the Spirit of Capitalism*, New York, Scribner's.

WEBSTER, F. and ROBINS, K. (1986) *Information Technology: A Luddite Analysis*, Norwood, NJ, Ablex.

WELLS, H.G. *World Brain*, Garden City, NY, Doubleday.

WHITE, HAYDEN (1987) *The Content of Form: Narrative Discourse and Historical Representation*, Baltimore: Johns Hopkins University Press.

WILLIAMS, R. (1958) *Culture and Society: 1780–1950*, New York, Harper Torchbooks.

WILLIAMS, R. (1976) *Keywords: A Vocabulary of Culture and Society*, New York, Oxford University Press.

WILLIAMS, R. (1983) *Towards 2000*, London, Chatto and Windus.

WINNER, L. (1977) *Autonomous Technology: Technics-out-of-Control as a Theme in Political Thought*, Cambridge, MA, MIT Press.

WINOGRAD, T. and FLORES, F. (1986) *Understanding Computers and Cognition: A New Foundation for Design*, Reading MA, Addison-Wesley.

WINTEROWD, W.R. (1989) *Culture and Politics of Literacy*, New York, Oxford.

WITTGENSTEIN, L. (1969) *On Certainty*, New York, Harper.

YANKELOVICH, N., MEYROWITZ, N.K. and VAN DAM, A. (1985) 'Reading and Writing the Electronic Book', *IEEE Computer*, **18**, pp. 15–30.

ZINSSER, W. (1983) *Writing with a Word Processor*, New York, Harper.

ZUBOFF, S. (1988) *In the Age of the Smart Machine: The Future of Work and Power*, New York, Basic.

Index

Adams, Henry 33–34, 42
Alschuler, Liora 69–70
Apple, Michael 26–27
Arnold, Matthew 12–13, 95
Arnold, Thomas 116
Aronowitz, Stanley 120
Arterton, F. Chris 132–133
Asimov, Isaac 81

Bakhtin, Mikhail 90–91
Balestri, Diane 57, 66
Barker, Thomas 81–82, 87, 89
Barrett, Edward 70–71, 87–89
Barthes, Roland 62–64, 65
Bartholomae, David 97
Batson, Trent 84, 116
Baudrillard, Jean 119
Begeman, Michael 71–72
Bell, Daniel 14, 18–19, 42
Bellah, Robert 131
Bentham, Jeremy 11, 20–21
Berger, Harry 67
Berlin, James 22, 99–101, 102, 104, 106, 107, 122
Bloom, Harold 97
Bolter, Jay 16, 39–40, 41, 49, 67–68, 69, 76, 79–80, 89, 118–119, 127
Booth, Wayne 32
Bowers, C.A. 82, 95, 120–121, 122–123
Brandt, Deborah 43, 46–47, 49
Brannon, Lil 31–33, 34, 41
Brontë, Charlotte 7–8, 103
Burns, Ken 73, 112
Bush, Vannevar 54–55, 56

Calhoun, Daniel 29–30
Calvino, Italo 64

Carlyle, Thomas 30, 48
Carroll, John 125
Cleveland, Harlan 41, 42
Coleridge, Samuel Taylor 52–53, 54, 55–56, 75
Conklin, Jeff 71–72
Cooper, Marilyn 82–83

Dewey, John 29–30, 47, 48
Durkheim, Émile x, 17–18

Eisenstein, Elizabeth 6
Elbow, Peter 129
Eldred, Janet 84
Eliot, T.S. 26
Ellul, Jacques 14
Emerson, Ralph Waldo 31
English Coalition 25, 27, 32–33, 47, 48, 126, 129

Fortune, Ron 66
Foster, E.M. 34
Foucault, Michel 11, 64–65, 106
Frey, Olivia 104
Friedenberg, Edgar 105

Gadamer, Hans-Georg 86
Gardner, Howard 127–130
Gallagher, Brian 89
Gere, Anne Ruggles 91, 95–97, 98–99, 100, 102, 103, 104, 107, 128
Gillespie, A. 133
Gilligan, Carol 86
Goff, Martyn 15
Good, Kenneth 130–132
Goody, Jack 9, 43

Gouldner, Alvin 6, 35–39, 40, 49, 93, 106, 123
Graff, Harvey 36–37, 39
Greenfield, Patricia 11

Haas, Christina 4
Habermas, Jürgen 17, 36, 38, 106, 118
Halio, Marcia Peoples 109–110, 111–112, 115, 127
Handa, Carolyn 12, 22, 91, 92, 95, 128
Havelock, Eric 9–10, 43, 58
Heath, Shirley Brice 44–46, 49, 126, 128
Heim, Michael 57
Hirsch, E.D. 23–26, 27–30, 32, 38, 39, 47, 48, 128
Horkheimer, Max 105
Horne, Haynes 17
Hypertext: and encyclopedias 52–54; and instruction 59–62; limits of, 69–80

Jameson, Fredric 78, 105, 118, 123, 130, 135–136
Jansen, Sue 86
Joyce, Michael 56, 67, 68, 69, 191

Kaplan, Nancy 112–113, 115, 116, 127
Kearney, Richard 69, 137, 138
Kemp, Fred 81–82, 87, 89
Kernan, Alfred 131–132, 134–135
Knoblauch, C.H. 31–33, 34, 41

Labov, William 43, 126
Landow, George 59–62, 66, 68, 79–80
Langston, M. Diane 116
Lanham, Richard 4, 12–13, 16, 18, 20–21, 30, 79–80, 114, 116, 117, 123, 127
Lasch, Christopher 105–106
LeFevre, Karen Burke 91, 92
Literacy, *see* Online Literacy; Print Literacy; Technology
Lockridge, Kenneth 29
Lucky, Robert 2, 19
Lyotard, François 13, 15, 16–17, 20, 120, 136, 137

McCorduck, Pamela 87
McHugh, Nancy 124–125, 126
McLuhan, Marshall 3
Mandeville, Bernard 28
Marx, Karl 120, 131
Maslow, Abraham 69
Mill, John Stuart 28, 40

Miller, Henry 32
Milton, John 7
Morgan, Thaïs 62
Mosco, Vincent 79
Moulthrop, Stuart 112–113, 115, 116, 127

Nelson, Ted 54, 55, 56–57, 61–62, 79, 81, 119

Ohmann, Richard 93
Olson, David 43
Olson, C. Paul 27
Ong, Walter 3, 34–35, 43, 60
Online literacy: as opposed to print literacy 16–17, 62–66, 112–113; and associative thinking 54–57; and critical thinking 66–69, 95–98; and community 83–87, 89–93, 98–101, 104–106; and consensus 106–108; in the workplace 101–103; graphic-based, 113–114
Orwell, George 8–10

Papert, Seymour 88
Paradis, James 87–89
Piaget, Jean 75, 97, 133
Pirsig, Robert 48–51, 86, 94, 128
Plato 2
Print literacy: and privacy, 6–11, 15–16; as totalizing force 11–14; in preindustrial society 27–30; as response to industrial society 30–35, 47–48; limits, 43–47, 48–51, 118–130; and collaboration 93–95
Provenzo, Eugene 80, 82

Raskin, Victor 24
Richardson, Samuel 6–7
Rheingold, Howard 85
Ricoeur, Paul 75
Robins K 133
Rose, Mike 124
Rosenblatt, Louise 34, 76, 95, 131
Roszak, Theodore 26, 27
Rousseau, Jacques 29

Saint Bonaventura 64
Sandberg-Diment, Erik 117
Santayana, George 124, 128, 131
Schumacker, E.F. 118–119
Scollon, Ron 126, 128

Scollon, Suzanne 126, 128
Selfe, Cynthia 66, 82–83
Shakespeare, William 9
Shallis, Michael 26
Sheridan, Richard 2–3
Shils, Edward 38, 132
Shneiderman, Ben 71, 72, 78
Slatin, John 74–75
Soltow, Lee 28
Steiner, George 10–11, 79, 121, 138
Stevens, Edward 28
Street, Brian 44
Stubbs, Michael 44

Taylor, Frederick 13–14
Technology: as source of literacy, 2–6,
    14–15, 18–22, 35–43, 130–138;
  as threat to literacy, 24–27
Trimbur, John 103, 104, 106–108, 128
Tuckman, Barbara 15–16
Tuman, Myron 31
Turkle, Sherry 83, 87
Twain, Mark 1

Ulam, Stanislau 19
Ulmer, Greg 12, 35, 134

Vidal, Gore 3

Watt, Ian 6–7, 9
Weber, Max 11, 36
Wells, H.G. 53–54, 121
White, Hayden 138
Williams, Raymond 5, 30, 94
Winner, Michael 35, 38
Winograd, Terry 119–120
Winterowd, Ross 31
Wittgenstein, Ludwig 100
Word processing: compared with typing
    1–2;
  limits of 57–58;
  with Mac compared with
    IBM-computers, 109–111
Writing instruction: 2, 3–4, 47–48,
    114–117;
  teacher-based 81–83;
  computer-based 87–89, *see also* Print
    literacy; Online literacy

Zinnser, William 1
Zuboff, Shoshana 101–103

DATE			